FIELD GUIDE TO

MAMMALS

OF SOUTHERN AFRICA

CHRIS & TILDE STUART

Struik Publishers
(a division of New Holland Publishing (South Africa) (Pty) Ltd)
Cornelis Struik House
80 McKenzie Street
Cape Town 8001
South Africa

New Holland Publishing is a member of Avusa Ltd

Visit us at **www.struik.co.za** and view over 40 000 unique African images available
to purchase at from our image bank at **www.imagesofafrica.co.za**

First published 1988
Second edition 1993
Third edition 2001
Fourth edition 2007

10 9 8 7 6 5 4 3 2

Fourth edition
Publishing manager: Pippa Parker
Managing editor: Helen de Villiers
Design manager: Janice Evans
Editor: Gill Gordon
Designers: Patricia Blom, Robin Cox
Cartographers: Robin Cox, Neil Bester, Patricia Blom, John Loubser
Illustrator (marine mammals): David C. Thorpe

Reproduction by Hirt & Carter Cape (Pty) Ltd
Printed and bound by Kyodo Printing Co (S'Pore) Pte Ltd

ISBN 978 1 77007 404 0

ACKNOWLEDGEMENTS

We gratefully acknowledge the help we have received over the years from friends and colleagues. No doubt many more names should appear below, and we ask pardon of those who assisted us in different ways but whose names have unintentionally escaped mention. Pierre Swanepoel and Lloyd Wingate of the Amathole Museum in King William's Town, Dr Naas Rautenbach of the Transvaal Museum, and the staff of the Iziko South African Museum are thanked for allowing us access to the mammal collections in their care.

Our sincere thanks for information, photographs and other assistance go to the following: Prof. Paul K. Anderson (University of Calgary); Dr Ric Bernard (Rhodes University); Dr Hu Berry; Dr Bill Branch (Port Elizabeth Museum); Dr John Carlyon; Dr Alan Channing (University of the Western Cape); Dr Jeremy David (Sea Fisheries Research Institute); Dr Nico Dippenaar; Anthony Duckworth and Laura Fielden (University of Natal); Patrick J. Frere (Langata Bird Sanctuary); Mike Griffin; Dr Hans Grobler; Dr Anthony Hall-Martin; Dr Graham Hickman; Niels Jacobsen; Howard Langley; Malan Lindeque; Ian Manning; Dr Daan Marais; Penny Meakin; Dr Gus Mills (SA National Parks); Peter le S. Milstein; Pam Newby; Harald Nicolay; Guy Palmer; Debbie Peake (for elephant skull measurments); Prof. Mike Perrin (University of Natal); Dr Graham Ross; Judith A. Rudnai; the late Dr Reay Smithers; Dr Steven Tischhauser; Tony Tomkinson; the late Dr H. van Rompaey; Alan Weaving; Viv Wilson (Chipangali Wildlife Trust); and Lloyd R. Wingate (Amathole Museum). Our special thanks go to Dr Merlin Tuttle, founder of Bat Conservation International, for his encouragement and photographs.

Finally, we should also like to express our appreciation to the present and former staff of Struik Publishers: in particular Peter Borchert and Eve Gracie for their support and advice at the start, John Comrie-Greig for editing the original manuscript, and Pippa Parker for successfully steering it through three subsequent editions.

Chris and Tilde Stuart
Loxton 2007

CONTENTS

INTRODUCTION

The mammal group is a small one when compared with the birds (8 900 species worldwide) or the fish (30 000 species worldwide). It contains between 4 000 and 4 500 living species, of which more than 350 are currently known to occur in the southern African subregion. Some of these, however, are known from very few, or even single, records. The richest period of mammal diversity was during the late Tertiary (2–5 million years ago), when an estimated three times as many mammal species roamed the earth than do so today.

Taxonomists are constantly revising and reassessing the scientific status of many mammals, particularly the smaller species such as bats, shrews and small rodents. This often results in scientific names being changed and, on occasion, new species being described; Juliana's Golden Mole, for example, was described from the former Transvaal in 1972 and the Long-tailed Forest Shrew from the southern coastal belt as recently as 1978. The bats are especially mobile, and it is very likely that additional species from this group will be discovered and added to the faunal complement of southern Africa in due course.

Mammals have a number of common characteristics that set them apart from other vertebrates: they breathe with lungs; they possess a four-chambered heart; they have three delicate bones in the middle ear; the females have mammary glands that produce milk for suckling the young; and nearly all species have a covering of body hair.

Major biotic zones of southern Africa

Many mammal species are restricted to one particular vegetation type or habitat, whereas others range over several.

The southern African subregion – defined as that part of the African continent and its coastal waters south of the Cunene and Zambezi rivers – can be divided into six major biotic zones, each differing in climate and vegetation. This does, however, present an oversimplified picture, and each of these zones can be further subdivided into many different habitat and vegetation types.

1. Desert
Desert is characterized by its very low rainfall (usually less than 100 mm per year) and sparse plant growth. Extensive areas may be devoid of any vegetation, being covered by sand-dunes or consisting of flat gravel plains and rugged hill country. Several species of mammal have evolved mechanisms that help them to survive in this harsh environment. In the southern African subregion, this biotic zone is represented by the Namib Desert of Namibia.

2. Arid (semi-desert) zone
Areas classed as 'arid' receive higher rainfall than true desert, but this rarely exceeds 500 mm per year. In southern Africa, rainfall is at its lowest in the west, gradually increasing towards the east. The Kalahari, Karoo, Bushmanland, Namaqualand and Damaraland fall within the arid zone. The southern section, namely Bushmanland, Namaqualand and the Karoo, consists mainly of extensive rocky plains and isolated hills and hill ranges, with a vegetation comprising low, woody shrubs and succulents. Much of the area is veined with river courses, which are vegetated along their banks with bushes and low trees. In the northern parts, for example, the Kalahari 'desert' of the Northern Cape and Botswana, sandy soils are more prevalent with low (often acacia) trees and bushes, and relatively

1. Desert

2. Arid (semi-desert) zone

3. Savanna woodland

4. Savanna grassland

5. Cape fynbos

6. Indigenous forest

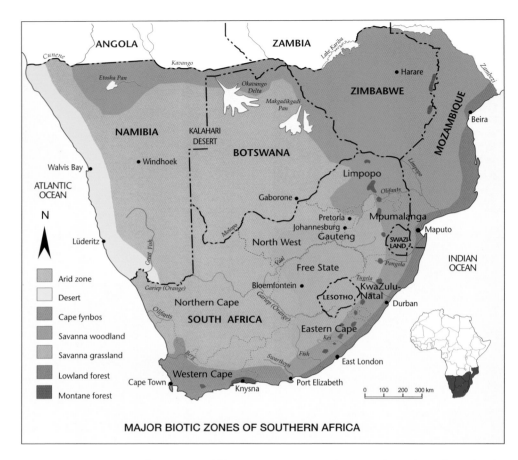

MAJOR BIOTIC ZONES OF SOUTHERN AFRICA

good grass cover. This zone once supported vast numbers of ungulates, but the free-roaming herds of Springbok, Red Hartebeest, Blue Wildebeest, Eland and Plains Zebra have diminished greatly and are now restricted to the more sparsely populated parts of Botswana.

3. Savanna woodland and 4. Savanna grassland

The savanna biome can be divided into two zones, namely savanna woodland mostly in the north, and savanna grassland in the south. Savanna woodland, which extends from Limpopo down the coastal belt of KwaZulu-Natal to the Eastern Cape, includes mopane woodland, thorn scrub (thicket) and dense woodland habitats in the east. Grass cover ranges from sparse to good. It is within this zone that many of the subregion's major game reserves are situated.

Savanna grassland consists largely of mixed grassland, with tree and shrub growth more or less restricted to the edges of water courses and to hills and more rugged terrain. Much of the formerly extensive savanna grassland of east-central South Africa has been destroyed by cultivation or modified by overgrazing.

Although falling within the larger savanna zone, the wetlands of the Okavango and Linyanti swamps deserve separate mention. The Okavango Swamp of north-western Botswana is the largest inland river delta in the world and southern Africa's most important wetland. The Linyanti Swamp is situated in eastern Caprivi, Namibia. These two areas are home to many species of water-adapted mammal, including Sitatunga, Lechwe and Hippopotamus. Both swamps are under increasing human pressure and there is an urgent need for careful resource management and conservation planning.

5. Cape fynbos
This small but significant zone is restricted to the Western and Eastern Cape provinces, and its vegetation can be broadly divided into mountain and lowland fynbos. This very limited area is so rich in plant species that it is classed as one of the world's six 'floristic kingdoms', although it covers only 0.04 per cent of the world's land surface area. The vegetation is dominated largely by evergreen shrubs and bushes. The fynbos zone has suffered more than any other in the subregion from agriculture and other human influences. It is not a mammal-rich region.

6. Indigenous (lowland and montane) forest
The sixth zone, indigenous forest, can be divided into Lowland Forest and Montane Forest. Poorly represented in southern Africa, it is restricted, in fragmented and widely scattered pockets, to the southern and eastern areas of South Africa, the eastern highlands of Zimbabwe and the adjacent areas of Mozambique. Several mammal species, such as the Giant Golden Mole and Sykes's Monkey, are found only in this habitat.

Using this field guide

Geographically, this book covers the area south of the Cunene River in the west and the Zambezi River in the east. The Atlantic Ocean laps the western seaboard, and the southern and eastern shores are bounded by the Indian Ocean.

The main purpose of a field guide is to enable the observer to identify mammals in the wild. While there should be little difficulty in identifying, to species level, the larger, medium-sized and some smaller mammals, one of the difficulties facing mammal-watchers is that many species are small and secretive, and therefore only rarely seen or difficult to find. Furthermore, many small species can be identified only by specialists with access to comparative study material of skins and skulls, usually through a museum. For some small species, identification is possible normally only to family and generic level; this applies particularly to golden moles, shrews, bats and small rodents, where positive identification may require expert examination of the skull, teeth and sometimes even the chromosomes. Where this is the case, it is pointed out in the text.

As the marine environment simply does not lend itself to easy observation, illustrations instead of photographs are used to depict most whales and dolphins.

Each species account is divided into sections under subheadings to enable the reader to look up any aspect which is of particular interest. Take care when identifying juvenile animals, as they may differ considerably from the adults. This applies particularly to the antelopes, where the subadults of one species may be easily confused with the adults of another species. Another thing to bear in mind is that a number of species possess one or more subspecies, or races, that differ from each other in colour, pattern or size. Where this is applicable, it is mentioned in the species account.

The tools of the mammal-watcher are simple: a good pair of binoculars, a notebook and pencil, and a suitable mammal reference book.

Mammal identification

Identification pointers

The main aids to identifying a species are summarized in each species account, and prominent features are highlighted under the heading 'Identification pointers'. Where one species is similar to, or could be confused with, another species, their distinguishing features are also mentioned (for example, the Side-striped and Black-backed Jackals).

Distribution

A glance at the distribution map will give a quick indication of a species' distribution within southern Africa. Remember that the scale of the maps is such that only general distribution patterns can be given. For example, although

SIX STEPS TO IDENTIFY A MAMMAL

Descriptions in this field guide concentrate on external features that will help with species identification. Follow the six steps below when identifying a mammal:

1. Decide to which group the mammal belongs. (Is it an antelope, or does it belong to the dog family, for instance?)
2. Estimate the shoulder height, total length and tail length if possible. (Is the tail shorter than the head and body? Are the ears long or short?)
3. Look for outstanding features. (Does it have white or black stripes, spots or a bushy tail?)
4. Check the distribution map to ascertain whether the animal occurs in the area.
5. Check the habitat preference of the mammal. (You will not see a Klipspringer bounding across open plains, or a Black-backed Jackal in dense forest.)
6. Make a note of specific behavioural traits that may aid in identification. (Did you see a large group together or just a few animals; was an individual digging a burrow?)

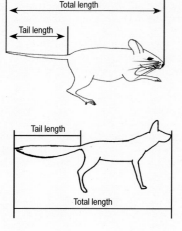

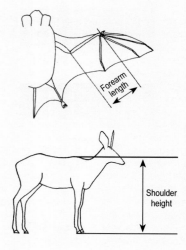

the Rock Hyrax (Dassie) is shown to have a continuous distribution, it can clearly only occur where suitable habitat is available. Always consult the notes on a species' habitat preference in conjunction with the distribution map.

Habitat
An indication is given in the text of the habitats favoured by each species. However, bear in mind that a species may be encountered within other habitats.

Behaviour
Behavioural characteristics that may aid in identification are given preference, but other aspects of interest are also mentioned.

Food and Reproduction
The notes under these headings may assist in identifying a mammal, but are usually given for general interest.

Spoor drawings
As a further aid to identification, spoor drawings have been provided for selected species. These show the tracks of species most likely to be encountered, or tracks that are particularly distinctive. 'Reading' tracks and signs adds a fascinating dimension to mammal-watching; a great deal of information may be gleaned without the animal itself being observed. The measurements given are the average for each species.

Measurements
The most useful measurement in the field identification of larger and medium-sized mammals is shoulder height. Other measurements are given as an aid to determining whether a mammal is 'small', 'medium-sized' or 'large', often when compared with an average human body, or a part of it, such as a hand or forearm. A useful method of learning to judge measurements is to cut pieces of wood into known lengths and place these at different distances. With practise, you should be able to apply these estimates to mammals in the field.

All measurements are metric, and it is important to note that average figures are given for each species. These measurements can vary considerably within a species and the figures given in this book should be taken only as a guide. In the case of antelope, two horn measurements are provided: the average length, and the record length as given in Rowland Ward's *African Records of Big Game*, the 'bible' of international hunting statistics.

The mysteries of changing taxonomy

In recent years, the use of modern techniques in mammal taxonomy has resulted in a number of changes in mammal classification. Some changes make good sense to us, a few do not, but there is no doubt that taxonomy is in a state of ongoing evolution. Cytogenetics, molecular technologies and protein electrophoresis are among the principal forces driving the taxonomic convulsions that are giving us a better understanding of the origins and roots of our mammalian fauna.

Where possible, this edition has incorporated these changes. However, the reader should be aware that, as research techniques continue to be refined, more changes will come into play. Taxonomy is a very fluid field of study that promises to produce much discussion and debate in the future.

Conservation and wildlife management

During the past 2 000 years, approximately 200 species of mammals and birds are believed to have become extinct; an average of one species every 10 years. This rate has accelerated, with many of these species having disappeared during the last hundred years. In southern Africa, one mammal species (Blue Antelope or Bluebuck, *Hippotragus leucophaeus*) and one subspecies (Quagga, *Equus quagga quagga*) have become extinct in recent times.

The Quagga once occurred in large herds on the southern and central plains of southern Africa, but was driven to extinction by hunting and by competition with domestic stock; the last Quagga died in Amsterdam Zoo in 1883. Present thinking is leaning towards the theory that the Quagga was simply the southernmost subspecies of the Plains (Burchell's) Zebra but, even if current research should prove this to be the case, the extinction of this distinctive subspecies is still inexcusable.

The Blue Antelope, on the other hand, was almost certainly a full species.

When the first European settlers arrived at the Cape of Good Hope in the mid-17th century, it would appear that this close relative of the Roan and Sable Antelopes was already declining in numbers and range. At that time it was restricted to the area now known as the Overberg in the Western Cape, although the fossil and sub-fossil record shows that it was once spread more widely along the coastal plain to the east and west. It is theorized that the decline of the Blue Antelope, like the Quagga, was a result of its having to compete for grazing with the sheep, goats and cattle of the indigenous people of the Cape, and was accelerated by the arrival of the colonists and their firearms. It finally disappeared around 1799–1800, gaining the dubious distinction of being the first mammal on the African continent recorded as becoming extinct in historic times.

The Cape Mountain Zebra, Bontebok, Black Wildebeest and Square-lipped Rhinoceros have all come perilously close to the brink of extinction. Fortunately, however, these once-numerous species were protected in good time, and their futures now seem secure. Regrettably, many species have been eradicated from their original ranges, and we will never again see elephant herds making their way across the sandy flats within sight of Cape Town, or hear lions roaring in the Nuweveld Mountains above Beaufort West. The Hook-lipped Rhinoceros was once found throughout southern Africa; today, it occurs only in a handful of sanctuaries in the north and east. Other species, such as Oribi,

Black Wildebeest (top) and Cape Mountain Zebra (above) are examples of sound conservation management.

Roan and Sable Antelopes, Wild Dog and Riverine Rabbit are all currently a cause for concern to conservationists.

Modern technology has frequently encouraged the wasteful and exploitative use of the natural environment. Apart from the deliberate hunting of wild mammals, probably the single greatest factor that has influenced wildlife in the subregion is the uncontrolled manner in which agriculture has modified or completely changed the character of many habitats and vegetation types.

Food cultivation, overgrazing, soil erosion and competition with domestic stock are all factors that have contributed to the decline of wild mammal populations.

Another issue is the trapping or poisoning of predators that include domestic animals in their diet. Because it is impossible to restrict control to just the species that has caused the damage, many thousands of non-target animals, including the Bat-eared Fox, Small Grey Mongoose and a variety of harmless rodents, are killed each year. Problem animal management (or 'vermin control' as it used to be called) is a field that deserves far greater attention in order to reduce the death toll among harmless species and to increase selectivity for the real problem animals.

The pivotal problem, of course, is human overpopulation and the resulting demands it places on the environment. Man creates or exacerbates pressure on the environment and, as a result, the mammal fauna is adversely affected. It is our responsibility to achieve a compromise between development and destruction that will allow man and nature to co-exist in harmony.

Although it is often difficult to balance economics and conservation, there is a growing awareness that wildlife can increasingly help to pay its way. Each year, southern Africa's vast, but diminishing, mammal resources draw tens of thousands of tourists to its reserves, wildlife sanctuaries and game-farms, creating a wide range of employment opportunities that boost local, regional and national coffers.

In the case of privately owned game-farms, some landowners have found that combining conservation initiatives with hunting concessions results in a profitable form of land use. Many such farms are situated on marginal agricultural land, with low livestock-carrying capacities. Game species, long adapted to these areas, are able to thrive without the costly dipping and dosing programmes associated with sheep, goat and cattle husbandry. In parts of northern South Africa and Namibia, this may be the only economically viable form of land use. However, many conservation-orientated people find the commercial aspects of wildlife utilization objectionable, and believe that man has a moral duty to protect, rather than to exploit, the environment and its biota. Although this is a morally correct standpoint, it is one that is becoming increasingly unrealistic. It would be difficult to convince a farmer to conserve large numbers of Springbok and Blesbok merely for the sake of conservation; if he cannot be assured of a cash return for his large game herds, he would go back to sheep- and goat-farming. By the same token, the suburban gardener cannot be expected to accept with equanimity the regular destruction of his potato patch by mole-rats.

Programmes to conserve the mammals of southern Africa are closely tied to habitat conservation. It is no good conserving a species, or group of species, if the habitat to which they are adapted is not also protected. But, in the last resort, mankind must also be convinced of the necessity of managing its own population and keeping it in check.

'Unwittingly for the most part, but right around the world, we are eliminating the panoply of life. We elbow species off the planet, we deny room to entire communities of nature, we domesticate the Earth. With growing energy and ingenuity, we surpass ourselves time and again in our efforts to exert dominion over fowl of the air and fish of the sea.

'We do all this in the name of human advancement. Yet instead of making better use of those lands we have already for our use, we proclaim our need to expand into every last corner of the Earth. Our response to natural environments has changed little for thousands of years. We dig them up, we chop them down, we burn them, we drain them, we pave them over, we poison them in order to mould them to our image. We homogenize the globe.

'Eventually we may achieve our aim, by eliminating every 'competitor' for living space on the crowded Earth. When the last creature has been accounted for, we shall have made ourselves masters of all creation. We shall look around, and we shall see nothing but each other. Alone at last.'

Norman Myers, *Environmental scientist and conservation philosopher*

FAMILY INTRODUCTIONS

The following are general accounts of the mammal families and subfamilies occurring in southern Africa.

■ GOLDEN MOLES | Order Afrosoricida

GOLDEN MOLES | Family Chrysochloridae (p30)

Eighteen species occur in southern Africa. Most are inadequately known as they are difficult to trap and are rarely seen because of their subterranean life-style; some are known only from very restricted geographical areas. They leave characteristic domed tunnels just below the soil surface, not the mounds or heaps normally pushed up by mole-rats. All golden moles are small (the largest has a total length of 23 cm), and have no external tail. The head is wedge-shaped, with a horny pad at the tip of the muzzle, which is used for burrowing. They are blind and their ears are merely small openings through the fur without pinnae. The hindlegs (with 5 digits each) are less developed than the forelegs (with 4 digits); the third digit of each forefoot carries a long, heavy claw to facilitate digging.

Sixteen species have smooth, dense, glossy fur but the two larger species have longer, coarse hair. As a group, the Golden moles have been aptly described as 'animated powder-puffs'. They show a marked preference for looser, sandy soils. They are not related to Rodent moles (family Bathyergidae, page 100).

Key features: Tail, eyes and ears not visible; glossy fur; surface tunnels; do not have pair of large incisors in upper and lower jaw.

■ SENGIS | Order Macroscelidea

SENGIS (ELEPHANT-SHREWS)
Family Macroscelididae (p34)

Eight species occur in the subregion. All are small (the largest has a head-and-body length of 19 cm) and characterized by the elongated, constantly twitching, trunk-like snout. The ears are rounded and prominent, and the eyes are large. Hindlegs and -feet are much longer than forelegs and -feet. The tail is about the same length as the head and body and is only sparsely haired. If disturbed, sengis can move very rapidly.

Key features: Small and mouse-like, with long, mobile trunk-like snout.

■ HEDGEHOGS & SHREWS | Order Eulipotyphla

HEDGEHOG | Family Erinaceidae (p38)

Only one species in the subregion. It is characterized by its small size (total length 22 cm), and the short, stiff spines on its back and sides. It has a pointed snout and a band of white hair across the forehead. The tail is not visible. Nocturnal.

Key features: Spine-covered back and sides; usually brownish in colour; curls up if threatened.

SHREWS | Family Soricidae (p40)

Seventeen species have been recorded from the subregion. All are small to very small (largest has head-and-body length of 12 cm) with a long, narrow and wedge-shaped muzzle (not as elongated and mobile as in sengis). The tail is usually shorter than the head-and-body length and the legs are short. The fur is short, soft and, in most species, dark in colour. Most species are associated with damp habitats. Some species are extremely difficult to identify in the field and careful examination of the teeth, skull and even chromosome structure is often required.
Key features: Small and mouse-like; long, wedge-shaped head; tiny eyes.

BATS | Order Chiroptera

All bats belong to the order Chiroptera, which is divided into two distinct suborders: the suborder Megachiroptera contains the fruit-eating bats, and the suborder Microchiroptera contains the insect-eating bats. At the present time eight species of fruit-bats and 67 species of insectivorous bats have been recorded as occurring in southern Africa, but it is highly probable that several more bat species will be added to the subregion's faunal list in the future, after more intensive biological surveying.

Bats are the only mammals capable of true flight. The forelimbs, with their greatly elongated fingers, have evolved into wings, over which the skin of the upper and lower surfaces has fused to form a very thin wing-membrane. This membrane extends along the side of the body to the ankles. When at rest, bats usually hang head-downwards, suspended by the claws of the hindfeet and with the wings either folded against the body, or enveloping it. The fruit-eating and insect-eating bats differ in several ways (see box below):

Character	Fruit-bat	Insectivorous bat
Size	Usually large	Usually small
Wing-claws	2*	1
Tail	Absent or short	Medium to long
Interfemoral (tail) membrane	Poorly developed	Usually well-developed
Ear tragus	Absent	Usually well-developed but absent in horseshoe bats
Eyes	Large	Small
Echolocation	Absent, except in *Rousettus aegyptiacus*	Present

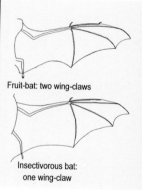

Fruit-bat: two wing-claws

Insectivorous bat: one wing-claw

(* in southern Africa)

Bats rely to a great extent on their hearing and this is particularly so in the case of the microchiropterans or insect-eating bats, which have perfected the art of echolocation. Their ears are extremely well developed and most microchiropteran species, with the exception of the horseshoe bats, have a small lobe, the tragus, in front of the ear opening. While in flight, insectivorous bats emit high-frequency sound waves through the mouth (e.g. the family Vespertilionidae) or nostrils (e.g. the family Hipposideridae). These clicks and bleeps are reflected by objects in the immediate vicinity of the bat and are picked up on the rebound by the bats' ears, thus providing information on obstacles and potential prey to the bat.

Anyone who has observed bats in flight will appreciate the rapidity with which they analyse and react to these 'messages'. The time between the emission of the call, the reception of the bounced echo and the bat's physical reaction to the stimulus may in fact be as little as one hundredth of a second. Among the fruit-bats, only the Egyptian Fruit-bat *Rousettus aegyptiacus* possesses the ability to echolocate; its clicks are made by the tongue, emitted through the mouth, and are of a lower frequency than those of insect-eating bats.

Fruit-bats | Suborder Megachiroptera | Family Pteropodidae (p46)

Eight species occur in the subregion but only three are regularly encountered. Dobson's Fruit-bat is known from only a single specimen collected in Botswana, and the validity of Angolan Epauletted Fruit-bat is not certain. Local bats that were previously assigned to Peter's Epauletted Fruit-Bat (*Epomophorus crypturus*) have been reassigned to Gambian Epauletted Fruit-Bat (*Epomophorus gambianus*).

All fruit-bats are large in size with pointed, dog-like heads. Their ears are fairly prominent but lack ear extensions or tragi. The tail is very short and the tail (interfemoral) membrane is indistinct (fig 1.1, below). Unlike the insectivorous bats, the fruit-bats have two claws on each wing. Two of the more common species have white tufts at the base of the ears and roost in trees; the Egyptian Fruit-bat lacks such white tufts and roosts in caves.

Key features: Large size; dog-like faces.

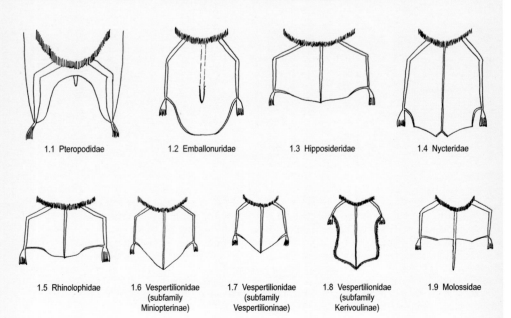

Figure 1: TAIL CONFORMATION IN DIFFERENT FAMILIES OF BATS (not to scale)

1.1 Pteropodidae

1.2 Emballonuridae

1.3 Hipposideridae

1.4 Nycteridae

1.5 Rhinolophidae

1.6 Vespertilionidae (subfamily Miniopterinae)

1.7 Vespertilionidae (subfamily Vespertilioninae)

1.8 Vespertilionidae (subfamily Kerivoulinae)

1.9 Molossidae

Insectivorous Bats | Suborder Microchiroptera (p50)

There are six families and more than 67 species of insectivorous bats in the subregion. Many species are difficult to separate without detailed examination. Unlike the fruit-bats, insectivorous bats have only one claw on each wing and they are generally much smaller in size. The conformation of the tail and the interfemoral membrane, which it helps to support, are useful diagnostic features at family level (see fig. 1, opposite).

SHEATH-TAILED & TOMB BATS | Family Emballonuridae (p50)

Three species occur in southern Africa. They are easily separated from other bats by the distinctive tail conformation: somewhat more than half of the tail is enclosed by the interfemoral membrane, the remainder being free. The tail-tip, however, does not reach the outer edge of the membrane as it does in the free-tailed bats (figs. 1.2 and 1.9, opposite). The eyes are larger than those of most insectivorous bats. They roost against a surface and never hang free.

Key features: Tail distinctive – partly free but not projecting beyond outer edge of membrane; simple face with no nose-leaves.

TRIDENT & LEAF-NOSED BATS | Family Hipposideridae (p52)

Four species occur in the subregion, two leaf-nosed bats and two trident bats (but note that the Trident Bat *Triaenops persicus* is usually called the Persian Leaf-nosed Bat). They are all similar in general appearance to horseshoe bats but can be separated from the latter by their more simple nose-leaves. Their tail conformation resembles that of horseshoe bats (figs. 1.3 and 1.5, opposite). Trident bats have a three-pronged process on the top edge of the nose-leaves. The leaf-nosed bats have large ears and tiny tragi. Commerson's Leaf-nosed Bat is one of the largest insect-eating bats in southern Africa. All species usually roost in caves.

Key features: Similar to horseshoe bats but nose-leaf structure simpler and less 'horseshoe'-like.

SLIT-FACED BATS | Family Nycteridae (p56)

Six species occur in the subregion, but only one has a wide distribution range. Bats of this family have disproportionately long ears (nearly 4 cm in the case of Egyptian Slit-faced Bat), which are parallel-sided and are held more or less vertically, unlike, for example, the ears of the long-eared bats (fig. 2.14, page 18), which are held at an angle of 45° to the head. There is a slit in the skin down the middle of the face which, when unfolded, reveals small nose-leaves. The terminal vertebra of the tail is bifurcated, giving a Y-tipped appearance, a feature diagnostic of this family (fig. 1.4). Slit-faced bats tend to roost singly or in small numbers, hanging free rather than pressed against a vertical surface. All six species in the subregion belong to the genus *Nycteris*.

Key features: Very long, vertically held ears; Y-shaped tail-tip; groove down middle of face.

HORSESHOE BATS | Family Rhinolophidae (p58)

The 10 species of horseshoe bat in the subregion are difficult to separate to species level. All have complex nose-leaves, which play an important role in echolocation. The plate-like or horseshoe-shaped main nose-leaf above the upper lip varies little in shape between the different species. Above the horseshoe, however, there is a protruding saddle-shaped outgrowth known as the sella, and in the region of the forehead is an erect, triangular fold of skin called the lancet (fig. 2.10, page 18). It is these outgrowths, together with the tooth structure, which allow taxonomists to distinguish the different species. The ears are prominent and widely separated, but have no tragi; the horseshoe bats are the only family of insectivorous bats to lack the tragus. The interfemoral membrane is more or less squared off between feet and tail-tip, as in the leaf-nosed and trident bats (figs. 1.5 and 1.3, opposite). Most species roost in caves and crevices and they hang free, not pressed against the walls of the roost. The wings are short and rounded and, when the bat is at rest, they envelop the body.

Key features: Horseshoe-shaped nose-leaf with projections; no tragus.

Figure 2: FACE AND EAR CONFORMATION OF DIFFERENT BAT GROUPS (not to scale)

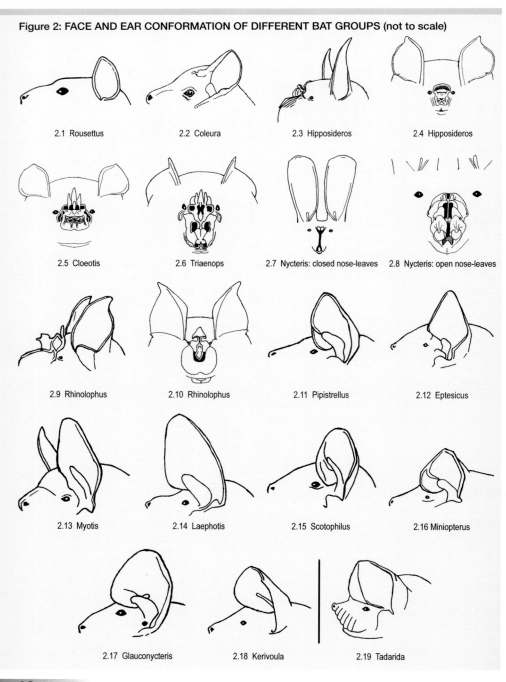

2.1 Rousettus

2.2 Coleura

2.3 Hipposideros

2.4 Hipposideros

2.5 Cloeotis

2.6 Triaenops

2.7 Nycteris: closed nose-leaves

2.8 Nycteris: open nose-leaves

2.9 Rhinolophus

2.10 Rhinolophus

2.11 Pipistrellus

2.12 Eptesicus

2.13 Myotis

2.14 Laephotis

2.15 Scotophilus

2.16 Miniopterus

2.17 Glauconycteris

2.18 Kerivoula

2.19 Tadarida

VESPER BATS | Family Vespertilionidae (p60)

By far the largest bat family in the southern African subregion, with at least 33 species recorded to date, although 11 species are known only from very few records. All vesper bats have simple mouse-like muzzles and lack any out-of-the-ordinary facial structures. Their ears are well developed and carry tragi, which vary in shape according to the species. The tail is completely enclosed by the interfemoral membrane, which tapers towards the tail-tip and projects backwards in a V-shape (figs. 1.6, 1.7, 1.8, page 16). The bats of this group are difficult to identify to species level.

Key features: Mouse-like faces; membrane extends to tail-tip in V-shape.

Long-fingered Bats | Subfamily Miniopterinae (p60)

Three species occur in southern Africa. The members of this subfamily are characterized by the second phalanx of the third digit being about three times as long as the first phalanx; in the other vesper bats it is not specially elongated. At present the three species can only be conclusively identified and separated by examination of various skull features, which is beyond the scope of this book.

Key feature: Second phalanx of third digit greatly elongated.

Various Vesper Bats | Subfamily Vespertilioninae (p62)

This subfamily contains 10 genera and 28 species. Members of two genera are relatively simple to place but the remainder are generally confusing and variable in appearance even within a single species. Many species occur only marginally in the subregion and are rarely encountered. The Butterfly Bat (page 68) has distinctive reticulated venation on the wings. The long-eared bats (*Laephotis*) are represented in the subregion by one to three species with very large ears which are held at an angle of 45° to the head (unlike, for example, the long ears of the slit-faced bats, which are held vertically). The hairy bats of the genus *Myotis* (page 62) can be separated from other vesper bats by their longer, more pointed muzzles and their soft, erect fur. Note, however, that the individual hairs are straight, not curled at the tip like those of the woolly bats.

Key feature: Mouse-like faces.

Woolly Bats | Subfamily Kerivoulinae (p74)

Two species occur. They are small and are characterized by a long, woolly coat, the individual hairs of which are curled at the tip, unlike that of the hairy bats (page 62). The interfemoral membrane is fringed with short hairs – a feature peculiar to this subfamily (see fig. 1.8, page 16).

Key features: Long, woolly hair; fringe of hair around tail membrane.

FREE-TAILED BATS | Family Molossidae (p74)

Of the 14 species recorded from the subregion, only four are regularly encountered. Members of the family are characterized by having the first third to half of the tail encased in the interfemoral membrane to its end, with the remainder of the tail projecting beyond the outer edge of the membrane (fig. 1.9, page 16). In the family Emballonuridae (page 50) the end of the tail is also free, but is shorter than the membrane and projects from the central area of the membrane at an angle (fig. 1.2, page 16). All but one species, the Large-eared Free-tailed Bat, have shortened faces and this is emphasized by the relatively large ears. A tragus is present but is small. Many species have distinctively wrinkled upper lips (and are often called bulldog bats; see fig. 2.19, opposite). The feet have a fringe of prominent hairs. The fur is short and flattened and usually dark brown or reddish-brown. Unlike most bats, free-tailed bats can scuttle around rapidly on walls and on the ground. Several species commonly roost in houses.

Key features: Partly free tail projecting beyond end of interfemoral membrane; wrinkled lips.

■ BABOONS, MONKEYS & BUSHBABIES
Order Primates

BABOONS & MONKEYS | Family Cercopithecidae (p78)

Three species occur in southern Africa. Two are long-tailed 'typical' monkeys – the Vervet Monkey, which is pale in colour and an open woodland dweller, and the Sykes's Monkey, darker in colour and a forest-dweller. Baboons are large in size, with dog-like muzzles, and have a marked kink in the tail about one-third of the way along its length. They are largely terrestrial but will readily climb trees. All are diurnal.

Key features: Unmistakable monkey-like appearance; diurnal.

GALAGOS (BUSHBABIES) | Family Galagidae (p84)

Three species, one of which is apparently restricted to Mozambique, occur in the subregion. All are small, slender animals, the largest being the Thick-tailed Bushbaby, with a total length of 75 cm, a long bushy tail, dense, soft fur and very large eyes. The ears are large, membranous and mobile. Its harsh, screaming call is often the only indication of its presence. The smaller species have long but less-bushy tails. All three species are nocturnal and largely arboreal.

Key features: Large eyes and ears; long furry tails; mainly arboreal; nocturnal.

■ PANGOLIN | Order Pholidota

PANGOLIN | Family Manidae (p86)

Only one species occurs in the subregion. It is quite unmistakable with its upperparts and sides covered entirely in large, hard, plate-like, brown scales.

Key feature: Body covered with large overlapping brown scales.

■ HARES & RABBITS | Order Lagomorpha

HARES & RABBITS | Family Leporidae (p88)

At least seven species occur naturally in the subregion and an eighth, the European Rabbit, has been introduced on a few offshore islands. All have short, fluffy tails but the two true hares have black-and-white tails while the rabbits have uniformly brown or reddish-brown tails. The true hares have long, well-developed hindlegs whereas those of the red rock rabbits and the Riverine Rabbit are less developed. The Riverine Rabbit is very rare and localized. All species are primarily nocturnal.

Key features: Unmistakable rabbit appearance; short, fluffy tails; long ears.

■ RODENTS | Order Rodentia

Only the rodents have the characteristic large pair of chisel-like incisor teeth at the front of both the upper and lower jaw (dassies have one pair of incisors above and two pairs below, see page 182). Rodents are very varied in size and appearance, from the 20 kg Porcupine to the 6 g Pygmy Mouse. Eighty-four species, belonging to nine families, occur in the subregion; four more have been introduced from other countries.

Key features: Two prominent pairs of large incisor teeth, one pair in upper jaw, one pair in lower jaw.

SQUIRRELS | Family Sciuridae (p92)

Five species of arboreal (tree-dwelling) and two species of partly fossorial (burrowing) squirrels occur in the subregion. They are characterized by having long, bushy tails. The arboreal species have soft hair and the burrowing species have coarse hair. Sometimes confused with much smaller (similarly bushy-tailed) dormice (page 98). All are diurnal (dormice are nocturnal).
Key features: Bushy tails; tail often held erect or curved forward over back.

DORMICE | Family Myoxidae (p98)

Four species have been recorded in the subregion. They are small, grey, mouse-like creatures with bushy, squirrel-like tails. They do not, however, sit erect or with tail raised like squirrels and they are all nocturnal in habit.
Key features: Greyish and mouse-like but with bushy tails; nocturnal.

SPRINGHARE | Family Pedetidae (p100)

This family contains two species, one in southern Africa and the other in East Africa. With its well-developed hindlegs, small forelegs and long bushy tail, it resembles a small kangaroo. Its eyes are large and its ears long. It lives in burrows in sandy soils and is nocturnal in habit.
Key features: Like miniature kangaroo; reddish-fawn colour; nocturnal.

MOLE-RATS | Family Bathyergidae (p100)

Six species of these burrowing rodents occur in the subregion. The largest is the Cape Dune Mole-rat, which has a mass of up to 750 g. The name 'mole-rat' is misleading, as these animals are neither moles nor rats. The eyes and ear openings are tiny but visible; the tail is very short and flattened. All species have short legs with long digging claws on the forefeet. They have a round, pig-like snout-tip. The fur is soft but not glossy as in golden moles (page 30). All species push up mounds or heaps of soil, unlike golden moles, which tend to raise long meandering ridges just under the soil surface.
Key features: Tiny eyes and ears; very short tail; pig-like snout-tip; obvious pair of incisor teeth; push 'mole-hills' in runs.

PORCUPINE | Family Hystricidae (p102)

Only one species occurs in southern Africa and it is unmistakable. It is the largest rodent in the subregion with a mass of up to 24 kg. The upperparts of its body are covered with long black-and-white banded flexible spines and rigid quills. It is nocturnal in habit.
Key features: Long black-and-white quills and spines; large size.

CANE-RATS | Family Thryonomyidae (p104)

Only two species found in the subregion. They are similar in general appearance with large, stocky bodies and short tails. The brown bristly body hair looks a little like short, soft quills. The Greater Cane-rat is widespread in the east where it inhabits reed-beds and other moist, well-vegetated areas; the Lesser Cane-rat will also use drier habitats. Both species are mainly nocturnal.
Key features: Large size; brown bristly, quill-like hair; moist habitats.

DASSIE RAT | Family Petromuridae (p106)

This family contains only one species, which is restricted to rocky habitats in the arid west of the subregion, north to Angola. It is somewhat squirrel-like in appearance but its tail is hairy rather than bushy. It is diurnal in habit.
Key features: Brown and squirrel-like, but tail not bushy; rocky habitat.

RATS & MICE | Family Muridae (p106)

Larger species are usually called rats and the smaller mice but there is no clear-cut distinction between the two terms. At least 64 species, in seven subfamilies and 24 genera, occur in the subregion. The majority of species are nocturnal. Three species, the House Rat, Brown Rat and the House Mouse, are alien to the subregion; they are cosmopolitan invaders associated with human settlements.

Key feature: Varied but typically mouse- and rat-like.

■ CARNIVORES | Order Carnivora

FOXES, JACKALS & WILD DOG | Family Canidae (p134)

Five canids occur in the subregion, ranging in size from the Bat-eared Fox to the Wild Dog. All have dog-like features – elongated muzzle, fairly long legs, prominent ears and variably bushy tails. They may have short hair (as in the Wild Dog) or long hair (as in the Bat-eared Fox) and all have non-retractile claws. They are mainly nocturnal in habit, except for the Wild Dog.

Key feature: Dog-like features.

OTTERS, BADGER, WEASEL & POLECAT

Family Mustelidae (p140)

Five species of mustelid are found in southern Africa. They are small to medium-sized carnivores. The two otter species are associated mainly with aquatic habitats, and have heavy, broad-based, rudder-like tails. Both the Striped Weasel, with its short legs and sinuous body, and the Striped Polecat, have distinctive black-and-white striping along the back, while the Honey Badger has silvery-coloured upperparts and black underparts. All species are mainly nocturnal.

Key features: Varied but distinctive group of carnivores: see species accounts.

MONGOOSES, GENETS & CIVETS | Families Herpestidae,

Viverridae and Nandiniidae (pp144, 158, 162)

These families are varied and have 18 southern African representatives: one civet, one palm civet, possibly four genets and 12 mongooses. They are small to medium-sized carnivores (260 g to 15 kg) with relatively long bodies and muzzles. Most species have medium to long, well-haired tails. The civets and genets are spotted. The mongooses and most civets are terrestrial (the Palm Civet is mainly arboreal) and the genets are at least partly arboreal. Most members of these families have nocturnal habits, but several mongooses are diurnal.

Key features: Varied but distinctive group of carnivores; long bodies, long muzzles and disproportionately short legs (except for the civet).

HYAENAS & AARDWOLF | Family Hyaenidae (pp162, 166)

(Family Protelidae often applied to Aardwolf)

Two species of Hyaena and the Aardwolf occur in the subregion. The hyaenas are moderately large carnivores but the Aardwolf is considerably smaller (and is often placed in its own family, the Protelidae). The Spotted Hyaena has a distinctive short, spotted coat and rounded ears, and its hindquarters are lower than its shoulders. The Aardwolf and Brown Hyaena have long hair, the former with vertical black body stripes. Predominantly nocturnal.

Key feature: Appear higher at the shoulder than at the rump.

CATS | Family Felidae (p168)

Seven species occur naturally in the subregion and an eighth, the domestic cat, takes readily to the wild. All are highly specialized carnivores with short muzzles and, except in the case of Cheetah, have fully retractile claws. They range in size

from the 1.5 kg Small Spotted Cat to the 225 kg Lion. Most smaller species are nocturnal, as is the Leopard, but the Lion is partly diurnal and the Cheetah predominantly so.
Key features: All have short muzzles and typically cat-like faces.

▌AARDVARK | Order Tubulidentata

AARDVARK | Family Orycteropodidae (p178)
There is only one species in this order. It cannot be confused with any other mammal, with its large size (up to 65 kg), arched back, long, pig-like snout and very heavy tail and legs. The ears are long and mule-like.
Key features: Large; pig-like; arched back; elongated snout.

▌ELEPHANT | Order Proboscidea

ELEPHANT | Family Elephantidae (p180)
A single species in the region and the largest land mammal. Unmistakable.

▌DASSIES (HYRAXES) | Order Hyracoidea

DASSIES (HYRAXES) | Family Procaviidae (p182)
At least two rock-dwelling and one tree-living species occur in the subregion. Small (up to 4.6 kg), stoutly built animals, with short legs, small rounded ears and no tail. The muzzle is pointed and they have well-developed incisors, one pair above and two pairs below. Rodents have one pair above, one pair below. Often called 'rock rabbits', although they have no relationship with rabbits.
Key features: Stocky build; tailless; small patch of different-coloured hair in centre of back.

▌ODD-TOED UNGULATES | Order Perissodactyla

ZEBRAS | Family Equidae (p188)
Two species occur in the subregion. Both are boldly striped in black and white but where Plains Zebra has a 'shadow' stripe in the white stripes, particularly on its hindquarters, this feature is absent in the Mountain Zebra. A dewlap on the throat and grid-iron pattern on the rump also distinguish the Mountain Zebra from the Plains Zebra.
Key features: Horse-like; striped in black and white.

RHINOCEROSES | Family Rhinocerotidae (p190)
The two species of the subregion are easy to separate on size and the structure of the lips. The Hook-lipped (Black) Rhinoceros is a browser with a hooked, prehensile upper lip; the Square-lipped (White) Rhinoceros is a grazer with broad, squared-off upper and lower lips. Both species carry two horns on the front of the head and are almost hairless.
Key features: Large size; two horns, one above the other on front of head.

EVEN-TOED UNGULATES

▌PIGS & HOGS | Order Suiformes | Family Suidae (p194)

Two species, Warthog and Bushpig, occur in southern Africa. Both are clearly recognizable as pigs. The head has a typically elongated, mobile snout, and the Warthog carries large, curved tusk-like canines. Separated largely by habitat – Warthog preferring open woodland savanna and Bushpig favouring denser cover. The Warthog is diurnal in habit and the Bushpig is nocturnal.
Key feature: Pig-like.

■ HIPPOPOTAMUS | Order **Whippomorpha**
Suborder Ancodonta

HIPPOPOTAMUSES | Family Hippopotamidae (p198)

Order Whippomorpha
includes Whales and
Dolphins (see page 26).

Only one of the two hippopotamus species occurs in the subregion. It is distinctively large with a massive head and a barrel-shaped body. It usually spends the day in water, emerging after dark to feed.
Key features: Large, barrel-shaped body; aquatic habitat.

■ EVEN-TOED UNGULATES | Order **Ruminantia**

GIRAFFE | Family Giraffidae (p200)
A single species, with greatly elongated neck and legs.
Key features: Unmistakable; large size and very long neck.

BUFFALO & ANTELOPES | Family Bovidae (p202)
This large family is represented in southern Africa by 33 indigenous species. All have cloven or centrally split hoofs. The males of all species carry horns, as do the females of slightly less than half of the species. Most live in herds of varying size but a number of the smaller species lead more solitary lives. There are ten subfamilies and tribes, as described below.
Key features: Cloven hoofs; all males carry horns.

There is some dispute
among taxonomists
as to whether the
subgroups of Bovidae
belong in subfamilies
or tribes. We have
supplied both.

Buffalo, Eland, Kudu, Nyala, Sitatunga, Bushbuck |
Subfamily Bovinae (Tribes Bovini and Tragelaphini) (p202)
Six species of this subfamily occur in the subregion. The Buffalo is unmistakable, uniformly coloured and cow-like. The other five species, known as tragelaphine antelopes, range from medium to very large in size. There is a crest of long hair, least noticeable in the Eland, along the neck and back. Only males of tragelaphine antelopes have horns – except for Eland where the females are also horned; horns are always spirally twisted and ridged at front and back; they are never ringed. Body colour varies from grey through to chestnut-brown but all tragelaphines have white stripes or spots to a greater or lesser extent, and thus differ from other antelopes.
Key features: Buffalo uniformly coloured and cow-like; colour generally variable but white spots or stripes usually present on body, unlike other antelope. Males of tragelaphine antelopes have spirally twisted horns (female Eland is the exception).

Roan, Sable & Gemsbok | Subfamily Antilopinae
(Tribe Hippotragini) (p212)
Three species of this subfamily occur in the subregion. They are large antelope with well-developed horns in both sexes. Horns are straight and rapier-like in the Gemsbok; sabre-like and backwardly curving in the other two species, and are distinctly ringed. All three species have a long, tufted tail and distinctive black-and-white facial markings.
Key features: Large size; distinctive horns; black-and-white facial markings.

Waterbuck, Lechwe, Puku, Reedbuck, Grey Rhebok
Subfamily Reduncinae (Tribe Reduncini) (p216)
Six species of this subfamily occur in the subregion. They range from medium to large in size. They are generally heavily built and only the males carry horns. These curve back, up and then forward, and are strongly ringed. The Grey Rhebok is restricted to South Africa, Swaziland and Lesotho. It is of medium size and only the male has short erect horns, ringed for about half their length.

Key features: Horn form of males; association with watery or damp habitats (except in case of Mountain Reedbuck). Rhebok has grey body; white underparts; straight, erect, short horns.

Wildebeest, Hartebeest, Bontebok/Blesbok & Tsessebe
Subfamily Alcelaphinae (Tribe Alcelaphini) (p224)
Six species of this subfamily occur in the subregion: two wildebeest, two hartebeest, the Tsessebe and the Bontebok/Blesbok. They are medium to large antelope, with shoulders higher than the rump and with a long, narrow face. Each species has a distinctive horn structure and both sexes have horns. They are usually found in herds on the open plains or ecotone (zone) of woodland and grassland.

Key features: Back slopes down towards rump; long faces.

Impala | Subfamily Aepycerotinae (Tribe Aepycerotini) (p232)
This subfamily has only one member, the Impala. It is of medium size and slender build. Only the males carry the slender, well-ringed, lyre-shaped horns. It is the only antelope with a tuft of black hair just above the ankle-joint of each hindleg.

Key features: Medium size; males with lyrate horns; characteristic tuft of black hair on each hindleg above ankle-joint.

Gazelles & Dwarf Antelope | (Tribe Antilopini; Tribe Oreotragini: Klipspringer; Tribe Neotragini: Suni) (p234)
Eight species of this subfamily (Springbok, Dik-dik, Steenbok, Oribi, Klipspringer, Suni, Cape Grysbok and Sharpe's Grysbok) occur in the subregion. The Springbok, whose male and female both carry horns, is placed in a separate tribe from the other seven species, only the males of which possess horns. Springbok congregate in herds but the other species live singly or in small family parties. The Steenbok, Oribi and Springbok prefer open habitat; the Klipspringer is found only in rocky areas; and the other four species show a preference for well-wooded or bushy habitats.

Key features: Small species, except for medium-sized Springbok. Diverse in habit and habitat. See species accounts.

Duikers | Subfamily Cephalophinae | (Tribe Cephalophini) (p244)
Three species of this subfamily occur in the subregion, of which two are forest or dense-bush dwellers while the third prefers more open bush country. The two forest species are small and have arched backs and short, back-pointing horns in both sexes. There is a distinct tuft of hair present between the horns of all species. The Common Duiker has a straight back and is longer in the leg; only the male carries horns. All three species have short tails. All usually occur solitarily or in pairs.

Key features: Small size; skulking habits; tuft of hair between ears.

DEER | Family Cervidae (p246)
Although several species of deer have been introduced to South Africa, only the Fallow Deer is numerous enough to warrant mention here. It has been widely distributed to game-farms and private estates throughout the country. Only the males carry the bony antlers, which are

shed and regrown annually. While growing, the antlers are covered by skin richly supplied with blood-vessels and are said to be 'in velvet'.

Key features: Males carry branched and palmate antlers for much of the year; females lack antlers; summer coat deep fawn with white spots.

MARINE MAMMALS

■ SEALS | **Order Carnivora**
(Although seals are classified in Order Carnivora, in this book they have been placed before Suborder Cetacea under a heading of convenience: 'Marine Mammals').

FUR SEALS | Family Otariidae (p248)
Three species of this family occur in the subregion, one as a resident, the others as rare vagrants. Their hind flippers can be turned forward under the body when moving on land. They possess small but clearly visible ears.

Key features: Hind flippers can be turned forwards on land; small ears present.

TRUE SEALS | Family Phocidae (p250)
Four species of 'true' seal occur as very rare vagrants off the southern African coastline. They lack external ears and their hind flippers cannot bend forward under the body. Southern Elephant Seal male has a prominent, bulbous proboscis.

Key features: Hind flippers cannot be turned forwards; no external ears.

■ WHALES & DOLPHINS | **Order Whippomorpha**
Suborder Cetacea

All of our 41 whales and dolphins – known collectively as cetaceans – fall into one of two infraorders: the Odontoceti, which includes the toothed whales and dolphins, and the Mysticeti, or baleen whales.

Hippopotamuses (see page 24) are also now included in Order Whippomorpha.

The toothed whales have a single nostril or blowhole, and the baleen whales have two. Whales and dolphins differ a great deal in shape, size, coloration and markings. In addition, as they are mammals, they must surface periodically to breathe and, in the case of the great whales, the 'blow' or spout can be used to aid identification (see page 28). The blow is not composed of water, as some people think, but is a cloud of vapour produced by condensation when the whale's warm breath – forcibly expelled on surfacing – comes into contact with the cooler air. Although baleen whales have two blowholes, not all produce a V-shaped spout; the rorquals, for example, tend to produce a single spout. All species have the ability to remain under water for long periods but the Sperm Whale is the master ot this art and is able to dive to great depths for up to 90 minutes.

The baleen whales are so-named from the great plates of baleen that hang from the roof of the mouth. Baleen is composed of keratin – the horny material of which human hair and fingernails are composed – and grows in long, thin, closely layered plates. The outer edges of the plates are smooth and the inner edges are frayed into interlocking strands. Baleen whales feed on plankton and can be separated into two groups, the 'gulpers' and the 'skimmers', each with different feeding behaviour. The gulpers take huge 'bites' of sea-water, then strain the plankton through the baleen plates by expelling the water through the sides of the mouth; the plankton residue is then licked off by the large tongue. The skimmers swim with their mouths open, filtering the water until enough plankton has accumulated on the baleen to be scraped off and swallowed. The Sei Whale uses a combination of both methods.

The toothed whales take a wide variety of food, which includes squid, fish and crustaceans. The only true flesh-eater is the Killer Whale.

Social behaviour in this interesting group is poorly known. Some species are thought to be solitary, others move in small groups or 'pods', while several species may congregate in schools of several hundreds or even thousands.

The toothed whales and dolphins, in particular, have highly developed communication faculties, based on the emission of clicks and whistles, some ranging beyond the limits of audible human perception. The Humpback Whale, which has been intensively studied, has an amazingly complex repertoire of sounds. The toothed whales also use their calls for echolocation, to pinpoint their fish and squid prey, but this ability has not yet been shown to exist in the baleen whales. There is no doubt that, as a group, the cetaceans are highly intelligent, but the level of their intelligence is still the subject of considerable debate and argument among scientists.

Whales and dolphins usually give birth to a single, well-developed young that can immediately follow its mother. Gestation periods vary between 9 and 16 months; relatively short when one considers the size of the adults. Young whales do not suckle; the milk is squirted directly into their mouths.

As whales and dolphins are usually only fleetingly seen, it is important to take note of the following points to assist in identification:
1. Overall size (length) – small, medium or large.
2. Dorsal fin – present or absent; size, shape and position.
3. Blow (air exhalation) – single or double spout; estimated height.
4. Tail flukes – shape; markings.
5. Body patterns or markings.
6. Body shape and general colour.
7. Jumping or breaching – the form it takes.
8. Presence of other whales and size of group or pod.

Baleen or Whalebone Whales | Infraorder Mysticeti
Nine species of baleen whales have been recorded off the coasts of southern Africa, ranging in size from the 6-metre-long Pygmy Right Whale to the 33-m Blue Whale – the largest mammal that has ever existed.

RORQUALS (PLEATED WHALES) | Family Balaenopteridae (p254)
Six of the seven baleen whales in southern African waters belong to this family. They are long, slender and streamlined and have flattened heads, pointed flippers and a small, back-curved dorsal fin set far back along the body. They are characterized by a large number of grooves or pleats running longitudinally from the throat and chest to the upper abdomen; these grooves allow for the massive expansions and contractions of the whale's mouth as it first engulfs its prey, then expels the water while sieving out the food organisms through the baleen plates. The other baleen whales (see below) have smooth, ungrooved throats.
Key features: Large size; back-curved dorsal fin; diagnostic longitudinal throat grooves.

RIGHT WHALES | Families Balaenidae and Neobalaenidae (p258)
The right whales, of which two species, the Southern Right and the Pygmy Right, occur in southern African waters, were so-called because they are slow-moving and hence were easily caught by the early whalers; when killed they floated, allowing the whalers to tow the carcasses to land. They were the 'right' whales to hunt. They are characterized by their large heads with arched jaw-line and smooth, ungrooved throat. The larger of the two species, the Southern Right Whale, has a smooth back lacking any fin or hump.
Key features: Large size; smooth, ungrooved throat; dorsal fin only in smaller of two species.

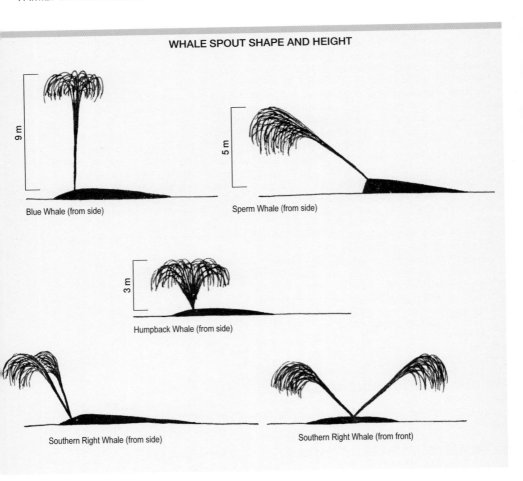

WHALE SPOUT SHAPE AND HEIGHT

9 m — Blue Whale (from side)

5 m — Sperm Whale (from side)

3 m — Humpback Whale (from side)

Southern Right Whale (from side)

Southern Right Whale (from front)

Toothed Whales & Dolphins | Infraorder Odontoceti

Thirty-one species of toothed whales and dolphins have been recorded off the coasts of southern Africa. The smallest of these appears to be Heaviside's Dolphin with a total length of 1.3 m. The largest is the Sperm Whale, with a total length of over 15 m. The two nasal cavities of the toothed whales fuse to form a single blowhole, unlike those of the baleen whales, which open separately (although situated together). All toothed whales have teeth, but the number is variable, from two in some of the beaked whales to over 120 in the Long-snouted Dolphin. In the beaked whales, the teeth of the females do not normally erupt through the gums.

BEAKED WHALES | Family Ziphiidae (p260)

Nine species of beaked whales have been recorded from southern African waters but most are known from very few specimens and sightings. All members of this family are distinguished by having two grooves on the throat, which converge (but do not meet) to form a V-shape, and the males have either one or two pairs of prominent teeth on the lower jaw and none in the upper jaw. The form, position and number of the teeth are important characteristics in identifying the different species. In all nine species, with the exception of Arnoux's Beaked Whale, the females are apparently toothless in that the teeth do not erupt from the gums. The flippers are small and the dorsal fin is usually prominent and set well back on the body. The tail-flukes do not have a central notch. All species are also characterized by a more or less developed bulbous swelling on the forehead and head, known as a 'melon'. Most are extremely difficult to identify to species level when seen at sea.

Key features: Between 4 and 9 m long; prominent 'beak' and bulbous forehead; prominent dorsal fin; one or two pairs of teeth in males only.

SPERM WHALES | Family Physeteridae (p266)

There is only one species in this family, and it is regularly recorded from subregion waters. It has a distinctly blunt and squared head. Functional teeth occur on the lower jaw but very rarely on the upper jaw. The head contains the spermaceti organ, whose white waxy product is believed to assist in regulating buoyancy when deep diving and perhaps also to focus sound used by the whales in echolocation.

Key features: Blunt, square head; dorsal fin present in two smaller species.

PYGMY & DWARF SPERM WHALES | Family Kogiidae (p266)

These small whales have well-developed spermaceti organs, as is found in their larger cousin, and distinct dorsal fins. Teeth are present only on the lower jaw.

Key features: Blunt, square head; dorsal fin present; small size.

WHALE DOLPHINS, PILOT WHALES, KILLER & FALSE KILLER WHALES | Family Delphinidae (p268)

Of the 20 species of this family recorded from the coastal waters of the subregion, only a handful are regularly seen close inshore. Lengths vary from 1.3 m to 8 m. All have long, more or less centrally situated dorsal fins, with the exception of the Southern Right Whale Dolphin, which lacks the fin. Members of the family are typically slender and sleek; nine species have a well-developed beak (mostly the smaller species), three have a short beak and seven have no beak and somewhat globose heads. All have numerous teeth in both jaws except for Risso's Dolphin, which lacks teeth in the upper jaw.

Key features: Numerous teeth in both jaws (except Risso's Dolphin); dorsal fin present (except Southern Right Whale Dolphin).

DUGONG | Order Sirenia

DUGONG | Family Dugongidae (p284)

One species occurs in the subregion. It is a marine but strictly coastal mammal with a long cigar-shaped body. Its forelimbs are paddle-like flippers and its boneless tail is broad and horizontally flattened. The snout is broad, rounded and well bristled. It could be confused with seals but the head shape is quite different. Less agile than seals.

Key features: Large (3-m) body; large blunt head; bristles around mouth.

GOLDEN MOLES | Order Afrosoricida

GOLDEN MOLES | Family Chrysochloridae

■ *Chrysospalax trevelyani*
■ *Chrysospalax villosus*
■ *Cryptochloris wintoni*
■ *Cryptochloris zyli*
■ *Chrysochloris visagiei*

■ *Chrysochloris asiatica*
■ *Eremitalpa granti*
■ *Carpitalpa arendsi*
■ *Chlorotalpa duthieae*

■ *Chlorotalpa sclateri*
■ *Calcochloris*
  obtusirostris
■ *Neamblysomus*
  gunningi
■ *Neamblysomus*
  julianae

The golden moles are endemic to Africa south of the Sahara, with 18 species occurring in southern Africa. Material records for several species are scanty, however, with Van Zyl's Golden Mole and Visagie's Golden Mole each being known from only a single specimen. The biology of all the golden moles is poorly known. They are all basically similar in appearance, with no visible eyes, no external ear pinnae and no external tails. The golden moles are not related to the rodent moles (mole-rats) (page 100). The latter are rodents, and have small but visible eyes, short tails, massively developed incisor teeth on both the upper and lower jaw and five claws on each forefoot.

■ **Giant Golden Mole** *Chrysospalax trevelyani*
Total length 23 cm; mass 538 g.
■ **Rough-haired Golden Mole** *Chrysospalax villosus*
Total length 15 cm; mass 125 g.
■ **De Winton's Golden Mole** *Cryptochloris wintoni*
Total length 9 cm.
■ **Van Zyl's Golden Mole** *Cryptochloris zyli*
Total length 8 cm.
■ **Cape Golden Mole** *Chrysochloris asiatica*
Total length 11 cm.
■ **Visagie's Golden Mole** *Chrysochloris visagiei* (cf. *C. asiatica*)
Total length 10,5 cm.
■ **Grant's Golden Mole** *Eremitalpa granti*
Total length 7 cm; mass 16–30 g.
■ **Arends's Golden Mole** *Carpitalpa arendsi*
Total length 12 cm; mass 40–76 g.
■ **Duthie's Golden Mole** *Chlorotalpa duthieae*
Total length 10 cm.
■ **Sclater's Golden Mole** *Chlorotalpa sclateri*
Total length 10 cm.
■ **Yellow Golden Mole** *Calcochloris obtusirostris*
Total length 10 cm; mass 20–30 g.
■ **Gunning's Golden Mole** *Neamblysomus gunningi*
Total length 12 cm.
■ **Juliana's Golden Mole** *Neamblysomus julianae*
Total length 10 cm; mass 21–23 g.
■ **Hottentot Golden Mole** *Amblysomus hottentotus*
Total length 13 cm; mass 75 g.

The genus *Amblysomus* has 5 recognized species, falling within the range of what used to be taken as just *Amblysomus hottentotus*. All are very similar in external appearance and their exact distribution limits have still to be defined. Use distribution map (see page 32) to aid identification.
■ **Fynbos Golden Mole** *Amblysomus corriae*
Range: Humansdorp to Cape Town
■ **Highveld Golden Mole** *Amblysomus septentrionalis*
Range: north-east Free State to south-east Mpumalanga
■ **Hottentot Golden Mole** *Amblysomus hottentotus*
Range: Eastern Cape into KwaZulu-Natal

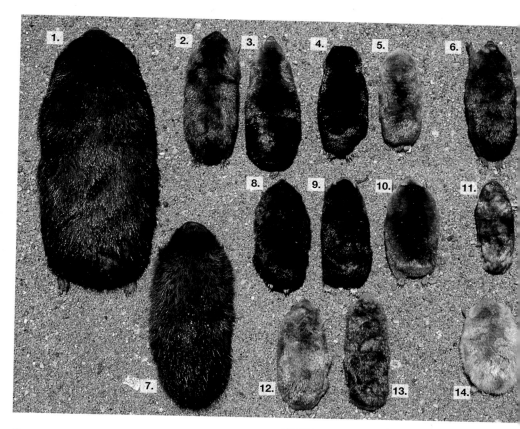

Key to Golden Mole skins

1. Giant Golden Mole
2. Cape Golden Mole
3. Hottentot Golden Mole
4. Gunning's Golden Mole
5. Zulu Golden Mole
6. Juliana's Golden Mole
7. Rough-haired Golden Mole

8. Arends's Golden Mole
9. Duthie's Golden Mole
10. Sclater's Golden Mole
11. Yellow Golden Mole
12. De Winton's Golden Mole
13. Van Zyl's Golden Mole
14. Grant's Golden Mole

Right: *Front foot of Golden Mole* (above) *and Mole-rat* (below), *showing difference in toes and claws.*

Grant's Golden Mole has a total length of just 7cm.

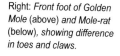

Giant Golden Mole

Grant's Golden Mole

31

■ *Amblysomus corriae*
■ *Amblysomus septentrionalis*
■ *Amblysomus hottentotus*
■ *Amblysomus marleyi*
■ *Amblysomus robustus*
□ *Amblysomus* spp. not yet determined
■ Area of overlap

■ **Marley's Golden Mole** *Amblysomus marleyi*
Range: Lebombo Mountains, northern KwaZulu-Natal
■ **Robust Golden Mole** *Amblysomus robustus*
Range: Steenkamps Range, eastern Mpumalanga
Identification pointers: All golden moles lack external tails, and have no visible eyes or external ears. Only two, the Giant and the Rough-haired Golden Moles, have long coarse hair; the others have soft, silky hair. The forefeet carry four claws, of which the third is particularly well developed. The teeth are small and pointed, unlike the heavy chisel-like teeth of the mole-rats. The snouts are tipped with a leathery pad and unlike the pig-like snout of the mole-rats. With the exception of a few species, the golden moles do not push up heaps or mounds like the mole-rats, but long, meandering ridges just under the surface.
Description: Only descriptions of the more widespread or distinctive species are given below:
Giant Golden Mole: Long, coarse hair; upperparts dark glossy-brown with paler underparts; small, light-coloured patches at sites of eyes and ears.
Rough-haired Golden Mole: Long, coarse hair; similar to Giant Golden Mole but has greyer underparts, and the sides of the face and top of the muzzle are pale grey.
De Winton's and Grant's Golden Moles: Both species are similar, their upperparts being pale yellowish to yellow-grey, with paler underparts.
Cape Golden Mole: Upperparts dark brown with changing sheen of purple, green and bronze; paler, duller underparts. Pale eye-spots, with pale-brown line running from each spot to pale-brown chin.
Sclater's Golden Mole: A rich glossy red-brown to dark brown above, with dull grey underparts with a reddish tinge; chin paler than rest of body.
Duthie's Golden Mole: Very dark, almost black, with distinct green sheen; pale, triangular cheek-patches.
Hottentot Golden Mole: Usually rich reddish-brown upperparts with bronze sheen; underparts lighter with grey tinge; cheeks very pale; top of muzzle greyish-brown. Wherever possible a specimen should be submitted to a natural history museum for confirmation of an identification. However, the use of the distribution maps will assist in narrowing down the number of species involved in any particular area.
Distribution: Consult the distribution maps as most species have very restricted distributions. For example, De Winton's Golden Mole is only known from Port Nolloth on the west coast of South Africa; Van Zyl's Golden Mole has also only been collected at one site on the west coast; Visagie's Golden Mole is known from a solitary specimen taken in the western Karoo. There is some doubt as to the validity of several of these species. Grant's Golden Mole is restricted to a narrow belt of sand-dunes in the Namib Desert. Both Gunning's Golden Mole and Juliana's Golden Mole also have extremely restricted distribution ranges.
Habitat: The Giant Golden Mole has a very patchy and limited distribution as it occurs only in the relict areas of indigenous high forest in the Eastern Cape. Gunning's Golden Mole is also associated with forested areas. By far the vast majority of species are associated with sandy soils, although the Hottentot Golden Mole, as well as a few other species, may also utilize clay or loamy soils. Duthie's Golden Mole has a broad habitat range, extending into montane areas. None of the species are able to cope with heavy clay soils.
Behaviour: All golden moles are subterranean dwellers, although foraging on the surface may be commoner than is generally believed. Certainly Grant's Golden Mole spends much of its nocturnal foraging time moving about above ground. Because of this habit, many fall prey to owls and other predators. As far as is

The Hottentot Golden Mole, as with most smaller golden moles, has a distinctive fur sheen.

The Cape Golden Mole has pale eye-spots, with a pale-brown line running to the chin.

known, all species have deeper-running, permanent tunnels, with the surface tunnels being purely for foraging. The Giant Golden Mole pushes mounds with soil removed from newly excavated burrows, in much the same way as the mole-rats. The Rough-haired Golden Mole creates both surface tunnels and loose mounds, the latter always having an opening.

Although some species may be nocturnal, at least several actively forage during the day. Where they occur in gardens they are usually considered a nuisance because of the soil disturbance but they are valuable allies as they eat large quantities of potentially harmful insects and other invertebrates. Virtually nothing is known about their social structure or general behaviour.

Food: All species feed on insects and other invertebrates. The Giant Golden Mole apparently feeds mainly on giant earthworms (*Microchaetus* spp.). Several (if not all) species also eat small reptiles, particularly legless lizards and worm-snakes that share their underground habitat.

Reproduction: From the meagre records it would seem that litters consist of either 1 or 2 young, born naked and helpless. Young are probably born during the rainy season when food is most abundant. At least some species have been recorded as breeding in cooler, drier months.

SENGIS (Elephant-shrews) | Order Macroscelidea

■ *Petrodromus*
  tetradactylus
■ *Macroscelides*
  proboscideus

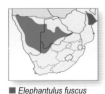

■ *Elephantulus fuscus*
■ *Elephantulus intufi*

■ *Elephantulus*
  brachyrhynchus
■ *Elephantulus rupestris*

SENGIS (ELEPHANT-SHREWS) | Family Macroscelididae

Elephant-shrews originally derived their name from their elongated, trunk-like snout, but the name is unfortunate and they are more correctly called Sengis, as they are not related to either elephants or shrews. The hindlegs and feet are considerably longer than the forelegs and -feet and rapid locomotion is achieved by a series of hops.

Four-toed Sengi *Petrodromus tetradactylus*
Total length 35 cm; tail 16 cm; mass 160–280 g.

Round-eared Sengi *Macroscelides proboscideus*
Total length 23 cm; tail 12 cm; mass 31–47 g.

Peters's Short-snouted Sengi *Elephantulus fuscus*
Total length 21 cm.

Short-snouted Sengi *Elephantulus brachyrhynchus*
Total length 21 cm; tail 10 cm; mass 44 g.

Western Rock Sengi *Elephantulus rupestris*
Total length 28 cm; tail 15 cm; mass 65 g.

Bushveld Sengi *Elephantulus intufi*
Total length 24 cm; tail 12 cm; mass 50 g.

Eastern Rock Sengi *Elephantulus myurus*
Total length 26 cm; tail 14 cm; mass 60 g.

Cape Rock Sengi *Elephantulus edwardii*
Total length 25 cm; tail 13 cm; mass 50 g.

Identification pointers: Elongated, highly mobile snout – nostrils at tip; large thin ears; tail fairly long and sparsely haired; large eyes. Apart from Four-toed Sengi and Round-eared Sengi, the other species are generally difficult to tell apart in the field. Use distribution maps; note habitat preferences.

Description: Four-toed Sengi easily distinguished by its large size. From head to base of tail the back is reddish-brown; sides are grey to grey-brown; white ring around eye; white patch at each ear base; underparts are white. Round-eared

Bushveld Sengi.

Four-toed Sengi.

Round-eared Sengi.

Short-snouted Sengi.

Eastern Rock Sengi.

Four-toed Sengi   Bushveld Sengi

■ *Elephantulus myurus*
■ *Elephantulus edwardii*

Sengi is one of smallest; variable in colour, but most commonly brownish-grey above, paler below; sometimes whitish-grey in colour; no white eye-ring. All other species have white or greyish-white rings around eyes. The three rock elephant-shrews, two short-snouted elephant-shrews, and the Bushveld Sengi have reddish-brown to brown patches at base of ears. Colour of upperparts varies considerably in all species. Underparts are always paler than the upperparts.

Distribution: See maps.

Habitat: Habitat preferences taken together with geographical locality are of considerable help in the identification of members of this group. The Four-toed Sengi is a forest species, associated with fairly dense undergrowth, usually in high-rainfall areas. Three species, the Eastern Rock Sengi, Cape Rock Sengi and Western Rock Sengi, are restricted to rocky environments and their distributions do not overlap. The Short-snouted Sengi, Peters's Short-snouted Sengi and the Bushveld Sengi occur in areas with sandy soils. Although the Eastern Rock Sengi and the Short-snouted Sengi occur in the same geographical areas, they are clearly separated by their habitat requirements.

Behaviour: All of the sengis are almost entirely diurnal, although the Round-eared Sengi may be partly nocturnal. They are all terrestrial and usually solitary, but in areas of high density, several animals may be observed in close proximity to one another. The rock-dwelling species keep to the shade of overhanging rocks and boulders during the hot midday hours, making occasional dashes to seize an insect. Those species relying more on bush or grass cover generally have regularly used pathways between shelters. The pathways tend to consist of evenly spaced, well-worn patches, a result of their rapid, hopping gait. Those species associated with sandy soil usually live in burrows. Although sengis are not particularly vocal, they do communicate regularly by rapid tapping of the hind feet to the ground. This serves to warn of the presence of a predator or other threat, as well as in conflict situations between individuals.

Food: All sengis eat insects and other invertebrates, with a marked preference for ants and termites. At least two of the rock-dwelling sengis will, on occasion, forage for insects attracted to the dung middens of Hyrax (Dassies) and Red Rock Rabbits (*Pronolagus*). In captivity, several species readily eat seed and other vegetable matter and it is possible that these items are included in their natural diet. Round-eared Sengis are known to eat a great deal of vegetation, including leaves, flowers and seeds. At certain times of the year this may make up between 50 and 90 per cent of their diet. Up to half the food intake of the Short-snouted Sengi is made up of plant parts, especially green leaves.

Reproduction: The young of all species are born fully haired with their eyes open and are able to move around shortly after birth. Litter of 1–2 young born usually in association with the rainy season, but some throughout the year. At least some species form monogamous pairs within greatly overlapping home ranges. The Cape Rock Sengi gives birth from November to January on the western escarpment of South Africa. By far the majority of females drop twins.

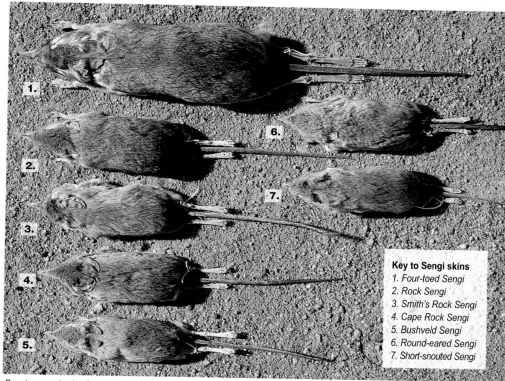

Key to Sengi skins
1. Four-toed Sengi
2. Rock Sengi
3. Smith's Rock Sengi
4. Cape Rock Sengi
5. Bushveld Sengi
6. Round-eared Sengi
7. Short-snouted Sengi

Sengis range in size from the 35-cm-long Four-toed Sengi to the 21-cm-long Short-snounted Sengi, as these skins show.

Western Rock Sengi.

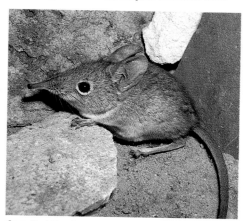

Cape Rock Sengi.

Western Rock Sengi

7 mm

Front   Back

37

HEDGEHOGS & SHREWS | Order Eulipotyphla

HEDGEHOGS | Family Erinaceidae

Atelerix frontalis

■ Southern African Hedgehog *Atelerix frontalis*

Total length 20 cm; tail 2 cm; mass 400 g.

Identification pointers: Small size; covered in short spines; pointed face; white stripe from ear to ear across forehead.

Description: The Hedgehog's upperparts are covered with short but strong sharp spines. These spines extend from the forehead and the area just in front of the ears over the back to the rump. Although there is some variation, the spines are usually white at the base and tip with a dark-brown or black band in between. The face, legs and tail are covered in dark to grey-brown hair. The underparts vary widely in colour from off-white to black. A prominent white band of hair extends across the forehead down beyond each ear. Contrary to popular belief, Hedgehogs have quite long legs, but this is only revealed when they move rapidly.

Distribution: Two populations, possibly linked, occur in southern Africa; one in Namibia and the other extending from the eastern part of the Eastern Cape north into Zimbabwe and eastern Botswana. However, recent records show that the Hedgehog occurs further west into the Northern Cape than previously thought, including the dry pan country from Van Wyksvlei to Brandvlei, between Bo-Karoo and the Kaiingveld. Outside the area covered by this field guide, it occurs in south-western Angola in a continuation of the Namibian population.

Habitat: Occurs in a wide variety of habitats, excluding desert and high-rainfall areas. To date it has not been recorded from regions receiving >800 mm of rain per year, as its habitat must provide suitable dry cover for lying up during the day.

Behaviour: Mainly nocturnal, although they are known to emerge during the day at the start of the rainy season. During the day they rest among dry vegetation or in the burrows of other species. Fixed resting-places are only used by females with young and by hibernating animals. At other times they use different sites. Hedgehogs hibernate chiefly between the winter months of May to July with peak activity occurring during the warmer, wetter months. They are nearly always solitary, only coming together to mate, or when a female is accompanied by young. The Hedgehog has an excellent sense of smell, as well as good hearing but its eyesight is poor. When disturbed or threatened it curls itself into a tight ball with the spines protecting the vulnerable head and underparts.

Food: The Hedgehog eats a wide variety of foods, including insects, millipedes, earthworms, mice, lizards, fungi and certain fruits. It eats approximately 30 per cent of its body weight in one night of feeding.

Reproduction: The young, weighing 9–11 g, are born during the summer months after a gestation period of about 35 days. Newborn Hedgehogs are blind and only the tips of the infant spines are visible. At about 6 weeks they have replaced the infant spines with a full covering of adult spines and it is at this time that they start to go foraging with the mother. Litters may contain 1–9 young, with an average of 4.

General: Although the spiny coat is adequate protection against many predators, including Lion, Hedgehogs are a favourite prey of Verreaux's (Giant) Eagle Owl (*Bubo lacteus*). Predation by humans for food or the alleged medicinal properties of the skin and spines occurs in some districts. Some areas have recorded a decline in Hedgehog numbers in recent years, due to a number of factors, including road mortality, predation by humans, capture for pets, detrimental agricultural practices and, possibly, climatic factors such as extended droughts.

The Southern African Hedgehog is mainly nocturnal, but is known to emerge during the day at the start of the rainy season.

When disturbed, the Hedgehog curls into a tight ball.

Some Hedgehogs have a pale patch below the eye.

Southern African Hedgehog

± 26 mm

Front   *Back*

39

SHREWS | Family Soricidae

Small, short-legged, mouse-like mammals, with long wedge-shaped snouts and very small eyes. Four genera – *Myosorex*, *Crocidura*, *Suncus* and *Sylvisorex* – with 18 species, are presently recognized as occurring in the subregion.

Forest Shrews Genus *Myosorex*

■ *Mysorex longicaudatus*
■ *Mysorex sclateri*

Mysorex cafer

Mysorex varius

Four species of forest shrew occur in southern Africa:
■ **Long-tailed Forest Shrew** *Myosorex longicaudatus*
Total length 15 cm; tail 6 cm.
■ **Dark-footed Forest Shrew** *Myosorex cafer*
Total length 12 cm; tail 4 cm; mass 9–16 g.
■ **Sclater's Forest Shrew** *Myosorex sclateri*
Total length 14 cm; tail 5 cm.
■ **Forest Shrew** *Myosorex varius*
Total length 12 cm; tail 4 cm; mass 12–16 g.
Identification pointers: Long-tailed Forest Shrew restricted to small area of southern South Africa; overlaps with Forest Shrew but has longer tail. Area of overlap of the two shorter-tailed species is limited to eastern coastal belt and the eastern escarpment of the north-east.

Description: Long-tailed Forest Shrew is dark brown to black in colour, with slightly paler underparts. Main distinguishing character is long tail which is black-brown above and slightly paler below. Forest Shrew and Dark-footed Forest Shrew are similar but it is possible to distinguish them where their ranges overlap in the Eastern Cape: there the Forest Shrew has more greyish underparts and the under-surface of its tail is paler than the upper-surface, while the Dark-footed Forest Shrew has browner underparts and a uniformly coloured tail. Although hairy, the short tail of the forest shrews lacks the long hairs or vibrissae found in the musk shrews and dwarf shrews.

Distribution: See 'Identification pointers' and maps.

Habitat: All species are associated with well-vegetated and moist areas, with the Long-tailed Forest Shrew found mainly in the transition zone between forest and fynbos. Although named 'forest shrews', they occur in a wide range of habitats.

Behaviour: Virtually nothing known about behaviour of Long-tailed Forest Shrew. As with all the other shrew species occurring in southern Africa, however, members of the genus *Myosorex* may be active at any time during the night or day. The Forest Shrew is an active digger, excavating shallow burrows, but it will also use holes dug by other species. In one study of the Forest Shrew, it was found that individuals caught at high altitude (to 1 900 m) were less aggressive than those caught at low altitudes (600 m). The reason for this is not clear.

Food: All four species are insectivorous but will take other invertebrates such as earthworms and small vertebrates, e.g. lizards and frogs.

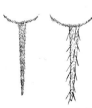

Forest Shrew tail (*left*) lacks the long hairs, or vibrissae, found in the tail of Musk and Dwarf shrews (*right*; see also pp 42 and 44).

Reproduction: The Forest Shrew and Dark-footed Forest Shrew mainly give birth in the summer months but in some areas in cooler months, to 2–4 naked young (1 g).

Note: Forest Shrews, also called Mouse Shrews, are believed to be among the most primitive of all African shrews. Evidence for this lies with their teeth and certain other anatomical features. Although at present only four *Myosorex* species are recognized for southern Africa, it seems highly likely that more will be described in the future.

Long-tailed Forest Shrew occurs in the transition zone between forest and fynbos.

The Forest Shrew feeds on a wide range of invertebrates, including earthworms, as pictured here.

Forest Shrew

7 mm

Front   Back

Long-tailed Forest Shrew

41

Musk Shrews Genus *Crocidura*

Nine species of musk shrew occur in southern Africa. Apart from the two largest species, the only way to distinguish one from another is by detailed examination of skull structure, dentition and chromosome composition.

■ *Crocidura occidentalis*
■ *Crocidura mariquensis*
■ Area of overlap

Crocidura fuscomurina

Crocidura cyanea

■ *Crocidura silacea*
■ *Crocidura flavescens*
■ *Crocidura luna*
■ Area of overlap

Crocidura hirta

■ **Giant Musk Shrew** *Crocidura occidentalis (olivieri)*
Total length 20 cm; tail 8 cm; mass 31–37 g.
■ **Swamp Musk Shrew** *Crocidura mariquensis*
Total length 13 cm; tail 5 cm; mass 10 g.
■ **Tiny Musk Shrew** *Crocidura fuscomurina*
Total length 10 cm; tail 4 cm; mass 6 g.
■ **Maquassie Musk Shrew** *Crocidura maquassiensis*
Total length 10 cm; tail 4 cm; mass 6 g.
■ **Reddish-grey Musk Shrew** *Crocidura cyanea*
Total length 13 cm; tail 5 cm; mass 9 g.
■ **Lesser Grey-brown Musk Shrew** *Crocidura silacea*
Total length 12 cm; tail 5 cm.
■ **Greater Red Musk Shrew** *Crocidura flavescens*
Total length 16 cm; tail 6 cm; mass 39 g.
■ **Greater Grey-brown Musk Shrew** *Crocidura luna*
Total length 14.5 cm; tail 5.5 cm.
■ **Lesser Red Musk Shrew** *Crocidura hirta*
Total length 13 cm; tail 4.5 cm; mass 15 g.

Identification pointers: Typical shrew appearance; prominent vibrissae on tail. Occupy wide range of habitats, so identification is aided by consulting distribution maps. Positive identification requires expert examination.

Description: Vary considerably in pelage colour, ranging from blackish-brown to greyish-fawn above, dark brown to pale grey below. Reddish-grey Musk Shrew, the most widespread, is greyish-red to reddish-brown on the upperparts depending on whether the specimen comes from western or eastern southern Africa; upper-surfaces of the feet are paler than the rest of the body. Swamp Musk Shrew is very dark brown to blackish-brown all over, including tail and upper-surface of feet. Giant and Greater Red Musk Shrews are distinguishable by their comparatively large size and pale-fawn to reddish-brown upperparts, with fawn-grey to off-white underparts. Lesser Red Musk Shrew is similar in appearance but smaller. Musk shrew tails are sparsely covered with fairly long vibrissae, a feature shared with dwarf shrews, but not with the Climbing Shrew or forest shrews.

Distribution: Greater Grey-brown Musk Shrew is restricted to Eastern Highlands of Zimbabwe and adjacent areas of Mozambique. Maquassie Musk Shrew is known only from a few scattered localities in eastern South Africa and Zimbabwe. Most widespread species is Reddish-grey Musk Shrew.

Habitat: Mostly found in association with moist habitats, although Reddish-grey Musk Shrew is also found in very dry areas. Lesser Red Musk Shrew also extends into drier areas. All species show a preference for dense, matted vegetation.

Behaviour: Musk shrews have alternating periods of activity and rest throughout the 24-hour cycle. Foraging is probably solitary in all species. They actively defend territories within fixed home ranges.

Food: Insects, other invertebrates and possibly small vertebrates.

Reproduction: Litters of 2–6 naked, helpless young in warm, wet summer months. Gestation period of Lesser Red is 18 days. Nothing known about reproduction of Maquassie, Lesser Grey-brown or Greater Grey-brown Musk Shrews.

Greater Grey-brown Musk Shrew.

Tiny Musk Shrew measures just 10 cm from nose to tail-tip.

Swamp Musk Shrew.

Reddish-grey Musk Shrew; note the vibrissae on snout.

Greater Red Musk Shrew.

Lesser Red Musk Shrew occurs in drier areas.

Greater Musk Shrew

Tiny Musk Shrew

43

Dwarf Shrews Genus *Suncus*

Three species of dwarf shrew occur in southern Africa:

Suncus lixus

■ **Greater Dwarf Shrew** *Suncus lixus*
Total length 11 cm; tail 4.5 cm; mass 8 g.
■ **Lesser Dwarf Shrew** *Suncus varilla*
Total length 9 cm; tail 3.3 cm; mass 6.5 g.
■ **Least Dwarf Shrew** *Suncus infinitesimus*
Total length 8 cm; tail 3 cm; mass 3.5 g.

Identification pointers: Very small size; could be confused with Tiny Musk Shrew where ranges overlap.

Description: Dwarf shrews are very small; only the Tiny Musk Shrew (total length 10 cm) and Maquassie Musk Shrew (10 cm) are as small as the Least and Lesser Dwarf Shrews. All three dwarf shrews are greyish-brown above with paler silver-fawn underparts; Lesser Dwarf Shrew has a clear demarcation between the colours of upper- and underparts but in the others the colours merge gradually. Upper-surfaces of feet are very pale or white in Greater and Lesser but somewhat darker in Least Dwarf Shrew. Body colouring of all species can vary considerably. Like musk shrews, but unlike forest shrews and the Climbing Shrew, dwarf shrews have long hairs (vibrissae) interspersed between shorter hairs of the tail.

Suncus varilla

Distribution: Although dwarf shrews have patchy distributions, this may be apparent rather than real as they are difficult to catch, and may be more common and widespread than present records indicate. The Lesser Dwarf Shrew is widespread in South Africa, whereas the other two species appear to have more limited distribution ranges and are absent from Namibia. All three extend into East Africa, with Least Dwarf Shrew widely distributed through sub-Saharan Africa.

Suncus infinitesimus

Habitat: The dwarf shrews, particularly the Greater Dwarf Shrew, occur in a broad range of habitats. The Least and the Lesser Dwarf Shrews are commonly found in association with termite-mounds, which provide shelter and probably also food.

Behaviour: Unknown.

Food: These shrews eat insects and probably other small invertebrates. In captivity the Greater Dwarf Shrew will readily attack grasshoppers equalling its own size.

Reproduction: Probably seasonal breeders and mainly during the rainy season. Two to four young per litter in at least two species.

Climbing Shrew Genus *Sylvisorex*

Sylvisorex megalura

■ **Climbing Shrew** *Sylvisorex megalura*
Total length 16 cm; tail 8.5 cm; mass 5–7 g.

Identification pointers: Thin tail longer than head and body; in southern Africa it is restricted to the eastern half of Zimbabwe.

Description: The only southern African shrew with a tail length greater than the length of the head and body. The upperparts are grey with a brownish tinge and underparts may be pale brown to off-white. The tail is long and thin, dark above and pale below.

Distribution: Only recorded from eastern Zimbabwe and adjacent Mozambique, but elsewhere in Africa occurs widely south of the Sahara.

Habitat: High-rainfall areas with dense scrub and grass cover.

Behaviour: Unknown.

Food: Unknown.

Reproduction: May breed throughout the year and mean litter size is 2.

The Lesser Dwarf Shrew, one of the smallest shrews, measures just 9 cm in length.

The Greater Dwarf Shrew is greyish brown above with silvery underparts.

Greater Dwarf Shrew

Least Dwarf Shrew

 Climbing Shrew

45

BATS | Order Chiroptera

FRUIT-BATS | Suborder Megachiroptera | Family Pteropodidae

Eight species of fruit-bat have been recorded from southern Africa. They may be divided into two groups based on the presence or absence of tufts of white hair at the base of the ears.

Eidolon helvum

Straw-coloured Fruit-bat *Eidolon helvum*

Total length 19 cm; forearm 11 cm; wingspan 75 cm; mass 300 g.

Identification pointers: Large size; dog-like face; no white tufts of hair at base of ears and no other obvious markings; black wings. Considerably larger than Egyptian Fruit-bat and with yellowish body fur, particularly on the shoulders and back.

Description: The Straw-coloured Fruit-bat is the largest bat in the subregion. Like other fruit-bats, it has a dog-like face. Wings long and tapered and are dark brown to black. General body colour is variable and may be dull yellow-brown to rich yellowish-brown. The underparts are always paler. The hindquarters and limbs are usually darker than the rest of the body. The tail is very short.

Distribution: This large bat occurs widely within southern Africa, although it is least likely to be encountered in drier areas. A migrant from the tropics, it is found from Guinea in West Africa through the Democratic Republic of Congo to Uganda, Kenya and Tanzania in East Africa. A colony of up to five million bats is present in north-eastern Zambia seasonally and recent records indicate that at least one breeding colony may be present in central Mozambique.

Habitat: Typically a species of tropical forest, but in southern Africa it even penetrates into the Namib Desert along wooded watercourses in search of ripe fruit.

Behaviour: In southern Africa it is usually encountered singly or in small groups, although in the tropics colonies may number well in excess of 100 000 individuals. Normally they hang in clusters of 10–50 animals in trees.

Food: It eats a wide range of both wild and cultivated fruit.

Reproduction: Does not breed in southern Africa.

Rousettus aegyptiacus

Lissonycteris angolensis

Egyptian Fruit-bat *Rousettus aegyptiacus*

Total length 15 cm; forearm 9.0–10.5 cm; wingspan 60 cm; mass 130 g.

Bocage's Fruit-bat *Lissonycteris angolensis*

Total length 12 cm; forearm 8.1–8.5 cm; wingspan 40 cm; mass 100 g.

Identification pointers: Neither species possesses white tufts at the base of the ears. Both species are large. Uniformly coloured upper- and underparts, but underparts always lighter in colour. Male of Bocage's has collar of stiff, orange-coloured hair on throat and side of neck; female's throat and neck are sparsely haired.

Description: Egyptian Fruit-bat plain-coloured without distinctive markings. Upperparts vary from dark brown to greyish-brown in colour, and underparts are grey. A paler, usually yellowish collar is present on the neck and the throat may have a brownish tinge. Round-tipped wings are dark brown or nearly black and tail is short. Bocage's is similar but is smaller and upperparts are usually richer brown. Male has distinctive brown-orange collar of stiff hairs on throat and sides of neck not found in male Egyptian Fruit-bat.

Egyptian Fruit-bats have a dog-like face and short tail.

Fruit-bats have two claws on each wing.

Egyptian Fruit-bats serve as plant pollinators.

Some Straw-coloured Fruit-bats, mainly males, have an orange 'collar'.

An Egyptian Fruit-bat skin showing short tail and narrow interfemoral membrane typical of the species.

Straw-coloured Fruit-bat

Bocage's Fruit-bat

47

Distribution: Egyptian Fruit-bat occurs from Cape Town eastwards through KwaZulu-Natal into Mozambique and inland to north-eastern South Africa and Zimbabwe. Also occurs widely through sub-Saharan Africa and north-eastwards to Egypt. Within the subregion, Bocage's Fruit-bat is only known from eastern Zimbabwe and the adjacent parts of Mozambique. The East African Little-collared Fruit-bat, *Myonycteris relicta*, is known from a single specimen collected in the Haroni Forest at the southern tip of Chimanimani Mountains on the Zimbabwe/Mozambique border.

Habitat: Forested areas or savanna and riverine woodland with plentiful supply of ripe fruit. A second essential prerequisite is the presence of caves or old mine-shafts to provide roosts.

Behaviour: Both species roost in caves during the day but the Egyptian Fruit-bat, being the only fruit-bat to echolocate, utilizes the darkest areas; it does, however, have good eyesight. Bocage's Fruit-bat is reliant on sight for orientation and will roost in the lighter areas of a cave; it also roosts in hollow trees. The Egyptian Fruit-bat may form colonies several thousands strong; Bocage's Fruit-bat colonies are small. Suitable roosting-caves may be several kilometres from feeding-grounds and caves may be vacated at certain times of the year when the bats need to travel too far in search of food.

Food: A wide range of soft fruit is eaten.

Reproduction: The single young of the Egyptian Fruit-bat is born after a gestation period of about 105 days from late winter (in the north) to early summer (in south). Nothing is known about the reproduction of Bocage's Fruit-bat in southern Africa.

■ *Epomophorus wahlbergi*
■ *Epomops dobsonii*

■ *Epomophorus gambianus*
■ *Epomophorus angolensis*

■ **Wahlberg's Epauletted Fruit-bat** *Epomophorus wahlbergi*
Males: total length 14 cm; forearm 8.4 cm; wingspan 50 cm; mass 70–160 g.
■ **Gambian Epauletted Fruit-bat** *Epomophorus gambianus*
Males: total length 15 cm; forearm 8.3 cm; wingspan 56 cm; mass 80–140g.
■ **Angolan Epauletted Fruit-bat** *Epomophorus angolensis*
Males: total length 16 cm; forearm 8.9 cm; wingspan 50 cm.
■ **Dobson's Fruit-bat** *Epomops dobsonii*
Males: total length 16 cm; forearm 8.5 cm.

Identification pointers: Large size; white hair tufts at ear bases; white or yellowish epaulettes on shoulders of males; uniformly coloured fur in various shades of brown, but lighter underparts. Dog-like faces.

Description: Distinguished by tufts of white hair at the base of the brown ears in both sexes, and by males having a glandular pouch on each shoulder covered in long white hair (or yellowish in the case of Dobson's Fruit-bat); when the pouch is spread, the light hair forms a prominent 'epaulette' – hence the group-name. Tails either absent or extremely short. Overall body colour of all four species is buff to brown with paler underparts, but colour can vary; Gambian Epauletted Fruit-bat, for example, can be yellowish-cream above and off-white below, while Wahlberg's tends to be darker brown on average. Wahlberg's and Gambian are quite common in our region (see maps) and often associate together. They are, however, difficult to separate in the field. The only certain way of distinguishing between the species of epauletted fruit-bats is by examining the number and situation of the transverse ridges on the palate.

Distribution: Wahlberg's Epauletted Fruit-bat largely restricted to the eastern coastal belt. It extends inland along watercourses in the north-east of South Africa and Zimbabwe. Gambian Epauletted Fruit-bat is largely restricted to the north-eastern part of subregion, with isolated records from the south-eastern coastal

Wahlberg's Epauletted Fruit-bat.

Epauletted Fruit-bats roost in trees.

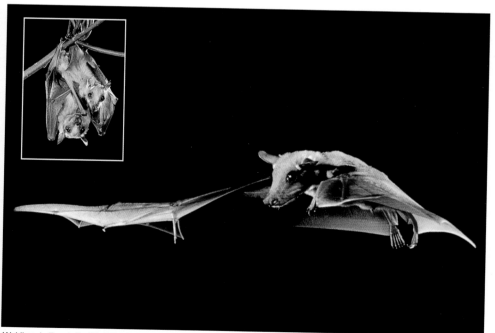

Wahlberg's Epauletted Fruit-bat in flight. Inset: *Gambian Epauletted Fruit-bat female with large young.*

area. The Angolan Epauletted Fruit-bat is restricted to south-western Angola and north-western Namibia. Dobson's Fruit-bat is known in our region from only one specimen from Chobe River in north-eastern Botswana.

Habitat: Forest and riverine woodland. May occasionally forage and roost away from the preferred woodland habitat, particularly in the case of the two commoner species; Wahlberg's, for example, commonly roosts in trees in parks and along busy streets in Mozambique's coastal cities.

Behaviour: Tree-roosters, with two commoner species coming together in noisy colonies with from a few to several hundred individuals.

Food: Most soft fruits, but possibly all species also feed from flowers.

Reproduction: Most young probably born in the early summer months.

INSECTIVOROUS BATS | Suborder Microchiroptera

SHEATH-TAILED & TOMB BATS | Family Emballonuridae

Bats of this family can be distinguished by the form of the tail, about one half of which is enclosed by the interfemoral membrane, the remainder not being attached to the membrane but not extending beyond it (fig. 1.2, page 16). They have simple faces without any projections or nose-leaves. The ears are triangular with rounded tips and each species has a different-shaped tragus.

Coleura afra

Taphozous mauritianus

Taphozous perforatus

■ **African Sheath-tailed Bat** *Coleura afra*
Total length 7 cm; wingspan 24 cm.
■ **Mauritian Tomb Bat** *Taphozous mauritianus*
Total length 10 cm; forearm 6 cm; wingspan 34 cm; mass 28 g.
■ **Egyptian Tomb Bat** *Taphozous perforatus*
Total length 10 cm; forearm 6 cm; wingspan 34 cm.

Identification pointers: Tail partly enclosed by membrane, with remainder free but not projecting beyond membrane (see fig. 1.2, page 16; compare with free-tailed bats, fig. 1.9). Much smaller size of Sheath-tailed Bat; Mauritian Tomb Bat with white underparts and wings; Egyptian Tomb Bat only outer two-thirds of wings white, remainder very dark; underparts light brown to grey with some white hairs on lower belly, but not all white as in Mauritian Tomb Bat.

Description: Tail as described above. Sheath-tailed Bat uniform brown body but slightly paler below and on wings. Mauritian Tomb Bat has grey upperparts, pure-white underparts and greyish-white wing-membranes. Males have a deep glandular sac in the throat; females have only shallow fold. Egyptian Tomb Bat has dark-brown upperparts and slightly paler underparts, although belly is usually off-white; only outer two-thirds of the wing-membranes white, inner third almost black. No throat gland.

Distribution: Sheath-tailed Bat occurs only in extreme north-east of subregion. Mauritian Tomb Bat restricted to southern and eastern coastal belt but extends inland into the north-east of South Africa and Zimbabwe, and to north of Botswana and the Caprivi Strip. Egyptian Tomb Bat only known from scattered localities in northern Botswana and Zimbabwe.

Habitat: Open woodland. Mauritian Tomb Bat frequently roosts in more exposed positions, such as outer walls of buildings and on tree-trunks; Egyptian Tomb Bat hides in dark cracks and crevices in caves or buildings.

Behaviour: Mauritian Tomb Bat usually roosts singly or in pairs and Egyptian Tomb Bat roosts in clusters of 6–10. Roost with belly flat against surface and, if

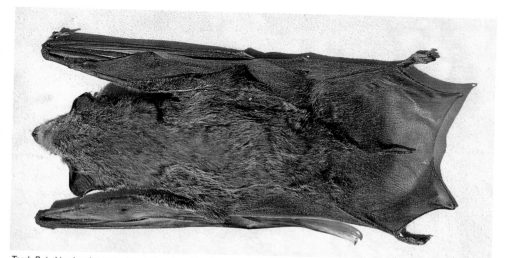

Tomb Bat skin showing part of the tail enclosed by the interfemoral membrane, with the remainder not extending beyond it.

The Mauritian Tomb Bat frequently roosts on tree trunks, or on the outer walls of buildings.

African Sheath-tailed Bat

Mauritian Tomb Bat
Egyptian Tomb Bat

disturbed, scuttles around a corner. Can detect movement from some distance away indicating that they have good eyesight in contrast to most other insect-eating bats. Sometimes hunt by day.

Food: Insects.

Reproduction: Tomb Bats give birth to a single young during summer. Sheath-tailed Bats probably similar.

TRIDENT & LEAF-NOSED BATS | Family Hipposideridae

This distinctive group of bats consists of three genera and four species in southern Africa, of which two have a single nose-leaf and two have three spear-shaped leaves mounted at the back of the main nose-leaf. These bats are sometimes also known as Roundleaf Bats.

Hipposideros commersoni

Hipposideros caffer

■ **Commerson's Leaf-nosed Bat** *Hipposideros commersoni*
Total length 15 cm; forearm 10 cm; wingspan up to 60 cm; mass 120 g.

■ **Sundevall's Leaf-nosed Bat** *Hipposideros caffer*
Total length 8 cm; forearm 5 cm; wingspan 20 cm; mass 8 g.

Identification pointers: Commerson's – very large; distinctive but simple nose-leaf, which lacks the triangular pointed process pointing backwards over the head typical of the horseshoe bats; short hair with overall pale-fawn appearance; males with white shoulder tufts; black feet. Sundevall's – small size; similar nose-leaf; colour variable; long woolly hair. Should not be confused with other bats (see Horseshoe Bats, p58 and tail diagrams, page 16).

Description: The two species can be easily separated by size difference. Have well-developed nose-leaves and are related to horseshoe bats; unlike the latter, however, they do not have the prominent triangular posterior nose-leaf processes. Ears are large, pointed and leaf-like. Commerson's has short hair, sandy-brown upperparts, but paler neck and head. Underparts also paler, with white, sparsely haired flanks; males have white tufts on sides of shoulders. Sundevall's is much smaller and its dorsal hair is long and woolly. Variable in colour, with some individuals being almost white (especially from Namibia) and others deep yellow-brown or dark grey-brown. Tail structure like horseshoe bats (fig. 1.3, page 16).

Distribution: Commerson's only occurs in the north of the subregion, but colonies numbering in the thousands have been recorded in Namibia and Zimbabwe, with one cave in Zimbabwe said to harbour as many as 100 000 individuals. Sundevall's has a similar range, but it extends further south, over much of north-eastern South Africa.

Habitat: Savanna woodland; roost in caves, mine-shafts, buildings.

Behaviour: Both species roost in colonies of hundreds of individuals, but Sundevall's sometimes in small groups of 2–3. Hang free at the roosts in clusters but not in contact with neighbours. Slow but agile fliers.

Food: Commerson's is believed to feed mainly on beetles, whereas Sundevall's takes mainly moths.

Reproduction: Both give birth to a single young in early summer, with nearly all Commersons' births in the region taking place in October.

Commerson's Leaf-nosed Bat roosts in caves, sometimes in very large colonies.

Sundevall's Leaf-nosed Bat is also a cave-dweller.

Leaf-nosed bat skin showing tail conformation.

Commerson's Leaf-nosed Bat.

Commerson's Leaf-nosed Bat

 Sundevall's Leaf-nosed Bat

Cloeotis percivali

■ Short-eared Trident Bat *Cloeotis percivali*
Total length 7 cm; forearm 3.5 cm; wingspan 15 cm; mass 5 g.
Identification pointers: Three-pointed process at top of nose-leaf – a feature shared only with the Persian Leaf-nosed Bat. Similar to the Persian Leaf-nosed Bat but total length only 7 cm to the latter's 14 cm.
Description: Distinctive three-pronged trident-like process at back of nose-leaf between eyes. Upperparts usually pale grey; underparts are grey-white to greyish-yellow; wings are dark. Face is whitish-yellow. Ears are small and almost hidden by long fur.
Distribution: Patchy distribution in north-east of subregion.
Habitat: Unknown. Roosts in caves and mine-shafts.
Behaviour: Colonies of several hundreds but also small groups. Roosts in darkest areas of caves or mines, hanging in tight clusters from roof.
Food: Insects, apparently mainly moths.
Reproduction: A single young is born in the early summer.

Triaenops persicus

■ Persian Leaf-nosed (or Trident) Bat *Triaenops persicus*
Total length 14 cm; forearm 5 cm; wingspan 35 cm; mass 12 g.
Identification pointers: Much larger than Short-eared Trident Bat. Three spear-shaped leaves at top of nose-leaf. Only known from extreme north-eastern corner of southern African subregion.
Description: Nose-leaf pitted with small cavities and folds; three large spear-shaped leaves mounted at back of nose-leaf. Ears are small, pointed and sharply notched on outer edge. Upperparts from light brown to reddish-brown; underparts paler and sides of face yellowish. Wings dark brown.
Distribution: Eastern Highlands of Zimbabwe and neighbouring Mozambique.
Habitat: Little known. Roosts in caves or old mines.
Behaviour: Usually forms large colonies. In roosting-caves hang from ceiling in clusters, but not touching one another. Have a slow, flapping flight.
Food: Insects.
Reproduction: Unknown.
General: The Trident and Leaf-nosed bats (Family Hipposideridae) are an Old World group of insect-eating bats. It is a large group with at least 69 species and 9 genera. They occupy tropical and subtropical regions of Africa, South Asia and Australia. The greatest diversity of species is in South Asia, but Africa is home to at least 17 different species.

The tiny Short-eared Trident Bat has a wingspan of 15 cm and weighs just 5 g on average.

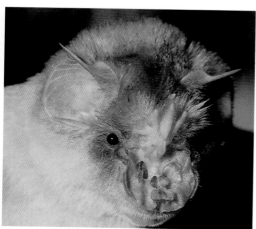

A Persian Leaf-nosed (Trident) Bat, showing the distinctive three-pronged trident-like process at the back of the nose-leaf between the eyes.

Short-eared Trident Bat

Persian Leaf-nosed Bat

SLIT-FACED BATS | Family Nycteridae

Immediately recognizable by the long, lobed slit that runs down the centre of the face; when this slit is opened nose-leaves can be seen. Slit-faced Bats possess ear tragi and have large, more or less straight- and parallel-sided ears. The wings are broad and rounded at the tips.

■ **Hairy Slit-faced Bat** *Nycteris hispida*
Total length 9 cm; forearm 4 cm; wingspan 28 cm; ear length 2.2 cm.
■ **Large Slit-faced Bat** *Nycteris grandis*
Total length 16 cm; forearm 6.5 cm; wing 35 cm; ear length 3.1 cm; mass 40 g.
■ **Wood's Slit-faced Bat** *Nycteris woodi*
Total length 9 cm; forearm 3.8 cm; ear length 3.2 cm.
■ **Greater Slit-faced Bat** *Nycteris macrotis*
Total length 11 cm; forearm 4.7 cm; ear length 2,9 cm; mass 12 g.
■ **Egyptian Slit-faced Bat** *Nycteris thebaica*
Total length 10 cm; forearm 4.7 cm; wing 24 cm; ear length 3.4 cm; mass 11 g.
■ **Vinson's Slit-faced Bat** *Nycteris vinsoni*
Total length 12.5 cm; forearm 5.1 cm; ear length 2.2 cm.

■ *Nycteris hispida*
■ *Nycteris grandis*

Nycteris woodi

■ *Nycteris macrotis*
■ *Nycteris vinsoni*

Nycteris thebaica

Identification pointers: Very long, erect ears; facial slit; bifurcated tail-tip. Most likely to encounter species of Egyptian Slit-faced Bat. Should not be confused with other bats, but see Long-eared Bats of the genus *Laephotis* (page 70).

Description: All slit-faced bats have long, rounded ears, a split running down the length of the face, a long tail bifurcated at the tip and wings rounded at the tip. Large Slit-faced Bat can be separated by its much larger size. Colour in all species is variable but upperparts are always darker than underparts. Large and Greater Slit-faced Bats usually have reddish-brown upperparts and greyer underparts. Egyptian Slit-faced Bat usually has light-brown upperparts (occasionally reddish-orange) and underparts that range from pale brown to dirty white.

Distribution: Vinson's Slit-faced Bat is known only from a single locality in Mozambique. The Greater Slit-faced Bat has only been collected in our subregion in eastern Zambezi Valley in Zimbabwe, but is widespread in equatorial Africa. The Hairy Slit-faced Bat has a limited distribution in eastern Zimbabwe and Mozambique but elsewhere occurs widely south of the Sahara. The Large Slit-faced Bat has a similar southern African distribution. Wood's Slit-faced Bat is known from several localities in Zimbabwe and south-eastern Zambia. The Egyptian Slit-faced Bat has a wide distribution, extending to Europe.

Habitat: Egyptian Slit-faced Bat has wide habitat tolerance, as has Hairy Slit-faced Bat, although latter avoids more arid areas. Large and Greater Slit-faced Bats show a preference for riverine woodland. Roosts include caves, buildings and among leaves in trees and bushes.

Behaviour: Although most species of slit-faced bat roost in small numbers and are often found roosting alone or in pairs, the Egyptian Slit-faced Bat sometimes forms roosts consisting of several hundred individuals. All are slow but highly efficient fliers. Insect and other prey is taken on the wing and even from the ground and vegetation and then carried to a regularly used perch to feed. Such perches may be recognized by the accumulation of non-edible parts such as moth wings and beetle elytra (horny front wings) on the ground below.

Food: Insects and other invertebrates are the usual prey but the Large Slit-faced Bat will also take vertebrate prey, including fish and frogs.

Reproduction: Egyptian Slit-faced Bat: a single young is born during the early summer months and is carried by the mother during feeding forays.

Hairy Slit-faced Bat.

Head of Egyptian Slit-faced Bat.

Slit-faced bat skin showing bifurcated tail-tip.

Slit-faced Bats sometimes roost in caves, but have a wide habitat tolerance.

Hairy Slit-faced Bat

Large Slit-faced Bat

■ *Rhinolophus fumigatus*
■ *Rhinolophus simulator*
■ Area of overlap

Rhinolophus clivosus

■ *Rhinolophus hildebrandtii*
■ *Rhinolophus capensis*
■ *Rhinolophus denti*

Rhinolophus darlingi

Rhinolophus landeri

■ *Rhinolophus blasii*
■ *Rhinolophus swinnyi*
■ Area of overlap

HORSESHOE BATS | Family Rhinolophidae

Horseshoe bats are characterized by having elaborate nose-leaves over the face between the mouth and forehead. Ten species have been recorded as occurring in southern Africa.

■ Hildebrandt's Horseshoe Bat *Rhinolophus hildebrandtii*
Total length 11 cm; forearm 6.5 cm; wingspan 39 cm; mass 27 g.
■ Rüppell's Horseshoe Bat *Rhinolophus fumigatus*
Total length 9.2 cm; forearm 5.0 cm; mass 14 g.
■ Geoffroy's Horseshoe Bat *Rhinolophus clivosus*
Total length 9.7 cm; forearm 5.4 cm; wingspan 32 cm; mass 17 g.
■ Darling's Horseshoe Bat *Rhinolophus darlingi*
Total length 8.5 cm; forearm 4.5 cm; mass 9 g.
■ Lander's Horseshoe Bat *Rhinolophus landeri*
Total length 8.0 cm; forearm 4.4 cm; mass 6 g.
■ Peak-saddle (Blasius's) Horseshoe Bat *Rhinolophus blasii*
Total length 7.6 cm; forearm 4.5 cm; mass 4 g.
■ Cape Horseshoe Bat *Rhinolophus capensis*
Total length 8.5 cm; forearm 4.8 cm; wingspan 30 cm.
■ Bushveld Horseshoe Bat *Rhinolophus simulator*
Total length 7.0 cm; forearm 4.3 cm; mass 8 g.
■ Dent's Horseshoe Bat *Rhinolophus denti*
Total length 7.0 cm; forearm 4.2 cm; wingspan 20 cm; mass 6 g.
■ Swinny's Horseshoe Bat *Rhinolophus swinnyi*
Total length 7.0 cm; forearm 4.3 cm; mass 7.5 g.

Identification pointers: Facial structure characteristic, with main nose-leaf base in form of horseshoe; large ears lacking tragi but with pronounced skin fold at ear-base. When at rest, wings wrap around the body.

Description: For the non-expert this is a very difficult group to identify to species level. Hildebrandt's Horseshoe Bat can be separated by its much larger size. Most species are variable in colour but Dent's Horseshoe Bat is usually pale brown or even cream above with off-white underparts and pale translucent brown wing-membranes edged with white. Swinny's Horseshoe Bat is similar in colour to Dent's Horseshoe Bat but lacks the white edging of the membranes. Another pale-coloured species is Darling's Horseshoe Bat, which has dull-grey upper- and pale-grey underparts and pale grey-brown wing-membranes. The Peak-saddle Horseshoe Bat is characterized by having long, woolly hair, which is very pale to white, with the palest area being at the back of the neck. The Bushveld Horseshoe Bat is dark brown above with contrasting greyish-white underparts. The other species have brown upperparts and usually lighter underparts. In all cases, however, careful examination of teeth, facial structures and forearm length is necessary for positive identification. Tail form is shown in fig. 1.5, page 16.

Distribution: Consult the distribution maps.

Habitat: Most species are associated with savanna. All are principally cave roosters but some use dark buildings; Hildebrandt's Horseshoe Bat utilizes tree hollows.

Behaviour: Rüppell's, Lander's, Peak-saddle and Swinny's Horseshoe Bats all roost in small numbers, whereas the other species may also roost in much larger colonies. Geoffroy's and Cape Horseshoe Bats are found numbering thousands in some roosts, where they hang free by the feet singly or in well-spaced groups.

Food: Insects.

Reproduction: The young are born singly in summer.

Geoffroy's Horseshoe Bat; orange phase.

Geoffroy's Horseshoe Bat.

Darling's Horseshoe Bat.

Rüppell's Horseshoe Bat; the elaborate nose-leaves are clearly evident.

Cape Horseshoe Bat.

Horseshoe bats roost with their wings wrapped around the body.

Horseshoe bat skin, showing squared-off tail.

Hildebrandt's Horseshoe Bat

Dent's Horseshoe Bat

59

VESPER BATS | Family Vespertilionidae

'Vesper Bat' is a group name for bats of the family Vespertilionidae, and includes the Long-fingered, Serotine, Hairy, Pipistrelle, Butterfly, Long-eared, House and Woolly bats. It is by far the largest bat family occurring in the subregion, with three subfamilies, 13 genera and about 30 species. Many can only be identified by examination of their dental and cranial characters. All have somewhat mouse-like faces without nose-leaves; the ears are widely separated and usually prominent. Ear tragi are present and are useful in identification. The tails are long and entirely enclosed in the interfemoral membrane (figs. 1.6, 1.7, 1.8, p16). With the exception of the Woolly and Hairy bats, all have short hair, which lies close to the body.

Long-fingered Bats Genus *Miniopterus* (Subfamily Miniopterinae)

Three species, which can only be distinguished on skull size, occur in southern Africa. The Greater Long-fingered Bat is only known from a few localities in the subregion, the Lesser is considered to be rare, and only Schreibers's Long-fingered Bat is common and widespread.

Miniopterus inflatus

Miniopterus fraterculus

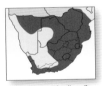

Miniopterus schreibersii

■ **Greater Long-fingered Bat** *Miniopterus inflatus*
Total length 11 cm; tail 5.5 cm; forearm 4.7 cm; mass 15 g.
■ **Lesser Long-fingered Bat** *Miniopterus fraterculus*
Total length 10 cm; tail 5.0 cm; forearm 4,2 cm.
■ **Schreibers's Long-fingered Bat** *Miniopterus schreibersii*
Total length 11 cm; tail 5.3 cm; forearm 4.5 cm; wingspan 28 cm; mass 10 g.
Identification pointers: All three very similar, with greatly elongated second phalanx of the third finger, which distinguishes them from all other bats of the family Vespertilionidae.

Description: All three species are variable in measurements and in colour; Schreibers's Long-fingered Bat, however, is usually dark-brown above and slightly paler below, with almost black wings and interfemoral membrane. This bat has recently been recognized as comprising several different species, and the population in southern Africa can probably be referred to as *Miniopterus natalensis*. The upperparts of the Lesser Long-fingered Bat are usually more reddish-brown, with black wing-membranes and dark-brown interfemoral membrane. The Greater Long-fingered Bat is similar but chocolate-brown above. In all species the wings are long and pointed and the ears are small and rounded.

Distribution: The Greater Long-fingered Bat is only known from a few localities in eastern Zimbabwe and northern Namibia, with scattered records from East Africa and the west coast of equatorial Africa. The Lesser Long-fingered Bat is restricted to the south and east of the region, with a few scattered localities from southern central Africa and Madagascar, but is rather uncommon throughout. Schreibers's Bat is widespread in the southern, eastern and northern parts of southern Africa. Elsewhere in Africa, Asia and Europe, genetic work has shown that other species are involved and accurate range limits are unknown.

Habitat: All three species roost in caves or mine-shafts although they will also roost in crevices and holes in trees. The type of surrounding vegetation seems to play no significant role in habitat selection.

Horseshoe bats tend to roost singly or in loose clusters.

Long-fingered bat skin, showing triangular tail conformation typical of Vesper Bats.

Schreibers's Long-fingered bats roost in caves or disused mine shafts, often in dense clusters.

Schreibers's Long-fingered Bat is dark-brown above.

Schreibers's Long-fingered Bat

Behaviour: Schreibers's Long-fingered Bat usually roosts in very large numbers, with over 100 000 individuals known to occur in a single roost. The other two Long-fingered species are frequently found in close association with Schreibers's Long-fingered Bat, but always in much smaller numbers. In the roosts they form very dense clusters. Schreibers's Long-fingered Bat females are subject to seasonal migrations to and from 'maternity' caves. Hibernation has been recorded in winter. They are rapid fliers.

Food: Insects.

Reproduction: A single young is born during the summer, particularly during November and December; the gestation period is eight months. The newborn young only remains clinging to the mother for a few hours and then it is left to hang independently from the rock among other juveniles.

Hairy Bats Genera *Myotis*, *Cistugo* (Subfamily Vespertilioninae)

The five species of the *Myotis*/*Cistugo* group in the southern African subregion can be separated from other Vesper Bats by their longer, more pointed muzzles, and their soft, erect fur.

■ *Myotis welwitschii*
■ *Cistugo seabrai*
■ *Myotis bocagei*

■ **Welwitsch's Hairy Bat** *Myotis welwitschii*
Total length 12 cm; tail 6.0 cm; forearm 5.5 cm; mass 14 g.
■ **Angolan Hairy Bat** *Cistugo seabrai*
Total length 8 cm; tail 3.5 cm; Forearm 3.2 cm.
■ **Lesueur's Hairy Bat** *Cistugo lesueuri*
Total length 9 cm; tail 4.3 cm; forearm 3,4 cm.
■ **Temminck's Hairy Bat** *Myotis tricolor*
Total length 11 cm; tail 5.0 cm; forearm 5.0 cm; wingspan 28 cm; mass 11 g.
■ **Rufous (Mouse-eared) Hairy Bat** *Myotis bocagei*
Total length 10 cm; tail 4.0 cm; forearm 4.0 cm; mass 7.0 g.

Cistugo lesueuri

Identification pointers: Fairly large ears; elongated muzzle; rich reddish-brown fur on upperparts of all except Lesueur's Hairy Bat; fur stands erect.

Description: Most hairy bats have similarly coloured upperparts of rich reddish brown, although this can be variable; the Angola Hairy Bat's upperparts may have a yellow tinge while Lesueur's Hairy Bat is honey-yellow. The underparts are usually off-white with a reddish-brown tinge except again for Lesueur's Hairy Bat where they are a light yellow-white. Welwitsch's Hairy Bat has bold red-and-black patterning on the wings and the interfemoral membrane is reddish-brown in colour and speckled with numerous small black spots; its ears are the same colour as the fur on the upperparts but are black around the edges. The wing-membranes of Temminck's Hairy Bat are dark brown and the interfemoral membrane has a covering of reddish-brown hair; its ears are brown. The rare Rufous Hairy Bat has virtually black ears, wing-membranes and interfemoral membrane. The wing- and interfemoral membranes of the Angola and Lesueur's Hairy Bats are dark brown.

Myotis tricolor

Distribution: The Rufous Hairy Bat is known from north-eastern South Africa and eastern Zimbabwe, but further north it appears quite common in the equatorial regions from the Democratic Republic of Congo to West Africa; there are, however, only a few East African records. Welwitsch's Hairy Bat is recorded from a few localities in north-eastern South Africa and Zimbabwe, and more widely in central Africa. The Angola Hairy Bat is restricted to the far west, from the Northern Cape Province through western Namibia to south-western Angola. Lesueur's Hairy Bat is only known from the Western Cape and adjacent parts of the Karoo.

Hairy bat skin, showing tail conformation.

Welwitsch's Hairy Bat has bold red-and-black patterning on the wings.

Temminck's Hairy Bat has reddish-brown upperparts and brown ears.

Rufous Hairy Bat favours open woodland habitats.

Temminck's Hairy Bat

Temminck's Hairy Bat is found along the southern and eastern areas of subregion and from there north to East Africa.

Habitat: Welwitsch's, Temminck's and Rufous Hairy Bats favour open woodland and savanna habitats, whereas the Angola Hairy Bat favours more arid, semi-desert areas. No information is available for Lesueur's Hairy Bat. Temminck's Hairy Bat is principally a cave-roosting species, preferring damp caves, whereas Welwitsch's and the Rufous Hairy Bats prefer to roost in hollow trees and among leaves. There is as yet no information on the roosting preferences of Lesueur's or the Angola Hairy Bats.

Behaviour: The hairy bats are slow fliers and they usually hunt within 5 m of the ground. Temminck's Hairy Bats live in small colonies and are subject to some local migration. The Rufous Hairy Bat is found singly or in pairs. Virtually nothing is known about the behavioural characteristics of the bats of this genus within their southern African range.

Food: Insects.

Reproduction: Temminck's Hairy Bat is recorded in the Western Cape as giving birth during October and November.

Serotine Bats Genera *Eptesicus, Neoromicia*
(Subfamily Vespertilioninae)

The serotine bats are all small, short-eared species, usually with brown fur. When examined in profile the front of the skull is almost straight. With the exception of Rendall's and Aloe Serotine Bats, it is usually not possible to make a positive identification of the other species in the field. The commonest and most widespread species is the Cape Serotine Bat. In recent years, these small bats have been something of a taxonomic 'football' but, with more refined genetic techniques we are gaining a fuller, if more confusing, understanding of their relationships. Ongoing research is likely to reveal more species, especially in under-collected regions of the continent.

Eptesicus hottentotus

Neoromicia capensis

Neoromicia nanus

▦ **Long-tailed Serotine Bat** *Eptesicus hottentotus*
Total length 11.5 cm; tail 4.7 cm; forearm 4.7 cm; mass 16.6 g.
▪ **Cape Serotine Bat** *Neoromicia capensis*
Total length 8.5 cm; forearm 3.3 cm; wingspan 24 cm; mass 6.5 g.
▪ **Banana Bat** *Neoromicia nanus*
Total length 7.5 cm; tail 3.6 cm; forearm 3.2 cm; wingspan 19 cm; mass 4 g.
▪ **Rendall's Serotine Bat** *Neoromicia rendalii*
Total length 8.8 cm; tail 3.8 cm; forearm 3.6 cm; mass 8.5 g.
▪ **Aloe Serotine Bat** *Neoromicia zuluensis*
Total length 8.0 cm; tail 3.5 cm; forearm 2.8 cm.

Identification pointers: Small size; relatively short ears; tail entirely enclosed by membrane; straight profile of head. See maps.

Description: With the exception of the Long-tailed Serotine Bat, the serotine bats are quite similar in size, most being 8–9 cm in total length. Rendall's Serotine Bat is easily recognized by the white wing-membranes, off-white interfemoral membrane and light-brown ears. The wing-membranes of the Aloe Serotine Bat are often edged with white. The Long-tailed Serotine Bat can be distinguished by its larger size and, in the eastern parts of its range, its body fur is almost black. All other species vary considerably, from light brown to dark brown, with slightly lighter underparts and dark brown wing-membranes. It is not possible to separate most of these species in the field.

Long-tailed Serotine Bat roosting in a crevice.

The Banana Bat has a mass of just 4 g.

Cape Serotine Bat.

The wing membranes of the Aloe Serotine Bat are often edged with white.

Cape Serotine Bat

Banana Bat

65

Neoromicia rendalii

Neoromicia zuluensis

Distribution: Within southern Africa, Rendall's Serotine Bat is only known from the far north-eastern fringes and a single record from KwaZulu-Natal; but it occurs widely in East and West Africa. The Long-tailed Serotine Bat has a disjunct distribution with one population along the west and south coast of the subregion, and another in Zimbabwe and adjacent Mozambique (extending into Malawi and eastern Zambia). The Aloe Serotine Bat is known from scattered localities in northern South Africa, northern Botswana, north and west Namibia, and Zambia. Cape Serotine Bats tend to be abundant and are found virtually throughout Africa.

Habitat: Serotine bats use a wide range of habitats, although Rendall's and Aloe Serotine Bats show a marked preference for open savanna woodland. They roost in a wide range of sites, including under bark and in roofs of buildings. Rendall's Serotine Bat also roosts in trees and bushes. The Long-tailed Serotine Bat makes use of caves, old mine-shafts and rock crevices. The Banana Bat shows a preference for moister forested areas, particularly where banana and strelitzia plants are found; this bat often roosts in the curled leaves of these plants.

Behaviour: The serotines roost in small numbers and, depending on the species, may be well hidden or hang in exposed clusters. The Banana Bat normally roosts in groups of 2 to 6 but solitary individuals are commonly encountered. Rendall's Serotine Bat is a low flier, often less than 2 m above the ground, whereas the Cape and Aloe Serotine Bats are relatively high fliers (the former usually between 10 and 20 m). As with most other bats, little is known about their behaviour.

Food: Insects. All species seem to take a wide range of flying insects, but there may be seasonal variations, especially during times of abundance.

Reproduction: Records indicate that some, and probably all, serotines give birth during the summer months. The Cape Serotine Bat may have single young, but twins are common, rarely triplets or quadruplets. Twins are also common in the Banana Bat and their young are weaned after about 8 weeks.

Pipistrelles Genera *Hypsugo*, *Pipistrellus* (Subfamily Vespertilioninae)

Four species of pipistrelle have been recorded from southern Africa. All are small and difficult to describe as they do not have outstanding features. They have tiny heads, the ears are not joined at the base (unlike some of the Free-tailed Bats, see page 74) and, in all cases, the forearms are less than 4 cm in length. Probably the most useful aid to separating the different species is the shape of the tragus, but this requires somewhat specialized knowledge.

■ *Hypsugo anchietai*
■ *Pipistrellus rueppelli*

Pipistrellus hesperidus

■ **Anchieta's Pipistrelle** *Hypsugo anchietai*
Total length 8.3 cm; tail 3.6 cm; forearm 3.2 cm; mass 4.6 g.
■ **African Pipistrelle** *Pipistrellus hesperidus*
Total length 8.6 cm; tail 3.4 cm; forearm 3.25 cm; mass 6 g.
■ **Rusty Pipistrelle** *Pipistrellus rusticus*
Total length 7.3 cm; tail 2.7 cm; forearm 2.8 cm; mass 4 g.
■ **Rüppell's Pipistrelle** *Pipistrellus rueppelli*
Total length 10.0 cm; tail 3.8 cm; forearm 3.4 cm; mass 7 g.

Identification pointers: Overall small size; Rüppell's Pipistrelle has pure-white underparts; tail in all cases completely enclosed by interfemoral membrane; distribution maps should be consulted.

Description: Rüppell's Pipistrelle is the most easily distinguished of the group because it is the only pipistrelle with pure-white underparts; its ears are dark brown and its upperparts are light brown; its tragus is long, pointed and knife-shaped. African

The African Pipistrelle roosts in rock crevices, as well as under roofs or loose bark.

The African Pipistrelle has a tiny head, with ears that are not joined at the base.

African Pipistrelle

Pipistrellus rusticus

and Rusty Pipistrelles are very similar, upperparts being fawn to reddish-brown and underparts paler. African Pipistrelle underparts are sometimes off-white. The wing-membranes of both species are very dark-brown to almost black, with a narrow white border around the margins in the African. The tragus of the African Pipistrelle is knife-shaped and that of the Rusty Pipistrelle is sickle-shaped.

Distribution: Anchieta's Pipistrelle is limited to the extreme east of South Africa and a small number of localities in Zimbabwe, but elsewhere occurs in a broad swathe across central Africa. The African Pipistrelle has a very broad sub-Saharan distribution, but in southern Africa it is mainly restricted to the eastern seaboard, extending inland in northern South Africa and Zimbabwe. The Rusty Pipistrelle is found from north-eastern South Africa and northern Botswana north to Zimbabwe, Zambia and Angola; there is an apparently separate population in Sudan and Ethiopia. Rüppell's Pipistrelle is distributed from Mozambique, Zimbabwe and northern Botswana northwards to the Sahel zone and to Egypt along the Nile Valley. There are isolated records from the Northern Cape and Limpopo provinces of South Africa.

Habitat: African Pipistrelles have a wide habitat tolerance, from oases in desert areas to the fringes of rain-forests, but close proximity to open water may be a limiting factor. The Rusty Pipistrelle shows a preference for savanna woodland and Rüppell's Pipistrelle is largely restricted to riverine woodland. There are few habitat records for Anchieta's Pipistrelle but they may show a preference for well-wooded areas with open surface water. Some, at least, roost behind the bark of trees and in narrow rock crevices.

Behaviour: African Pipistrelles roost in small numbers, usually in groups of up to 10 or 12. All pipistrelles are slow but acrobatic fliers, emerging at dusk to hunt.

Food: Insects.

Reproduction: The single young of the African Pipistrelle are born during the warm, wet summer months. This seasonality in births probably applies to all pipistrelles in the subregion when insect prey is most abundant.

Glauconycteris variegata

■ **Butterfly Bat** *Glauconycteris variegata* **(Subfamily Vespertilioninae)**
Total length 11 cm; tail 4.7 cm; forearm 4.5 cm; wingspan 28 cm; mass 13 g.
Identification pointers: Overall pale yellow or fawn appearance; yellowish wing-membranes with numerous black lines forming a reticulated pattern. Resembles no other species.

Description: This is a very pretty bat and should not be mistaken for any other species. Its name derives from the reticulated pattern on the wing-membranes, which bears a fanciful resemblance to the veins of a butterfly's wings. The ground colour of the wing-membranes is yellowish-brown, overlaid with black lines. The upperparts range from nearly white to yellowish-fawn and the underparts are paler than the upperparts. The ears are small and similar in colour to the upperparts.

Distribution: In southern Africa it only occurs in the extreme north and north-east, although it does extend down the east coast as far as KwaZulu-Natal.

Habitat: Bushveld and open savanna. Roosts among leaves in trees and bushes and in the thatch of abandoned huts.

Behaviour: The Butterfly Bat leaves its roost early in the evening to hunt and is a high flier. It roosts in pairs or in very small numbers.

Food: Insects.

Reproduction: Nothing recorded for subregion.

The Rusty Pipistrelle shows a preference for savanna woodland and occurs in northern South Africa and Zimbabwe.

Anchieta's Pipistrelle.

The Butterfly Bat has uniquely patterned wings, and is yellowish in colour.

Rüppell's Pipistrelle has pure-white underparts.

Butterfly Bat

Long-eared Bats Genus *Laephotis* (Subfamily Vespertilioninae)
There are three small bats of the genus *Laephotis* in southern Africa. All are extremely rare, and information on their biology is sparse or lacking entirely.

Laephotis namibensis

Laephotis botswanae

Laephotis wintoni

■ **Namib Long-eared Bat** *Laephotis namibensis*
Total length 10.5 cm; tail 4.6 cm; ear 2.4 cm; forearm 3.8 cm.
■ **Botswana Long-eared Bat** *Laephotis botswanae*
Total length 9.2 cm; tail 4.2 cm; ear 2.1 cm; forearm 3.6 cm; mass 6 g.
■ **De Winton's Long-eared Bat** *Laephotis wintoni*
Total length 8.5 cm; tail 4.5 cm; forearm 3.8 cm.
Identification pointers: Small size; the long ears, situated at 45° angle to the face, are about one-third of the head-and-body length. Easily confused with Slit-faced Bats (see page 56), but the latter hold their ears almost vertically and the slit in the face is prominent.
Description: Long-eared Bats have unusually long ears about one-third of the head-and-body length. The species can be separated on the shape of the tragus. The ears stand out sideways at an angle of 45° to the head and are not held almost vertically as in larger slit-faced bats (see page 56). All have short faces and lack facial decoration in the form of nose-leaves. General body colour is light to very light brown, with slightly paler underparts. Wing-membranes are light brown.
Distribution: The Namib and De Winton's Long-eared Bats are each known only from a few localities in the subregion (see map). The Botswana Long-eared Bat has been recorded in the subregion from northern Botswana and Zimbabwe and from Punda Maria in Limpopo Province, South Africa.
Habitat: The two specimens of the Namib Long-eared Bat were taken in the wooded bed of the section of the Kuiseb River, which penetrates the Namib Desert. De Winton's was taken in fynbos scrub on a rocky hill area near Algeria Forest Station in the Western Cape's Cedarberg range; the Botswana Long-eared Bat is associated with open woodland in the vicinity of rivers.
Behaviour: Unknown.
Food: Insects.
Reproduction: Unknown.

Scotoecus albofuscus

■ **Thomas's (Light-winged Lesser) House Bat**
Scotoecus albofuscus (Subfamily Vespertilioninae)
Total length 7 cm; forearm 3 cm; mass 4.5 g.
Three bat species of the genus *Scotoecus* are now added to the faunal list for southern Africa: Light-winged Lesser House Bat *S. albofuscus* (also known as Thomas's House Bat); White-bellied Lesser House Bat *S. albigula*; and Hinde's Lesser House Bat *S. hindei*. They are known from single localities in Mozambique within the region, with an additional record for *S. albofuscus* from KwaZulu-Natal, South Africa. All are tiny bats (forearm <4.6 cm) and have to be examined in detail – tragus, skull, teeth and penis – to be sure of an identity.
   Thomas's Flat-headed Bat *Mimetillus moloneyi*, recorded from Zinave National Park in Mozambique, also within the subregion, is another tiny species, with a forearm length of less than 3.1 cm and very narrow, short wings. Detailed examination of the tragus and skull is required to obtain identity.

The ears, held at an angle to the face, take up about one-third of the head-and-body length of Long-eared Bats, as depicted here by the Botswana Long-eared Bat.

De Winton's Long-eared Bat is known only from a few localities.

De Winton's Long-eared Bat

Thomas's House Bat

Nycticeinops schlieffenii

Schlieffen's Bat *Nycticeinops schlieffenii* (Subfamily Vespertilioninae)
Total length 7.5 cm; tail 3 cm; forearm 3 cm; wingspan 18 cm; mass 4.5 g.
Identification pointers: Fawn or reddish-brown upperparts; dark-brown wing-membranes; fairly large, rounded ears; very small.
Description: No outstanding features. Ears are large and rounded, wing-membranes dark brown and fur of upperparts is pale fawn to dark reddish-brown. Underparts lighter than upperparts. Smallest bat in subregion.
Distribution: Restricted to northern and north-eastern areas of subregion.
Habitat: Open woodland. Roosts in crevices in hollow trees and buildings.
Behaviour: Hunts early in evening; flies jerkily. Roosts alone or in large numbers.
Food: Insects.
Reproduction: Births recorded in November.

Yellow House Bats Genus *Scotophilus* (Subfamily Vespertilioninae)
Solidly built bats, with bluntish heads and short ears; ear tragus is long and pointed. Fur is woolly and soft with a distinct sheen. Recent records indicate that a fourth species, the White-bellied Yellow House Bat *Scotophilus leucogaster*, may be present in northern Namibia. Wide distribution in African tropics.

Scotophilus nigrita

Giant Yellow House Bat (Schreber's Yellow Bat)
Scotophilus nigrita Total length 18 cm; tail 7.7 cm; forearm 7.7 cm.
Yellow House Bat (African Yellow Bat) *Scotophilus dinganii*
Total length 13 cm; tail 5.3 cm; forearm 5.5 cm; wingspan 30 cm; mass 27 g.
Lesser Yellow House Bat (Greenish Yellow Bat) *Scotophilus viridis*
Total length 12 cm; tail 4.6 cm; forearm 4.8 cm; wingspan 28 cm; mass 16 g.
Identification pointers: Variable colouring but usually yellow or yellowish-brown on upperparts and often on underparts.

Scotophilus dinganii

Description: Body colour in this genus is not necessarily yellow. The Yellow House Bat, however, usually has distinctive yellowish or orange-yellow underparts although its upperparts are olive-brown to russet-brown. The Lesser Yellow House Bat has light or dark yellow-brown upperparts and white to grey-white underparts. The Giant Yellow House Bat may be dark red-brown to yellow- or grey-brown above, and pale yellow to white below. In all species wing-membranes are translucent dark brown. Best field criterion to separate Yellow and Lesser Yellow House Bats is the smaller size of the latter.
Distribution: The Giant Yellow House Bat has only been recorded three times from the subregion. The other two species are restricted to the northern and north-eastern areas of southern Africa.

Scotophilus viridis

Habitat: Savanna woodland, with Lesser Yellow showing preference for riverine vegetation and high-rainfall areas. The Yellow House Bat often roosts in buildings, as well as hollow trees. Lesser Yellow roosts in hollow trees, changing its roosting location every few days, perhaps to avoid predation.
Behaviour: Very little known. The Yellow House Bat roosts in small groups of up to a dozen individuals, although several such groups may utilize the same roost. When roosting they crawl into crevices. They are fast, low fliers.
Food: Insects.
Reproduction: Yellow and Lesser Yellow House Bats give birth in summer to litters of 1–3 young.

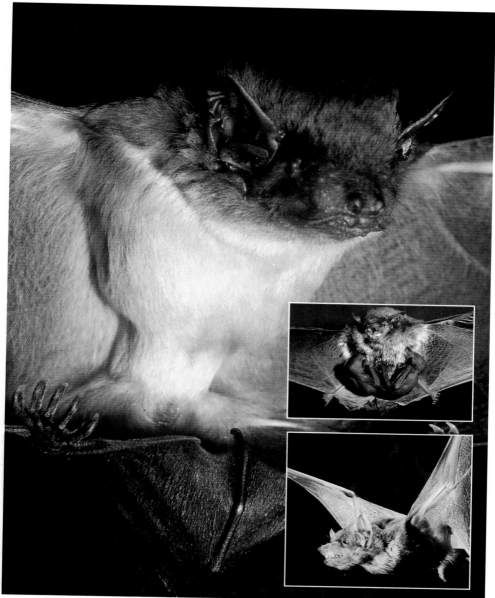

The Yellow House Bat, also known as the African Yellow Bat has a total length of about 13 cm.
Inset top: *Schlieffen's Bat with young.* Inset bottom: *Lesser Yellow House Bat (Greenish Yellow Bat).*

Schlieffen's Bat

Yellow House Bat

Woolly Bats Genus *Kerivoula* (Subfamily Kerivoulinae)

Immediately recognizable by their long, erect, soft, curly-tipped hair. (The long, erect hair of Hairy Bats, genus *Myotis*, page 62, is straight and not curled at the tips.) Woolly Bats are also distinguished by fringe of hair around the interfemoral membrane (fig. 1.8, page 16). There are only two species in southern Africa.

Kerivoula argentata

Kerivoula lanosa

■ **Damara Woolly Bat** *Kerivoula argentata*
Total length 9.5 cm; forearm 3.7 cm; wingspan 25 cm; mass 8 g.
■ **Lesser Woolly Bat** *Kerivoula lanosa*
Total length 7.8 cm; tail 3.8 cm; forearm 3.4 cm; mass 7 g.
Identification pointers: Woolly, erect hair; noticeable fringe of short hair around margin of interfemoral membrane (fig. 1.8, page 16).
Description: Easily recognized by erect curly hair and characteristic fringe of hair along edge of interfemoral membrane. Ears are funnel-shaped with long pointed tragus. Upperparts of Damara Woolly Bat are rich brown in colour and grey-flecked, and the underparts are greyish-brown. Upperparts of Lesser Woolly Bat are lighter brown but also have a grizzled appearance; underparts are very pale. In both species the wing-membranes are brown.
Distribution: Damara Woolly Bat is only known in the subregion from the northern and eastern areas. The less abundant Lesser Woolly Bat is known from a few records in southern and central Africa.
Habitat: Well-watered savanna woodland. Roost in clusters of dead leaves, under bark, under roofs and in deserted weaver-bird nests.
Behaviour: Roost singly, in pairs or in small groups. Damara Woolly Bat is a late-emerging species, with low, slow and erratic flight.
Food: Insects.
Reproduction: Nothing is known from the subregion for either species.

FREE-TAILED BATS | Family Molossidae

Also called Mastiff or Wrinkle-lipped Bats, in reference to their dog-like faces and heavily wrinkled upper lip. Distinctive family characteristic is the tail, of which only half or less is enclosed by the interfemoral membrane, the remainder projecting beyond the membrane (fig. 1.9, page 16). Ears are large, have a small tragus and are approximately equal in length and width. Hair is short, smooth and lies close to body. Most species are dark-brown to reddish-brown. Of the 14 species in subregion, 10 are known from very few specimens or are considered to be rare.

■ *Otomops martiensseni*
■ *Mormopterus*
   acetabulosus
■ *Chaerephon ansorgei*

■ *Sauromys petrophilus*
■ *Tadarida lobata*
■ *Mops condylurus*

■ **Large-eared Free-tailed Bat** *Otomops martiensseni*
Total length 14 cm; tail 4.5 cm; forearm 7.0 cm; mass 33 g.
■ **Flat-headed Free-tailed Bat** *Sauromys petrophilus*
Total length 11 cm; tail 4.0 cm; forearm 4.5 cm; wingspan 26 cm; mass 13 g.
■ **Natal Free-tailed Bat** *Mormopterus acetabulosus*
■ **African Free-tailed Bat** *Tadarida ventralis*
Total length 14 cm; tail 5.5 cm; forearm 6.2 cm.
■ **Egyptian Free-tailed Bat** *Tadarida aegyptiaca*
Total length 11 cm; tail 3.8 cm; forearm 4.8 cm; wingspan 30 cm; mass 15 g.
■ **Kenyan Big-eared Free-tailed Bat** *Tadarida lobata*
Forearm 6.3 cm.
■ **Madagascar Free-tailed Bat** *Tadarida fulminans*
Total length 14 cm; tail 5.5 cm; forearm 6.0 cm; mass 32 g.

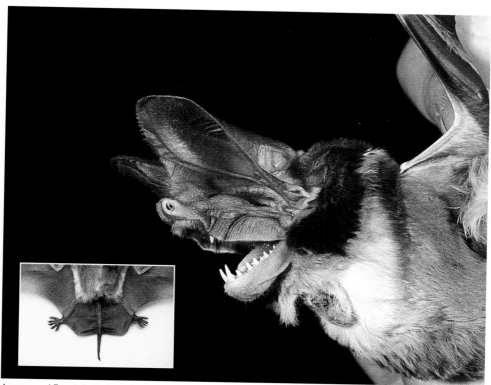

Large-eared Free-tailed Bat: each enlarged ear has a row of small spines along its forward edge. Note the gland on the upper chest. Inset: *The tail character that gives these bats their name.*

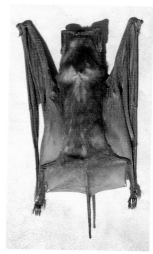

Lesser Woolly Bat.

Woolly bat skin, showing the fringe of hair around the tail membrane.

Free-tailed bat skin; the free tail is clearly evident.

Tadarida aegyptiaca

■ *Tadarida ventralis*
■ *Tadarida fulminans*

■ *Chaerephon pumila*
■ *Chaerephon nigeriae*
■ *Area of overlap*

■ *Chaerephon chapini*
■ *Chaerephon bivittata*
■ *Mops midas*

■ **Ansorge's Free-tailed Bat** *Chaerephon ansorgei*
Total length 10 cm; tail 3.6 cm; forearm 4.3 cm.
■ **Little Free-tailed Bat** *Chaerephon pumila*
Total length 9 cm; tail 3.6 cm; forearm 3.8 cm; wingspan 24 cm; mass 11 g.
■ **Nigerian Free-tailed Bat** *Chaerephon nigeriae*
Total length 10 cm; tail 3.5 cm; forearm 4.9 cm.
■ **Pale (Chapin's) Free-tailed Bat** *Chaerephon chapini*
Total length 15 cm; tail 3.1 cm; forearm 3.6 cm.
■ **Spotted Free-tailed Bat** *Chaerephon bivittata*
Total length 11 cm; tail 3.7 cm; forearm 4.7 cm; mass 15 g.
■ **Angola Free-tailed Bat** *Mops condylurus*
Total length 12 cm; tail 4.0 cm; forearm 5.0 cm; mass 22 g.
■ **Midas Free-tailed Bat** *Mops midas*
Total length 14 cm; tail 5.0 cm; forearm 6.0 cm; wingspan 45 cm; mass 50 g.
Identification pointers: All species have part of tail extending beyond limits of the interfemoral membrane (fig. 1.9, page 16). Except for Large-eared Free-tailed Bat (whose long ears extend along face plane), the ears are large and rounded and may or may not be joined by flap of skin across forehead. Most have wrinkled upper lips.
Description: Large-eared Free-tailed Bat is easy to distinguish from other Free-tailed Bats by very long ears attached along length of face; no tragus or antitragus. Upperparts are dark brown with paler band across shoulders; underparts also dark brown. Band of white hair runs along each side of the body from shoulder to knee. Flat-headed Free-tailed Bat is characterized by its flattened head which enables it to crawl into narrow crevices. Largest species, Midas Free-tailed Bat, has white-flecked dark-brown upperparts and slightly paler underparts. Bands of white hair run from the forearm to the thigh. Angola Free-tailed Bat is typically dark brown above, with tawny throat, grey-brown upper chest, and off-white abdomen. Nigerian and Pale Free-tailed Bats have crests of erectile hair on top of head. The crest of the latter is longer, its wing-membranes are white and interfemoral membrane is dark brown. Tail and wing-membranes of the Nigerian Free-tailed Bat are off-white. Little Free-tailed Bat is smallest and identified by band of white hair on wing-membrane from wing to thigh. Egyptian Free-tailed Bat is common and widespread. It has no outstanding features except that a pale neck yoke, present in most species, is absent. The only certain way of identifying most Free-tailed Bats, however, is by detailed examination of the teeth.
Distribution: See maps.
Habitat: Usually associated with open woodland and riverine vegetation, but Egyptian and Little Free-tailed Bats occur in a wide range of habitats. Most species utilize natural roosts such as rock crevices, caves, hollow trees or behind loose bark of dead trees. Midas, Little and Egyptian Free-tailed Bats also use man-made structures, such as brickwork crannies or overlapping sheets of corrugated-iron roofing. They have the ability to withstand high temperatures (>40°C) for long periods, often roosting under metal roof-sheeting too hot for the human hand.
Behaviour: Usually gregarious: Angola Free-tailed Bat forms colonies of several hundred individuals, but Flat-headed averages 4 and Spotted averages 6. Unlike other bats they prefer to move into cover when disturbed at the roost, rather than take to wing. They usually roost packed tightly together and the larger colonies can produce a considerable noise. High and rapid fliers.
Food: Insects.
Reproduction: Single young, born in summer, is thought to be the rule.

Angola Free-tailed Bat is typically dark-brown above, with a tawny throat, grey-brown upper chest and off-white abdomen. It forms colonies of several hundred individuals.

Egyptian Free-tailed Bat is the most common and wide-spread of the free-tailed bats in the region. Most species are dark-brown to reddish-brown, with short, smooth hair.

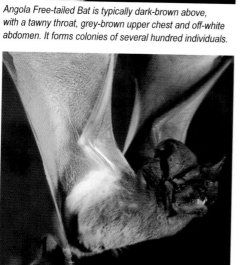

Like most free-tailed bats, Ansorge's Free-tailed Bat has large, rounded ears. Their wrinkled upper lips and dog-like face has led to them also being called Mastiff or Wrinkle-lipped Bats.

Little Free-tailed Bat has a wingspan of about 24 cm.

Little Free-tailed Bat

Midas Free-tailed Bat

77

BABOONS, MONKEYS & GALAGOS |
Order Primates

BABOONS & MONKEYS | Family Cercopithecidae

Papio cynocephalus ursinus

■ **Savanna Baboon** *Papio cynocephalus ursinus*
Male: total length 120–160 cm; tail 60–85 cm; mass 25–45 (average 32) kg.
Female: total length 100–120 cm; tail 50–60 cm; mass 12–20 (average 16) kg.
Identification pointers: Fairly large size; long, dog-like snout in adults; uniform grey to grey-brown colour; males considerably larger than females; apparently 'broken' tail; nearly always in troops, very rarely solitary males.
Note: The Savanna Baboon that occurs in the area covered by this book was long considered to be *Papio ursinus*, later changed to a subspecies of *Papio cynocephalus*. This latter includes the Chacma (*ursinus*), Yellow (*cynocephalus*), Olive (*anubis*) and, possibly, the Guinea (*papio*). The Hamadryas (*Papio hamadryas*) of Ethiopia and Arabia was set as a separate species. However, recent thinking has now placed all these baboons as subspecies of *Papio hamadryas*. As this classification may still change, we have retained the *cynocephalus* option.
Description: The largest primate (other than man) in southern Africa. It is relatively slender and lightly built, although adult males have powerfully built shoulders and heads. When the baboon is on all fours the shoulders stand higher than the rump. The long, somewhat dog-like muzzle is particularly pronounced in the males. The body is covered by coarse hair, which may be light greyish-yellow through to dark grey-brown, but coat colour is variable, even within a troop. Only the male has a mane of long blackish hair on the neck and shoulders. Hair on the upper surface of the hands and feet is dark brown to black. Characteristic of the baboon is the posture of the long tail; the first third of the tail is held upwards and the remainder droops downwards, giving it a 'broken' appearance. Males have a single, hard pad of naked grey skin that extends across both buttocks, but the female has one smaller pad on each buttock. During gestation the skin around the female buttock pads is bright scarlet while at the onset of the menstrual cycle the skin distends enormously into rather unsightly swollen red protuberances.
Distribution: Occurs widely in southern Africa in suitable habitat.
Habitat: Wide habitat tolerance but it requires rocky cliffs or tall trees to which to retreat at night or when threatened. Drinking water is essential. It inhabits mountains, hill ranges and riverine woodland.
Behaviour: A highly gregarious and social species that lives in troops of 15 to sometimes 100 or more. Within a baboon troop all adult males are dominant over all females. Adult males have a strict rank order and only dominant males mate with oestrous or receptive females, although subordinate males do mate with young females and those that are not in oestrus. It is only in their fifth year that the males become dominant over the females. The dominant male determines when the troop will move. The females and infants remain closest to this male, with the non-breeding females staying close to the subordinate males. Youngsters and subadults move around the edges of the troop. Water sources are visited each day. Very vocal and the bark or 'bogom' of the adult male is a common day-time sound of the hills and savanna of southern Africa. Baboons are considered to be strictly diurnal, retreating to tree or cliff roosts before sunset. However, we have encountered baboons foraging on the ground at, or near, full moon, on several occasions, although they were never more than a few metres from roosts. This behaviour is the exception rather than the rule.

Young baboons are carried jockey-fashion by their mothers; the 'broken tail' appearance is typical of Savanna Baboons.
Inset: *Female baboon, showing typical dog-like muzzle.*

A family of Savanna baboons, with the larger male in the foreground.

Savanna Baboon

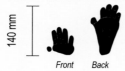

140 mm

Front   Back

Food: Omnivorous. Digs for roots and bulbs, eats wild fruit, seeds, leaves and flowers, insects and other invertebrates. Raids cultivated crops. Will eat young antelope, hares, mice and birds if encountered. In rocky areas a feeding baboon troop leaves a trail of overturned stones and small rocks.

Reproduction: The birth of the Savanna Baboon's single offspring may take place at any time of the year. When a female comes into oestrus the 'sexual skin' on the buttocks becomes red and considerably swollen. This is completely natural and is not a result of injury or sickness as is often thought. The gestation period is 6 months. The newborn infant is black with a pink face and for the first few weeks clings to its mother's chest; as it grows older, however, it rides on her back.

Cercopithecus
pygerythrus

■ Vervet Monkey *Cercopithecus pygerythrus*

Male: total length 100–130 cm; tail 60–75 cm; mass 4–8 (average 5.5) kg.
Female: total length 95–110 cm; tail 48–65 cm; mass 3.5–5 (average 4.0) kg.
Identification pointers: Typical monkey appearance; grizzled grey hair on head, back and flanks; black face with rim of pale to white hair; long tail; lives in troops. Habitat usually separates this species from the Sykes's Monkey.
Note: There is uncertainty as to whether the Vervet monkey should be called *Chlorocebus aethiops* or *Cercopithecus pygerythrus*. Until clarity is reached, we have retained the latter. Several of the subspecies occurring elsewhere in Africa may, in fact, be found to be distinct species.

Description: A well-known animal with its grizzled grey, fairly long, coarse hair and typical monkey appearance. Its underparts are paler than its upperparts and are frequently white. The face is short-haired and black, with a rim of white hair across the forehead and down the sides of the cheeks. The hands and feet are black. Several subspecies occur in southern Africa, with some variation in colour: animals from northern Namibia usually have very pale feet and hands, while the subspecies in the Tete district of Mozambique has a reddish back. The general hair colour varies from area to area but this monkey is unlikely to be confused with any other species. The adult male has a distinctive bright blue scrotum.

Distribution: Northern and eastern parts of southern Africa, extending along the southern coast as far west as Mossel Bay. It extends into otherwise inhospitable areas along rivers, including the Gariep (Orange) River as far west as its estuary, and along wooded streams in the Great Karoo. In recent years, small troops (up to 15 individuals) have established themselves in suitable locations in many parts of the Karoo, including near the authors' village; to get there, they must have crossed up to 20 km of open plain, utilizing wooded water courses. They are widespread throughout central and East Africa with the exception of equatorial forest.

Habitat: This is a monkey of savanna and riverine woodland.

Behaviour: Vervet monkeys live in troops of up to 20 or more. The formation of large groups will generally be associated with an abundant food source or water. They are completely diurnal and sleep at night in trees or more rarely on cliffs. A distinct 'pecking order' or hierarchy is well established in each troop. They forage in a well-defined home range, spending much of their time on the ground. They frequently raid crops and gardens and are in consequence heavily persecuted.

Food: Although Vervet Monkeys are mainly vegetarian, they also eat a wide range of invertebrates and small vertebrates such as nestling birds. Fruits, flowers, leaves, gum and seeds form the bulk of their food.

Reproduction: A single young, weighing some 300–400 g, born after a gestation period of about 165 days, at any time of the year, although in some areas there seems to be a birth peak at certain times.

A single young is born after a gestation of some 165 days.

Male Vervet Monkey with a bright blue scrotum.

The Vervet Monkey's underparts are pale, frequently white.

The black face and white forehead is characteristic.

Vervet Monkey

60 mm

Front

Back

74 mm

Cercopithecus albogularis

■ Sykes's Monkey *Cercopithecus albogularis*

Male: total length 1.4 m; tail 80 cm; mass 8–10 kg.
Female: total length 1.2 m; tail 70 cm; mass 4–5 kg.

Identification pointers: Typical monkey appearance; much darker than Vervet Monkey, being black on legs, shoulders and last two-thirds of tail length; long hair on cheeks; brown (not black) face. Forest habitat usually separates it from the more open areas occupied by the Vervet Monkey.

Note: In southern Africa, Sykes's Monkey is often referred to as the Samango, or Blue, Monkey. The name Sykes's Monkey is most extensively used in East Africa. Many subspecies/races have been described across its extensive African range.

Description: A fairly large forest species with dark-brown face, and white only on lips and throat. Hair on legs and shoulders is dark brown or black, but rest of the back and sides is grizzled grey-brown, browner towards the tail. Long tail is black for the last two-thirds of its length. Long hair stands out on cheeks and forehead. Underparts are paler than upperparts, usually off-white with a suffusion of light brown.

Two subspecies are recognized from southern Africa: *C. albogularis erythrarchus* is restricted to the coastal forests of Maputaland in northern KwaZulu-Natal (north of the Imfolozi River), extending into Mozambique, Malawi and Zimbabwe, with isolated populations occuring in the Soutpansberg range and other Afromontane forests on the Eastern escarpment of Limpopo and Mpumalanga. *C. albogularis labiatus* is found in the forests of the Eastern Cape (from the vicinity of Pirie Forest) and northwards to the KwaZulu-Natal Midlands. The ranges of the two subspecies do not overlap, making for easy separation. *C. a. erythrarchus* has a black tail with patches of orange-red on the lower buttock area and around the anus. In *C. a. labiatus*, the tail is dark above but the basal third is paler to off-white below and there are no red hairs.

Distribution: Isolated populations are found in forest and forest pockets extending from Eastern Cape to KwaZulu-Natal, Mpumalanga and the southern slopes of the Soutpansberg mountains; also found in eastern Zimbabwe and Mozambique. A small isolated population was recently discovered in the Masebe River Gorge on the Makgabeng Plateau to the south of the Soutpansberg and Blouberg ranges. This riparian forest is very narrow and sided by steep cliffs and extends for just over 10 km. Of interest is that these monkeys regularly use the cliffs and rock ledges to move between trees.

Habitat: High forest, forest margins and riverine gallery forest; may forage in more open woodland but always close to forest.

Behaviour: Lives in troops up to 30 strong, although most are smaller than this. More arboreal than Vervet Monkey. During the hottest hours of the day it rests in deep shade. As with most monkeys, the Sykes's is a vocal species with a range of different calls. The males have a very loud, far-carrying bark sounding superficially like 'jack'. Calling and their crashing progress through trees is often all that is revealed of their presence.

Food: Feeds on a wide range of plants, including fruits, flowers, gum, leaves and seeds. Debarks young trees in softwood plantations, so is not popular with foresters. Sometimes eats insects; only rarely predates on birds and small mammals.

Reproduction: Normally single, almost black young born during summer.

The forest-dwelling Sykes's, or Samango, Monkey has a very restricted distribution in southern Africa.

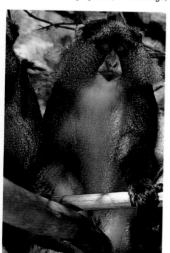

Sykes's Monkey in the forests of the Soutpansberg, Limpopo Province.

Sykes's Monkey has relatively long hair.

Sykes's Monkey

80 mm

Front

Back

GALAGOS (BUSHBABIES) | Family Galagidae

*Otolemur (Galago)
crassicaudatus*

■ Thick-tailed (Greater) Galago *Otolemur (Galago) crassicaudatus*
Total length 70–80 cm; tail 35–45 cm; mass 1–1.5 kg.

Identification pointers: Superficially cat-like when seen on the ground and tail usually held erect; uniformly grey to grey-brown; long, fairly bushy tail, same colour as body; large thin ears and large eyes; harrowing and unnerving screaming call made at night; usually seen in trees.

Description: Much larger than Southern Lesser Galago (see below), with which it is sometimes confused. On ground it is somewhat cat-like, but hindquarters are higher than shoulder region and the long tail is held high off ground, or erect. Hair of upperparts and tail is woolly, fine and grey-brown. Underparts are lighter in colour than upperparts. Characteristic features are the very large, rounded, thin ears and large eyes, which shine red in torchlight.

Distribution: Restricted to the far eastern parts of southern Africa, but occur widely in central Africa and East Africa.

Habitat: Forest, woodland (sometimes dry) and wooded riverine margins.

Behaviour: Nocturnal, spending the day sleeping among dense vegetation tangles in trees or in self-constructed nests. Rest together in groups numbering 2–6 but usually forage alone at night. A group has a fixed home range of several hectares, within which are a number of resting-sites. Frequently forage on the ground. An obvious sign of their presence is a loud screaming call, like that of a baby in distress. They also use urine and gland secretions to communicate with other individuals. They urinate on the soles/palms of feet and then transfer the urine to the ground as they walk. Both sexes have a scent-gland on the front of the chest which is rubbed against branches and other individuals.

Food: Fruit and tree gum, particularly of acacias; also insects, reptiles, birds.

Reproduction: In the south give birth in November; in Zimbabwe and Zambia give birth in August and September. Usually 2 young are born after a gestation period of about 130 days.

Galago moholi

■ Southern Lesser Galago (Bushbaby) *Galago moholi*
Total length 30–40 cm; tail 20–25 cm; mass 120–210 g (average 150 g).

Identification pointers: Small size with long fluffy tail; large, mobile, thin ears; large, forward-facing eyes; prodigious jumping ability and arboreal habits. Compare with Thick-tailed Galago where distributions overlap.

The name South African Galago is sometimes used for this species but, as it also occurs in Central Africa, we prefer to use Southern Lesser Galago, or Bushbaby.

Description: The Southern Lesser Galago (Bushbaby) is considerably smaller than the Thick-tailed Galago, with which it is frequently confused. The fine woolly, greyish to grey-brown hair extends onto the fluffy tail, which is slightly longer than the head and body. The ears are large, thin and rounded and extremely mobile. The eyes are very large, forward-pointing and ringed with black, and the head is small and rounded with a short snout.

Distribution: In our subregion this species is restricted to the northern and north-eastern parts. Closely related species are widely distributed in woodland areas of central, East and West Africa but are absent from equatorial forests.

Habitat: Woodland savanna, particularly acacia and riverine woodland.

Behaviour: The Southern Lesser Galago is nocturnal and feeds mostly in trees but it does descend to the ground to forage. Family groups of 2–8 sleep together but they usually forage alone or in very loose association. Although they construct

The Thick-tailed Galago, the largest galago species in the region, is nocturnal, resting during the day and foraging at night. Inset: *This species will forage on the ground, seeking insects and small reptiles.*

The Southern Lesser Galago (Bushbaby) has very large eyes and large, thin, mobile ears.

Thick-tailed Galago

50 mm

Front

Southern Lesser Galago

30 mm

Front

85

their own nests of leaves, they will also lie up in dense creeper tangles or in holes. They are territorial and groups occupy home ranges of about 3 ha, but this will vary according to food availability. They jump considerable distances from branch to branch and tree to tree. They are vocal animals with a wide range of calls, from low croaking to chittering and grunts.

Food: The gum or exuding sap of trees, particularly acacias, is very important in their diet but they also eat insects, which they catch with their hands.

Reproduction: After a gestation period of slightly more than 120 days, 1 or 2 young are born. At birth they weigh about 9 g, the eyes are open and they are well-haired. Females may have two litters a year, in early and late summer. The young are carried by the female when she forages but are left clinging to branches while she moves about in the vicinity.

Galagoides granti

■ Grant's Galago *Galagoides granti*
Total length 37–42 cm; tail 21–25 cm; mass 165 g.
Identification pointers: As for Southern Lesser Galago.
Description: Slightly larger than Southern Lesser Galago and browner in colour. Calls differ from those of the last species.

Distribution: In the subregion, restricted to Mozambique coastal plain to an altitude of about 200 m, extending inland to the eastern border with Zimbabwe.

Behaviour: When jumping, they land with either the front feet, or all four feet, whereas Southern Lesser Galago normally lands hindfeet first. The territorial male often lies up with one or two females, unlike the Southern Lesser Galago where males sleep apart from the females.

Food: Mainly insects, other invertebrates, small vertebrates and fruits; very rarely tree gum.

Reproduction: Probably similar to Southern Lesser Galago.

PANGOLINS | Order Pholidota | Family Manidae

Manis temminckii

■ Ground Pangolin *Manis temminckii*
Total length 70–140 cm; tail 30–45 cm; mass 5–16 kg.
Identification pointers: Unmistakable; covered in large brown overlapping scales. Small head, heavy hindquarters and tail; small forelegs.
Description: This cannot be mistaken for any other species. Large, brown scales composed of agglutinated hair cover the upperparts, sides and tail. Smaller scales cover outer sides of legs and top of head. Underparts sparsely covered with hair. Head disproportionately small and pointed. It has powerfully built hindlegs, short forelegs and a long, heavy tail. Walks on hindlegs, occasionally using tail and forelegs for balance.

Distribution: Wide distribution in subregion north of Gariep (Orange) River.

Habitat: Habitats range from low to high rainfall areas, including open grassland, woodland and rocky hills, but excluding forest and desert.

Behaviour: Solitary and mainly nocturnal, although occasionally diurnal. May try to run away when threatened but usually curls into ball to protect the head and underparts. May dig own burrows, but readily uses those dug by other species, or simply curls up among dense vegetation.

Food: Only eats certain species of ants and termites. Scratches superficially into nests close to the surface, under plant debris and animal dung.

Reproduction: Single young apparently normally born in winter.

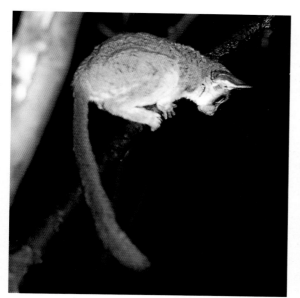

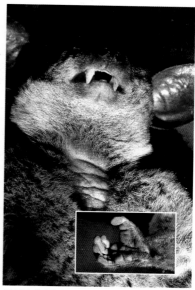

The Southern Lesser Galago is also known as the South African Galago, or Bushbaby; note the long, bushy tail.

Thick-tailed Galago uses its chest gland to mark territory. Inset: *Hand, showing opposable thumb.*

The Pangolin is also known as a Scaly Anteater. Inset: *Pangolins curl into a ball for protection when they feel threatened.*

Grant's Galago

60 mm

Back

Ground Pangolin

HARES & RABBITS | Order **Lagomorpha** | Family Leporidae

Two species of hare and five species of rabbit occur naturally in southern Africa. The European Rabbit (*Oryctolagus cuniculus*) occurs on eight small offshore islands, to which it was introduced by man.

Lepus capensis

Lepus saxatilis

■ **Cape Hare** *Lepus capensis*
Total length 45–60 cm; tail 7–14 cm; mass 1.4–2.5 kg.
■ **Scrub Hare** *Lepus saxatilis*
Total length 45–65 cm; tail 7–17 cm; mass 1.5–4.5 kg.
The Scrub Hare and the Cape Hare vary considerably in size from area to area, although the former is generally larger than the latter.
Identification pointers: Both species have long ears, and the hindlegs are much longer than the forelegs. The tail is black above, white below. See also distribution maps and habitat requirements.
Description: Both species of hare have long ears, long, well-developed hindlegs and a short fluffy tail. The body hair is fine and soft.

	Cape Hare	Scrub Hare
Upperparts	Varies; light brown and black- flecked; whitish-grey in north	Brown-grey to grey; black-flecked
Underparts	Chest not white; abdomen white; in north may be completely white	White throughout
Face	Yellowish on nose and cheeks; pale grey in northern animals	Lighter (whitish or buff) on sides of face and around eyes
Nuchal patch (on nape of neck behind ears)	Brownish-pink; pale grey in northern animals	Reddish-brown

Distribution: Cape Hare has a wide distribution in the western and central areas of southern Africa with isolated populations in the north (Botswana) and east (Limpopo Province and southern Mozambique). Scrub Hare is found throughout southern Africa, with the exception of the Namib Desert.
Habitat: Cape Hare prefers drier, open habitat; Scrub Hare occurs in woodland and scrub cover with grass. Scrub Hare is commonly seen in cultivated areas. Normally the Scrub Hare is not seen in completely open grassland and the Cape Hare is not found in dense scrub or woodland; there is some overlap, however.
Behaviour: Both species nocturnal but some early morning and late afternoon activity may occur. Both lie up in 'forms' (shallow indentations in the ground made by the body), with those of Scrub Hare being in more substantial cover. They rely on their camouflage when approached, only getting up and running off at the last minute. Normally zigzag, often at high speed.
Food: Predominantly grazers but will feed on other plants.
Reproduction: Young born at any time of the year. Cape Hare may have as many as four litters per year. Gestation period about 42 days; 1–3 leverets are born fully haired and with open eyes and can move about soon after birth.

Cape Hare upperparts are whitish-grey in the north-west.

Most, but not all, Scrub Hares have a white forehead spot.

Scrub Hare upperparts are brown-grey to grey.

Underside of Scrub Hare foot is covered in hair.

European rabbits have been introduced to a number of offshore islands.

Scrub Hare's natural colouring enables it to blend easily into the undergrowth.

Scrub Hare
Cape Hare

300 mm

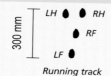

LH ● ● RH

● RF

LF ●

Running track

Red Rock Rabbits Genus *Pronolagus*

Four species occur in the subregion. Based on DNA sequencing, Hewitt's Red Rock Rabbit is recognized as occuring in the Western and Eastern Cape, but cannot be separated from Smith's Red Rock Rabbit in the field.

Pronolagus randensis

■ **Jameson's Red Rock Rabbit** *Pronolagus randensis*
Total length 48–63 cm; tail 6–13 cm; mass 1.8–3.0 kg.
■ **Natal Red Rock Rabbit** *Pronolagus crassicaudatus*
Total length 50–67 cm; tail 3–11 cm; mass 2.4–3.0 kg.
■ **Hewitt's Red Rock Rabbit** *Pronolagus saundersiae*
■ **Smith's Red Rock Rabbit** *Pronolagus rupestris*
Total length 43–65 cm; tail 5–11 cm; mass 1.3–2.0 kg.

Identification pointers: Different red rock rabbits can be identified from distribution maps, except where there is overlap. They can also be separated from the two hare species and the Riverine Rabbit by their much shorter ears.

Description: All rabbit-like and all are similar in appearance. Their distribution ranges only overlap marginally, however, and therefore use of distribution maps is very important. Coloration can be variable but usually the back and sides are reddish-brown, grizzled with black. Underparts of all species range from pinkish-brown to reddish-brown.

Pronolagus crassicaudatus

Pronolagus rupestris
P. saundersiae
(These two red rock rabbits are identical in appearance and cannot be separated in the field.)

	Jameson's	**Natal**	**Smith's**
Rump and back legs	Lighter than back and sides	Bright red-brown	Bright red-brown
Tail	Red-brown, black tip	Uniform red-brown; no black tip	Dark to red-brown; black tip
Face and neck	Head light grey, brown-flecked	Grey-white band from chin along lower jaw and to back of neck	Sides of face greyish

Distribution: See distribution maps.
Habitat: Rocky habitats from isolated outcrops to mountain ranges.
Behaviour: Essentially nocturnal, but may feed on overcast days. Normally rest up in rock crevices or in dense vegetation cover. Usually single.
Food: Predominantly grazers, but Jameson's eats leaves of woody plants.
Reproduction: Young (1–2 per litter) are probably born hairless and helpless in cup-shaped nest lined with soft hair from the female's underparts.

'Latrine' sites with heaps of lozenge-shaped pellets are characteristic of areas inhabited by red rock rabbits.
Inset: *Juvenile Smith's Red Rock Rabbit.*

Jameson's Red Rock Rabbitt, one of the few known photographs of this little-known species. Note the dark-coloured tail.
Inset: *Red rock rabbit skins (l. to r.): Smith's, Natal, Jameson's and Riverine Rabbit.*

Red Rock Rabbits

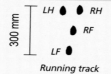

300 mm

LH ● ● RH
● RF
LF ●
Running track

Bunolagus monticularis

■ **Riverine Rabbit** *Bunolagus monticularis*
Total length 52 cm; tail 9 cm; mass ± 1.5–1.9 kg.
An endangered species, but numbers probably not as low as previously thought.
Scattered populations, mainly in the districts of Victoria West, Fraserburg and
Beaufort West; also recently discovered near Touwsrivier and in Little Karoo.
Identification pointers: Similar to red rock rabbits, but ears much longer
and upperparts drab grey; differs from the two hares in having more or less
uniformly coloured grey-brown tail, not black and white. Dark-brown stripe
along lower jaw towards ear base only found in this species; white eye-ring.
Description: Similar to the red rock rabbits but has longer, more hare-like ears.
White ring around eye and dark-brown stripe down the side of the lower jaw,
extending to ear base. Upperparts grizzled grey; nuchal patch deep red-brown;
tail short, fluffy and grey-brown, somewhat darker towards the tip.
Distribution: Central districts of Karoo, South Africa.
Habitat: Dense riverine bush in arid areas.
Behaviour: Little known but home range is 10–15 ha.
Food: Mainly browse, but also grass when fresh.
Reproduction: Apparently one 50 g young born in nest in shallow burrow.

RODENTS | Order Rodentia
Rodents are characterized by the pair of large, chisel-like, continuously growing
incisors in both jaws. Currently, 84 species have been recorded from subregion
(four introduced), ranging in size from the 6 g Pygmy Mouse to 20 kg Porcupine.

SQUIRRELS | Family Sciuridae
Of the seven species in the subregion, five are arboreal and two terrestrial. The
Grey Squirrel is an alien introduced from North America via the United Kingdom.

Xerus inauris

■ **Southern African Ground Squirrel** *Xerus inauris*
Total length 40–50 cm; tail 19–25 cm; mass 500–1 000 g (average 650 g).
Identification pointers: Terrestrial, lives in burrows; white stripe down each
side; long bushy tail; very small ears. Nearly impossible to distinguish from
Damara Ground Squirrel where ranges overlap, but incisors of latter species
are orange; those of Ground Squirrel are white. Occasionally confused with the
Suricate (page 156) but latter species lacks the bushy tail or side stripes.
Description: Easily identifiable species, being entirely terrestrial yet typically
squirrel-like. Upperparts usually cinnamon-brown, some animals more grey-brown.
Single white stripe runs along each side of body from shoulder to thigh. Underparts
are white tinged with light brown in mid-belly. Coarse hair; white incisors.
Distribution: Endemic to the arid areas of southern Africa.
Habitat: Open areas with sparse cover and usually a hard substrate.
Behaviour: Gregarious diurnal species occuring in groups of 5 to 30. It excavates
extensive burrow-systems. Females and young remain in close proximity to the
burrows but males live in separate burrow systems, moving from colony to colony.
Frequently stands on its hindlegs to enhance its view of the surrounding area. Its
bushy tail is often held over the body and head when the squirrel feeds, to act as
a sunshade. Burrow-systems often shared with Suricate and Yellow Mongoose.
Food: Grass, roots, seeds and bulbs; also insects, particularly termites.
Reproduction: Gestation ±45 days. 1–3 naked, helpless young, weighing ±20 g,
born any time of year, in a burrow from which they emerge at about 6 weeks.

The seriously endangered Riverine Rabbit.

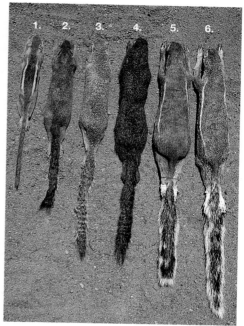

Greyish form of the Southern African Ground Squirrel.

Key to Squirrel skins:
1. *Striped Tree Squirrel*
2. *Tree Squirrel*
3. *Red Squirrel*
4. *Sun Squirrel*
5. *Southern African Ground Squirrel*
6. *Damara Ground Squirrel.*

More usual brown form of Southern African Ground Squirrel; note tail being used as a sunshade.

Southern African Ground Squirrel eats a variety of grass, roots, bulbs and seeds; sometimes small insects.

Riverine Rabbit

60 mm
Front   Back

Southern African
Ground Squirrel

Xerus princeps

Damara Ground Squirrel *Xerus princeps*
Species very similar to Southern African Ground Squirrel in appearance. It is more closely associated with rocky hills and mountainous country, is solitary, lives in pairs or female with young. Unlike the other species, it will readily climb into low bushes to feed. They seem to be seasonal breeders with 1–3 young being dropped during the cooler winter months. Largely restricted to the Namibian escarpment and where this extends into south-western Angola, but recently found to occur in the Richtersveld in north-western South Africa.

Heliosciurus mutabilis

Sun Squirrel *Heliosciurus mutabilis*
Total length 40–55 cm; tail 20–30 cm; mass 300–480 g.
Identification pointers: Subregion's largest arboreal squirrel; variable in colour but usually grizzled light brown; bushy, narrowly banded tail. Compare with Red Bush Squirrel (see below).
Description: The largest indigenous, arboreal squirrel occurring in southern Africa. Varies considerably in colour but the upperparts are usually grizzled light brown. In parts of Zimbabwe, it can be black above while in other areas it is reddish. The underparts are pale fawn to white. The tail has a series of narrow, indistinct whitish bands.
Distribution: Restricted in southern Africa to the forests of eastern Zimbabwe and Mozambique. It is widely, if patchily, distributed in East Africa and westwards through the equatorial forest areas into West Africa.
Habitat: Forested areas at both high and low elevations, including riverine forest.
Behaviour: Diurnal, occuring singly or in pairs. Most activity is restricted to early morning and late afternoon. It is often observed basking in the sun, stretched out on branches. In areas where its distribution overlaps with the Red Squirrel, it tends to utilize the higher canopy zone. As is common with most arboreal squirrels, it is quite vocal, giving vent to clucking calls accompanied by frequent tail-flicking.
Food: It takes a wide range of plant food but it will also eat insects and possibly smaller vertebrates such as lizards and birds.
Reproduction: All that is known with any certainty is that litters consist of 1–4 young and are probably produced in summer.

Paraxerus palliatus

Red Bush Squirrel *Paraxerus palliatus*
Total length 35–40 cm; tail 17–20 cm; mass 200–380 g.
Identification pointers: Dark-grey to black upperparts; underparts and tail reddish or yellowish. Compare with Sun Squirrel where range overlaps.
Description: The upperparts are grizzled dark grey to black and the underparts, sides of face, feet and tail are usually reddish or yellowish. As the most brightly coloured of all our squirrels, it should not be mistaken for any other.
Distribution: Confined to Mozambique and extreme eastern parts of Zimbabwe but there are two isolated populations in KwaZulu-Natal. Beyond the subregion it extends into East Africa.
Habitat: Forest habitats, including coastal dune and montane forests.
Behaviour: Diurnal, usually solitary except when female is accompanied by young. A male, female and small young may be observed in a loose association. Very vocal species with a range of different calls, usually accompanied by tail-flicking.
Food: It takes a wide range of plant food, including fruits, berries and some insects.
Reproduction: 1 or 2 young, each weighing about 14 g, are born after a gestation period of between 60 and 65 days. As with other squirrel species, the young are born hairless and blind. Births occur mainly during the wet season.

Damara Ground Squirrel. Inset: *The Sun Squirrel is active in the morning and late afternoon.*

Skins of arboreal tree squirrels (l. to r.): Sun Squirrel (two colour phases), Red Bush Squirrel, Striped Tree Squirrel.

Sun Squirrel	Damara Ground Squirrel	Red Bush Squirrel

95

Funisciurus congicus

■ **Striped Tree Squirrel** *Funisciurus congicus*
Total length 30 cm; tail 17 cm; mass 110 g.
Identification pointers: Small size; white side stripe; only found in northern Namibia. Could be confused with Tree Squirrel but the latter does not have white body stripe. Tail held over back.
Description: Smallest squirrel in subregion. Upperparts pale yellow-brown; underparts paler or off-white. Single white stripe runs down side from neck to base of long bushy tail. A darker stripe runs below the white stripe.
Distribution: Restricted to north-western Namibia.
Habitat: Dense woodland, near watercourses and rocky outcrops.
Behaviour: Diurnal and arboreal, but descends to the ground to forage. It lives in small family groups. Resting-sites are in tree-holes and its nest or 'drey' is constructed from leaves and twigs in the fork of a branch. Only indigenous squirrel to construct a drey.
Food: A wide range of plant food but also insects.
Reproduction: Two young are born in a tree-hole or drey with most births taking place either at the onset or at the end of the rains.

Paraxerus cepapi

■ **Tree Squirrel** *Paraxerus cepapi*
Total length 35 cm; tail 16 cm; mass 100–260 g.
Identification pointers: Small size; uniformly greyish or yellowish-brown upperparts; no distinctive markings. Most widespread of all our tree squirrels.
Description: Very variable in size and colour. In general, animals from western areas are greyer and eastern animals are more yellow-brown. Underparts range from fawn to white. Body has a generally grizzled appearance.
Distribution: Occurs widely in north and north-eastern parts of southern Africa.
Habitat: A wide variety of woodland habitats but not true high forest.
Behaviour: Although it is usually seen singly or in mother/young groups, a number of animals live in loose association. The adult male or males in a group will defend a territory against incursions by other squirrels. As with other squirrel species it is very vocal. Equally at home foraging in trees and on the ground.
Food: A wide variety of plant food and also insects. Will cache surplus food.
Reproduction: After a gestation period of about 55 days, 1–3 young, each weighing about 10 g, are born in a leaf-lined tree-hole, mostly in summer.

■ **Grey Squirrel** *Sciurus carolinensis* (Introduced)
Total length 50 cm; tail 22 cm; mass 600 g.
Identification pointers: Restricted to south-western Cape, where it is the only squirrel. Uniform grey-brown or silvery-grey upperparts, white underparts.
Description: This large squirrel has a summer coat that is generally brownish-grey in colour, but after the moult the winter coat is silvery-grey. The underparts are white to off-white. The tail is long and bushy.
Sciurus carolinensis
Distribution: Native to North America. In subregion it is restricted to alien pine plantations and oak trees in extreme south-western South Africa.
Habitat: Oak woodland, pine plantations and suburban gardens.
Behaviour: Normally solitary or in mother/young family groups but several may be seen feeding in close proximity. Makes use of tree-holes but also constructs dreys. Although arboreal, it spends large amounts of time on the ground foraging.
Food: Acorns, pine seeds, cultivated fruits, fungi, insects, young birds, birds' eggs.
Reproduction: All year round but birth peaks in August and January. Gestation 45 days; 1–4 young each weigh about 15 g at birth.

Tree Squirrels (main picture and inset) *are equally at home in trees or foraging on the ground.*

Tree Squirrels colour varies in different regions. *Inset: Grey Squirrel is confined to the south-western Cape.*

Striped Tree
Squirrel

Tree Squirrel

Front   Back

46 mm

Grey Squirrel

97

DORMICE | Family Myoxidae

Four species of dormouse occur in southern Africa, but the Lesser Savanna Dormouse is considered by some authorities to be merely a smaller form of the Woodland Dormouse. Because of their bushy tails they are sometimes mistaken for squirrels but they differ in being much smaller in size and nocturnal in habit.

Graphiurus ocularis

■ **Spectacled Dormouse** *Graphiurus ocularis*
Total length 25 cm; tail 10 cm; mass 80 g.
■ **Rock Dormouse** *Graphiurus platyops*
Total length 18 cm; tail 7 cm; mass 45 g.
■ **Woodland Dormouse** *Graphiurus murinus*
Total length 16 cm; tail 7 cm; mass 30 g.
■ **Lesser Savanna Dormouse** *Graphiurus kelleni*
Total length 14 cm; tail 6 cm.

Graphiurus platyops

Identification pointers: See distribution maps and habitat descriptions. Distinct black-and-white facial markings and larger size distinguish Spectacled Dormouse; Rock Dormouse distinguished by flattened skull and rocky habitat; the Woodland and Lesser Savanna Dormice smallest in size and most frequently seen. All generally greyish in colour with bushy, squirrel-like tails.

Description: Dormice have bushy, squirrel-like tails, fairly short muzzles, small ears and soft fur. Hair colour is grey to silvery-grey. Spectacled Dormouse is most distinctive, not only because of its relatively large size but also for black, white and grey facial markings. A dark ring surrounds each eye (the 'spectacles'), and a dark line runs from the sides of the muzzle onto the shoulders. Lips, cheeks, underparts and upper-surfaces of the hands and feet are white. Tail is usually rimmed and tipped with white. Rock Dormouse also has a dark facial pattern but much less distinct than Spectacled Dormouse. Its bushy pale-grey tail is usually white-tipped. The underparts are grey. An interesting feature of this dormouse is the somewhat flattened skull, an adaptation to living in narrow rock crevices. Although Woodland Dormouse lacks distinctive facial markings, cheeks, lips and underparts are either white or greyish-white; tail may or may not be white-tipped. Lesser Savanna Dormouse is very similar to Woodland Dormouse.

Graphiurus murinus
Graphiurus kelleni

Distribution: Spectacled Dormouse is restricted to western South Africa. The Rock Dormouse occurs in two widely separated populations, one in the west and the other in the east. The Woodland Dormouse has a wide distribution in northern and eastern areas and narrowly along the southern coastal belt; it is difficult to separate from the Lesser Savanna Dormouse (see combined distribution map).

Habitat: Both the Spectacled and Rock Dormice are associated with rocky habitats but the Spectacled Dormouse also utilizes trees and buildings. The Woodland Dormouse is a woodland savanna and bush species but it is also frequently found in association with man-made structures.

Behaviour: All are nocturnal and are agile climbers. Woodland Dormouse may construct substantial nests of grass, leaves and lichen and may become quite tame where it lives in close association with man. Both Spectacled and Rock Dormice appear to be solitary but several Woodland Dormice may share the same nest. Northern Hemisphere dormice hibernate in winter; local species appear either to hibernate or, at least, become more sluggish during cold periods.

Food: Seeds, other plant material, insects and other invertebrates.

Reproduction: Virtually nothing is known about this aspect of dormouse biology, but indications are that young are born during the summer. Spectacled Dormouse has litters of 4–6 young every six months under optimum conditions.

Spectacled Dormouse has distinct facial markings. Inset (top to bottom): *Woodland, Rock and Spectacled Dormouse skins.*

A young Woodland Dormouse just out of the nest.

The Woodland Dormouse uses lichen to construct its nest.

Spectacled Dormouse

 Lesser Savanna Dormouse

SPRINGHARES | Family Pedetidae

Pedetes capensis

■ **Springhare** *Pedetes capensis*
The East African springhare population, now known to be a separate species, *Pedetes surdaster*, differs from the South African species in relatively minor anatomical and cytogenic details; but, unlike its southern relative, it occupies communal burrow systems.
Total length 75–85 cm; tail 35–45 cm; mass 2.5–3.8 kg.
Identification pointers: Kangaroo-like appearance; long, powerful hindlegs; long well-haired tail with black tip; ears and eyes fairly large. Nocturnal and found in habitats with sandy soils.
Description: A true rodent despite its name. Kangaroo-like, with long, powerfully built hindlegs and short, lightly built forelegs. Hindfeet have three large nails and forefeet have five long, pointed claws for digging. Progresses by hopping; forelegs only used while feeding. Tail long, bushy and black towards tip. Ears long and pointed; eyes large. General colour of upperparts is yellowish or reddish-fawn and underparts are off-white to pale fawn.
Distribution: Widespread, although absent from Western Cape and Namibian coastal belt, as well as the extreme north-eastern parts of southern Africa. Absent from the Rift Valley of central Africa but occurs again in East Africa.
Habitat: Compacted sandy soils with short vegetation cover. It will colonize sandy areas along river-banks where these pass through unsuitable habitat.
Behaviour: Nocturnal, terrestrial and apparently not territorial. Although several burrows, housing several individuals, may be situated in close proximity, each burrow is occupied by a single animal or a female with young. Two types of hole are dug: a sloping one which is most frequently used, and a vertical escape-burrow. Burrows may be blocked with sand if the Springhare is in occupation. Its eyes shine brightly in torchlight.
Food: Grass, grass-roots and other plants. Cultivated crops.
Reproduction: A single young, weighing approximately 300 g, may be born at any time of the year. Juvenile emerges 6–7 weeks after birth.

RODENT MOLES (MOLE-RATS) | Family Bathyergidae
Six species of mole-rat occur in southern Africa, two of which are restricted to the extreme west of South Africa.

■ *Bathyergus suillus*
■ *Bathyergus janetta*

Cryptomys hottentotus

■ **Cape Dune Mole-rat** *Bathyergus suillus*
Total length 32 cm; tail 5 cm; mass 650–890 g (> 2 kg).
■ **Namaqua Dune Mole-rat** *Bathyergus janetta*
Total length 25 cm; tail 4 cm; mass 340–470 g.
■ **Common (African) Mole-rat** *Cryptomys hottentotus*
Total length 15 cm; tail 2 cm; mass 100–150 g.
■ **Damara Mole-rat** *Cryptomys damarensis*
Total length 15 cm; tail 2 cm; mass 100–150 g.
■ **Mashona Mole-rat** *Cryptomys darlingi*
Mass 64 g.
■ **Cape Mole-rat** *Georychus capensis*
Total length 20 cm; tail 3 cm; mass 180 g.
Identification pointers: Large size distinguishes Cape Dune Mole-rat and Namaqua Dune Mole-rat; small size and uniform colouring of Common Mole-rat; Cape, Damara and Mashona Mole-rats nearly always have white patch on

The Springhare has powerful hindlegs and short forelegs.

The Springhare's long tail has a bushy black tip.

The Cape Dune Mole-rat is the largest mole-rat species.

Namaqua Dune Mole-rat has dull to silvery-grey fur.

Common, or African, Mole-rat can be greyish-fawn.

Mole-rat skins (l. to r.) Common Mole-rat, Cape Mole-rat, Namaqua Dune Mole-rat, Cape Dune Mole-rat.

Springhare

38 mm

Back feet in soft sand

Cape Dune Mole-rat

Damara Mole-rat

■ *Cryptomys damarensis*
■ *Cryptomys darlingi*

Georychus capensis

top of head but Cape also has other black-and-white head markings and is larger, and can be separated on range. Consult the distribution maps.

Description: All have soft fur, short tails, large, rounded heads, well-developed and prominent incisors, and tiny eyes and ears. Legs are short and forefeet each carry four long claws for digging. Snouts are flattened and somewhat pig-like. Cape Dune Mole-rat is largest with cinnamon to pale-fawn upperparts tinged with grey underparts and white chin and muzzle. Namaqua Dune Mole-rat differs from Cape Dune Mole-rat in having dull- to silvery-grey fur with broad, darker band extending down back from base of neck to rump. There is usually a white ring around the eyes. Tail brown above and white below. Common Mole-rat variable but usually greyish-fawn to dark brown without any distinguishing markings. Cape Mole-rat is easily distinguished from the other species because of black-and-white markings on head; general body colour brown to reddish-brown with greyish underparts.

Distribution: See distribution maps. Mashona Mole-rat restricted to northern Zimbabwe and probably adjacent Mozambique. Similar to Damara Mole-rat.

Habitat: Sandy soils but Common Mole-rat also occupies a wide range of other soils with the exception of heavy clay.

Behaviour: Fossorial, digging extensive underground burrow-systems marked on the surface by mounds of earth. Digging is undertaken by well-developed incisors, then using the feet to shovel loosened earth out of the way. Most digging follows rain. Within burrow systems of most, if not all, species, there are usually chambers that serve for food storage. All our mole-rats are believed to live in small to large colonies. Some, such as the Damara Mole-rat, have a complex social system that may be similar to that of the Naked Mole-rat of East Africa. A reproductive pair is dominant over the colony and these animals are larger than other group members.

Food: Vegetarian, eating mostly roots, bulbs and tubers. A nuisance in gardens and agricultural areas.

Reproduction: The young of the Cape Dune Mole-rat are born in the summer months and the usual litter size is 3–4. Common Mole-rats may have as many as 6 young per litter in summer; Damara Mole-rats are seasonal breeders and the dominant female only produces 2–3 young per litter. Cape Mole-rats have 4–10 pups per litter in summer.

PORCUPINE | Family Hystricidae

■ **Cape Porcupine** *Hystrix africaeaustralis*
Total length 75–100 cm; tail 10–15 cm; mass 10–24 kg.
Identification pointers: Unmistakable with body-covering of long quills banded in black-and-white. Confusion sometimes arises between this species and the Southern African Hedgehog but the latter is much smaller, is brown rather than black and white, and has very short spines.
Description: By far the largest rodent occurring in southern Africa; unmistakable with its protective covering of long quills banded in black and white. The sides, neck, head and underparts are covered in dark, coarse hair. A crest of long, erectile, coarse hairs extending from the top of the head, down the neck and onto the shoulders, is raised when the animal is alarmed or angry. The head and snout are broad, with small eyes and short, rounded ears. Legs are short and stout, with heavily clawed feet. Quills are easily detached and are frequently found lying on

Hystrix africaeaustralis

Mashona Mole-rat has a large rounded head, well-developed insicors and tiny ears and eyes.

Cape Mole-rat has black-and-white markings on the head.

Cape Porcupine has distinctive black-and-white banded quills.

Cape Porcupine

70 mm

Front   Back

trails and pathways. The tail is short and carries a number of hollow, open-ended quills which act as warning rattles when vibrated together.
Distribution: Occurs virtually throughout subregion, except Namib Desert.
Habitat: Wide range but preference for more broken country.
Behaviour: Solitary porcupines are most commonly seen but pairs and family parties will also be encountered. It is nocturnal and during the day it lies up in caves, among rocks, in burrows (either its own or those of other species) or even among dense vegetation. A common feature of well-used porcupine shelters is the accumulation of gnawed bones. It is generally believed that Cape Porcupines gnaw these bones both for their mineral content and to sharpen the long incisors. Within its home range, it makes use of regular pathways, along which are numerous shallow excavations exposing plant roots and bulbs. Although several porcupines may share a shelter, foraging is usually a solitary activity.
Food: Roots, bulbs, tubers and the bark of trees, as well as cultivated crops such as potatoes and pumpkins. It has been recorded as eating from animal carcasses, and it is often caught in traps baited with meat set to catch carnivores.
Reproduction: Litters from 1–4 (usually 1 or 2) young, each weighing from 300–450 g, are born usually in summer; they are well developed at birth and move around within a few hours.

CANE-RATS | Family Thryonomyidae
Two species of cane-rat occur in southern Africa.

Thryonomys swinderianus

Thryonomys gregorianus

■ **Greater Cane-rat** *Thryonomys swinderianus*
Total length 65–80 cm; tail 15–20 cm; mass 3.0–5.0 kg.
■ **Lesser Cane-rat** *Thryonomys gregorianus*
Total length 40–60 cm; tail 12–18 cm; mass 1.5–2.5 kg.
Identification pointers: Large size; dark-brown speckled hair; short tail; stout appearance. The Lesser Cane-rat has very limited distribution in southern Africa (see Habitat, maps).
Description: Large, coarse-haired, stockily built rodents with short tails. Two species differ only in size and in positioning of grooves on incisor teeth: grooves of Greater run close to inner edge of teeth; those of Lesser Cane-rat more evenly spaced over front surface of incisors. Upperparts and sides are generally dark speckled brown, underparts range from off-white to greyish-brown. The body hair falls out readily if an animal is handled. On the face, a fleshy pad, used in aggressive butting bouts, extends beyond the nostrils.
Distribution: Both widely distributed in Africa but in subregion Lesser Cane-rat is restricted to parts of southern Zimbabwe and adjacent areas of Mozambique; Greater Cane-rat occurs in extreme north and east.
Habitat: Occurs in reed-beds and dense vegetation near water; Lesser Cane-rat utilizes drier habitats.
Behaviour: Predominantly nocturnal although also crepuscular. Tend to forage alone, but they do, however, live in loosely associated groups. Distinct runs are formed within feeding areas and these are characterized by small piles of cut grass or reed segments along their length. Hunted for their meat and regarded as a delicacy.
Food: Mostly roots, leaves, stems and shoots of grasses, reeds and sedges. Greater Cane-rat can be a problem in sugar-cane areas.
Reproduction: Young of Greater Cane-rat born between August and December with a litter of 4 (up to 8). Mass at birth 80–190 g. Nothing is known about the reproduction of the Lesser Cane-rat.

The Greater Cane-rat is a coarse-haired, stockily-built rodent.

Head of Greater Cane-rat, showing the brown and rust-speckled coat, as well as the distinctive nose-pad.

Greater Cane-rat

Lesser Cane-rat

DASSIE RAT | Family Petromuridae

These rodents are neither dassies nor rats, so their common name is unfortunate. Efforts should be made to rather use the local Khoisan name, *Noki*.

Petromus typicus

■ Dassie Rat *Petromus typicus*

Total length 30 cm; tail 14 cm; mass 160–250 g.

Identification pointers: Squirrel-like appearance; tail very hairy but not bushy; general colour brown; rocky habitat; diurnal.

Description: Somewhat squirrel-like in appearance but although its tail is hairy, it is not bushy. Grizzled grey-brown to brown with hindquarters usually being more uniformly brown. Underparts vary from off-white to yellowish-brown. Head is somewhat flattened and ears are small.

Distribution: Largely restricted to the Namibian escarpment but the range extends southwards into the north-west of South Africa.

Habitat: Restricted to rocky areas, including isolated rock outcrops.

Behaviour: Pairs or family groups occupy rock crevices. It is active by day although much of its activity is restricted to early morning and late afternoon; it will, however, move about in shade even during the hottest part of the day. It is frequently observed basking in the early-morning sun, much like its namesake, the dassie. When feeding, it usually plucks a leaf or twig and takes it to shelter to feed. Like dassies, the Dassie Rat urinates at specific sites, which become stained yellowish-white. When handled, they readily and easily shed substantial tufts of hair. This may be a way to escape predators that do not take a firm grip.

Food: The Dassie Rat is vegetarian and eats a wide variety of plant food, with a preference for leaves and flowers; seeds and fruits to a lesser extent.

Reproduction: One to three fully-haired young born after a 90-day gestation. The well-developed young are dropped in rock crevices, mainly in summer.

RATS & MICE | Family Muridae

At least 64 species of rats and mice, all belonging to the Muridae, are recorded as occurring in southern Africa. The four species below are characterized by having wholly or partially white tails; the first three have short tails.

Zelotomys woosnami

■ Woosnam's Desert Rat *Zelotomys woosnami*

Total length 24 cm; tail 11 cm; mass 55 g.

Identification pointers: Tail and upper surface of feet white; tail slightly shorter than head-and-body length. Range does not overlap with White-tailed Mouse, which is similar but has much shorter tail. See Pouched Mouse (p108).

Description: Easily identifiable with its pale-grey black-flecked upperparts, paler sides and creamy-white underparts. Tail and top of feet are white.

Distribution: North-central and north-western areas of subregion.

Habitat: Arid areas with sandy soil and sparse vegetation.

Behaviour: Nocturnal. Makes own burrows or uses those dug by other species.

Food: Mainly seeds but also insects and possibly small vertebrates.

Reproduction: Litters of up to 11 young are born in summer.

The Dassie Rat's tail is hairy, but not bushy. Inset: *A Dassie Rat midden with dried urine and droppings.*

The Dassie Rat has a flat head, an adaptation that allows it to enter narrow rock crevices.

Woosnam's Desert Rat

 Dassie Rat

Mystromys albicaudatus

■ White-tailed Mouse *Mystromys albicaudatus*

Total length 22 cm; tail 6 cm; mass 75–110 g.

Identification pointers: Grey-brown body and short white tail. See Woosnam's Desert Rat (page 106), but latter has proportionally longer tail. Pouched Mouse has short tail but not pure white.

Description: Most characteristic feature is short white tail. Upperparts grey to greybrown flecked with black; underparts greyish-white. Upper surfaces of feet white.

Distribution: Swaziland, Lesotho, southern and eastern South Africa.

Habitat: Grassland and heath but also Karoo vegetation.

Behaviour: Nocturnal and lives in burrows and cracks in ground.

Food: Seeds, green plant material and insects.

Reproduction: Litter of 2–5 young. Gestation period 37 days. Breeds throughout the year.

Saccostomus campestris

■ Pouched Mouse *Saccostomus campestris*

Total length 15–16 cm; tail 5 cm; mass 45 g.

Identification pointers: Dumpy appearance (similar to the domestic hamster); short tail; large cheek-pouches for food transport.

Description: Round, fat body, with soft, silky-grey or greyish-brown fur. Underparts and lower face white. Tail length is much less than head-and-body length. Variable in size and colour.

Distribution: Widespread in southern Africa, absent from true desert.

Habitat: Wide habitat tolerance but prefers soft, particularly sandy soils. Can be found in open or dense vegetation and in rocky areas.

Behaviour: It leads a generally solitary existence, although it may live in loose colonies. It digs its own burrows but also utilizes burrows excavated by other species. Where other shelter is not available, it will use termite-mounds, logs and rock piles. One of the principal characteristics of this species is its ability to carry large quantities of food in the cheek-pouches. The food is carried in these pouches to the shelter or burrow, where it can be eaten in relative safety from predators. Compared with most other rodents, it is slow-moving and quite easy to catch by hand. It is nocturnal and terrestrial.

Food: Chiefly seeds, small wild fruits; occasionally insects, depending on season.

Reproduction: 2–10 fully haired young, each weighing less than 3 g, are born in the wet summer months, after a gestation period of about 20 days.

■ Gambian Giant Rat *Cricetomys gambianus*

Total length 80 cm; tail 42 cm; mass 1–3 kg.

Identification pointers: Large size; long naked tail which is white towards tip; dark ring around eye and long thin ears. The superficially similar House Rat is smaller and lacks white on the tail.

Cricetomys gambianus

Description: Largest 'rat-like' rodent in subregion. Distinctive long whip-like tail that is white for slightly less than half of its length towards the tip. Upperparts grey to grey-brown; underparts lighter. Hair around eyes is dark. Ears are large, thin and mobile.

Distribution: Extreme north-eastern areas of subregion but isolated populations occur in the Soutpansberg and southern Zimbabwe. This large rat has a very wide sub-Saharan range, occuring right across West Africa and large swathes of Central and East Africa, but absent from the equatorial forest belt. Records indicate that it does not occur in areas receiving less than 800 mm of rain a year.

Habitat: Forest and woodland but occasionally urban areas.

White-tailed Mouse has grey-white upperparts.

Pouched Mouse has a round, fat body.

Skins of small mice with white or pale tails (l. to r.): Pouched Mouse, White-tailed Mouse, Woosnam's Desert Rat.

Gambian Giant Rat; note the dark ring around the eye.

White-tailed Mouse

Pouched Mouse

29 mm

Front   Back

Gambian Giant Rat

Behaviour: Mainly nocturnal but if undisturbed can be diurnal. Digs own burrow but also makes use of holes, hollow trees and piles of plant debris. Surplus food is carried in cheek-pouches to store. When a burrow is occupied, it is usually closed from the inside. Placid and generally harmless.

Food: Fruits, roots and seeds (including cultivated crops); occasionally insectivorous.

Reproduction: 2–4 young, each weighing about 20 g, are born in summer. The gestation period is about 28 days (some authors have noted that it may be as much as 42 days). Unusually for rodents, the young remain in the burrow for at least 40 days before beginning to forage, and leave the nest for good at about 80 days.

Fat mice Genus *Steatomys*

Steatomys pratensis

■ **Fat Mouse** *Steatomys pratensis*
Total length 13 cm; tail 5 cm; mass 26 g.
■ **Tiny Fat Mouse** *Steatomys parvus*
Total length 12 cm; tail 4 cm; mass 18 g.
■ **Krebs's Fat Mouse** *Steatomys krebsii*
Total length 13 cm; tail 5 cm; mass 24 g.

Identification pointers: Quite small size; dumpy appearance; short tail; white to off-white below; upper surface of feet white.

Description: All three species of fat mice show considerable size and colour variation. The Fat Mouse itself is usually rusty-brown above and white below; its tail is darker above than below. The Tiny Fat Mouse is rufous-grey above with off-white underparts. In the Botswanan part of its range, the tail is pure white but, in the separate KwaZulu-Natal population, it is brown above and white below. Krebs's Fat Mouse is ochre-yellow above and white below, with a similar colour division on its tail. The upper-surfaces of the feet in all three species are white, although the hindfeet of Krebs's Fat Mouse are yellowish-buff.

Steatomys parvus

Distribution: All three species have patchy distributions, with ranges that overlap in some areas. The only species occurring in south-western and southern South Africa is Krebs's Fat Mouse. The Fat Mouse occurs widely south of the Sahara but the other two species are more restricted in their distribution.

Habitat: Usually found over sandy substrates. Sometimes in cultivated lands.

Behaviour: Nocturnal, terrestrial and apparently live singly or in pairs. They live in burrows which they dig themselves. An interesting characteristic of the fat mice is their ability to lay down very thick fat deposits under the skin and around the body organs. They are also able to reduce the body temperature and decrease food intake. This has obvious advantages during droughts and other times of food shortage. Unlike the Pouched Mouse, the fat mice do not have cheek-pouches, but they do carry food to the burrow.

Steatomys krebsii

Food: The fat mice are primarily seed-eaters but they have also been recorded as digging up and eating bulbs. Insects are also eaten occasionally.

Reproduction: Little known. The Fat Mouse apparently gives birth during summer. Although litters of 1–9 young have been recorded, litters of 3–4 are more usual. Reproduction features are probably similar in all three species.

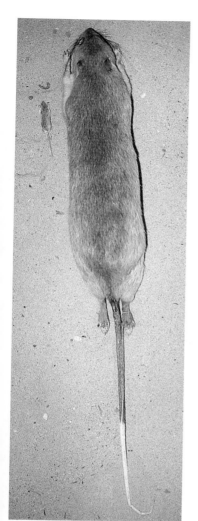

Pygmy Mouse and Gambian Giant Rat.

Foot of Gambian Giant Rat.

Fat Mouse is usually rusty-brown above and white below.

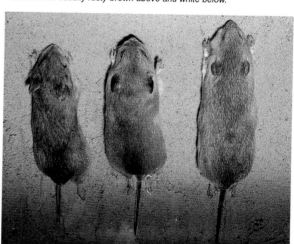

Fat Mouse skins (l. to r.): Tiny Fat Mouse, Fat Mouse, Krebs's Fat Mouse.

Fat Mouse

Tiny Fat Mouse

Krebs's Fat Mouse

111

■ *Dendromus nyikae*
■ *Dendromus mesomelas*

Dendromus melanotis

Dendromus mystacalis

Climbing Mice Genus *Dendromus*
Four species of climbing mice occur in the subregion.

■ **Nyika Climbing Mouse** *Dendromus nyikae*
Total length 16 cm; tail 9 cm; mass 15 g.
■ **Grey Climbing Mouse** *Dendromus melanotis*
Total length 15 cm; tail 8 cm; mass 8 g.
■ **Brants's Climbing Mouse** *Dendromus mesomelas*
Total length 17 cm; tail 10 cm; mass 14 g.
■ **Chestnut Climbing Mouse** *Dendromus mystacalis*
Total length 15 cm; tail 8 cm; mass 8 g.
Identification pointers: In all cases the tail is longer than the head-and-body length and a dark dorsal stripe is present.
Description: All species have a dark, diffused, dorsal stripe and a long, thin tail. Grey Climbing Mouse has ash-grey fur; others are reddish-brown to chestnut-coloured. Underparts are white to off-white.
Distribution: See maps.
Habitat: Tall grass and rank vegetation.
Behaviour: Nocturnal. Good climbers with semi-prehensile tails and toes adapted for clinging to grass-stalks. Grey, Chestnut Climbing Mice build small, ball-shaped nests of fine grass just above ground, and use burrows dug by other species.
Food: Seeds and insects.
Reproduction: Litters of 2–8 born in summer.

Malacothrix typica

■ **Large-eared or Gerbil Mouse** *Malacothrix typica*
Total length 11 cm; tail 3.5 cm; mass 15–20 g.
Identification pointers: Dark patterning on back and head; large ears; short tail. Should not be confused with any other species.
Description: Characterized by dark patterning on the back and head, and by large ears. Upperparts pale grey to reddish-brown; underparts grey or white.
Distribution: Drier central and western areas of subregion.
Habitat: Short grass habitats over hard soils.
Behaviour: Nocturnal. By day, shelters in deep, self-excavated burrows.
Food: Green plant material as well as seeds, occasionally insects.
Reproduction: Summer litters of 2–8 (usually 4). Birth mass 1 g.

GERBILS | Subfamily Gerbillinae
Nine species in three genera occur in southern Africa.

Desmodillus auricularis

■ **Cape Short-tailed Gerbil** *Desmodillus auricularis*
Total length 20 cm; tail 9 cm; mass 50 g.
Identification pointers: Tail shorter than head and body and relatively thick; diagnostic white patch at base of each ear. Soles of feet hairy.
Description: Dumpy appearance and only gerbil with tail shorter than head-and-body length. Upperparts vary from reddish-brown to grey-brown, but species is easily distinguishable by prominent white patch at base of ear.
Distribution: Widespread in the drier western areas.
Habitat: Hard ground with grass or karoid bush. Not sandy soils.
Behaviour: Nocturnal. It digs its own burrows and lives singly or in pairs.
Food: Seeds, mostly of grasses; some green plant parts.
Reproduction: Year-round litters consisting of 1–7 young, but usually 4.

Climbing mouse skins (l. to r.): Chestnut Climbing Mouse, Brants's Climbing Mouse, Grey Climbing Mouse.

Brants's Climbing Mouse in a typical habitat.

Large-eared or Gerbil Mouse has dark patterning on the head and back, large ears and a short tail.

Cape Short-tailed Gerbil; the upperparts vary in colour from reddish-brown to grey-brown.

Nyika Climbing Mouse, Grey Climbing Mouse, Brants's Climbing Mouse, Chestnut Climbing Mouse, Large-eared or Gerbil Mouse

Cape Short-tailed Gerbil

113

Hairy-footed Gerbils Genus *Gerbillurus*

Gerbillurus paeba

■ **Hairy-footed Gerbil** *Gerbillurus paeba*
Total length 20 cm; tail 11 cm; mass 25 g.
■ **Brush-tailed Hairy-footed Gerbil** *Gerbillurus vallinus*
Total length 20 cm; tail 12 cm; mass 35 g.
■ **Dune Hairy-footed Gerbil** *Gerbillurus tytonis*
Total length 22 cm; tail 12 cm; mass 27 g.
■ **Setzer's Hairy-footed Gerbil** *Gerbillurus setzeri*
Total length 23 cm; tail 12 cm; mass 38 g.

Identification pointers: Fairly small size; long tails – three species with tufts of longish hair at tip; large hindfeet with hairy soles; Setzer's and Dune with white patches above eyes and at ear-bases.

■ *Gerbillurus vallinus*
■ *Gerbillurus setzeri*

Description: Hairy-footed Gerbil has small tuft of long hair at tail-tip; Brush-tailed Hairy-footed Gerbil has a prominent tassel. Colour variable but Hairy-footed Gerbil commonly reddish-brown or greyish-red; Brush-tailed Hairy-footed Gerbil reddish-brown to dark grey-brown. Both have white underparts but Brush-tailed Hairy-footed Gerbil also has white forelegs. Setzer's and Dune Hairy-footed Gerbils have white spot just above eye and behind ear. Both have tufts of longish hair at tip of tail. Soles of feet hairy, unlike naked soles of Tatera gerbils.

Distribution: See maps.

Gerbillurus tytonis

Habitat: Sandy soils in arid areas, although Hairy-footed Gerbil extends into moister environment of southern coastal zone.

Behaviour: All species probably nocturnal, excavate their own burrows. Brush-tailed Hairy-footed Gerbil lives in colonies, Hairy-footed Gerbil apparently in smaller groups.

Food: Omnivores mainly, taking seeds, green plant material and insects.

Reproduction: Hairy-footed Gerbil has litter of 2–5 young.

The Tatera Group Genus *Tatera*

Tatera leucogaster

■ **Bushveld Gerbil** *Tatera leucogaster*
Total length 28 cm; tail 15 cm; mass 70 g.
■ **Cape Gerbil** *Tatera afra*
Total length 30 cm; tail 15 cm; mass 100 g.
■ **Highveld Gerbil** *Tatera brantsii*
Total length 28 cm; tail 14 cm; mass 80 g.
■ **Gorongoza Gerbil** *Tatera inclusa*
Total length 32 cm; tail 16 cm; mass 120 g.

Identification pointers: Fairly large size; tails about same length as head and body; well-developed hindlegs and feet; ears greater length than width; eyes quite large. Soles of feet are naked (see *Gerbillurus* above).

■ *Tatera afra*
■ *Tatera brantsii*
■ *Tatera inclusa*

Description: All have white underparts, but eastern form of Highveld Gerbil is greyish-white underneath. Bushveld Gerbil has distinct dark line along upperside of tail and tip is never white. Its upperparts are most commonly reddish-brown, bright and silky. Many Highveld Gerbils have white-tipped tails. Cape Gerbil's long, woolly hair is usually pale fawn and mottled with brown. Its tail is uniform in colour. Gorongoza Gerbil dark brown; tail dark brown above, white underneath; some have white tip to tail.

Distribution: See maps.

Setzer's Hairy-footed Gerbil; note the large hindfeet.

Hairy-footed Gerbil is reddish-brown in colour.

Cape Gerbil has long, woolly hair.

Highveld Gerbil is greyish-brown underneath.

Gerbil skins (l. to r.): Cape Gerbil, Highveld Gerbil, Bushveld Gerbil, Short-tailed Gerbil, Brush-tailed Hairy-footed Gerbil, Hairy-footed Gerbil.

Brush-tailed Hairy-footed Gerbil; note the tuft of longish hair at the tip of the tail.

Bushveld Gerbil has variable coloured upperparts, usually reddish-brown to yellow-brown.

Brush-tailed Hairy-footed Gerbil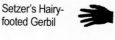

Setzer's Hairy-footed Gerbil

Bushveld Gerbil

  Gorongoza Gerbil

115

Habitat: All species are found on sandy soils with the two widespread species being found in a wide variety of habitats.
Behaviour: Nocturnal; dig own burrows and live in loosely knit colonies.
Food: Grass-seed but also other plant food. Partly insectivorous.
Reproduction: Litter sizes of the Highveld Gerbil vary from 1–5 (usually 3); the Bushveld Gerbil has 2–9 with an average of 5.

Spiny Mice Genus *Acomys*

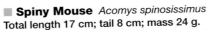

■ *Acomys spinosissimus*
■ *Acomys subspinosus*

■ **Spiny Mouse** *Acomys spinosissimus*
Total length 17 cm; tail 8 cm; mass 24 g.
■ **Cape Spiny Mouse** *Acomys subspinosus*
Total length 17 cm; tail 8 cm; mass 22 g.
Identification pointers: Spiny hairs on back; white underparts.
Description: Unmistakable with their dorsal covering of spiny hairs. Upperparts of Spiny Mouse are reddish-grey and those of Cape Spiny Mouse are dark grey-brown. Both species have white underparts.
Distribution: In subregion Spiny Mouse restricted to north-eastern parts. Cape Spiny Mouse only occurs in Western Cape.
Habitat: Rocky habitats but also woodland and other associations.
Behaviour: Nocturnal, but can be active in early morning and late afternoon in shadows cast by rocks. Live singly or in small groups.
Food: Seeds and green plant material; also insects, millipedes and snails.
Reproduction: Spiny Mice litters of 2–5 are born during summer.

Rock Mice Genera *Aethomys* and *Micaelamys*

Five species occur in southern Africa; the Silinda Rat (*Aethomys silindensis*) is known only from a few specimens collected in eastern Zimbabwe.

Micaelamys namaquensis

Aethomys chrysophilus
Aethomys ineptus

■ **Namaqua Rock Mouse** *Micaelamys namaquensis*
Total length 26 cm; tail 15 cm; mass 50 g.
■ **Grant's Rock Mouse** *Micaelamys granti*
Total length 20 cm; tail 10 cm; mass 40 g.
■ **Red Veld Rat** *Aethomys chrysophilus* (includes Tete Veld Rat, *A. ineptus*)
Total length 28 cm; tail 15 cm; mass 75 g.
■ **Silinda Rat** *Aethomys silindensis*
Total length 35 cm; tail 18 cm.
Identification pointers: Nondescript; typically rat-like; long, well-scaled tail; underparts lighter than upperparts. See distribution maps.
Description: Both Namaqua Rock Mouse and Red Veld Rat have a tail that is longer than the head and body; Grant's Rock Mouse has a tail equal in length to that of the head and body. The tail of Red Veld Rat is shorter, thicker and more heavily scaled than that of Namaqua Rock Mouse. Coloration is very variable but in general Grant's Rock Mouse is dark grey-brown above and grey below with a dark-coloured tail. The Namaqua Rock Mouse has reddish-brown to yellowish-fawn upperparts, often pencilled with black, and the underparts are white to greyish-white. As its name implies, Red Veld Rat is usually reddish-brown, but is also pencilled with black; the underparts are grey-white.

■ *Micaelamys granti*
■ *Aethomys silindensis*

Spiny Mouse has a covering of spiny hairs.

Cape Spiny Mouse has grey-brown upperparts.

Namaqua Rock Mouse (reddish-brown form).

Grant's Rock Mouse is dark-grey above, lighter below.

Namaqua Rock Mouse (yellow-fawn form).

Rock Mouse skins (top to bottom): *Namaqua Rock Mouse, Red Veld Rat, Grant's Rock Mouse.*

Red Veld Rat is reddish-brown with grey-white underparts.

Spiny Mouse
Cape Spiny Mouse

Grant's Rock Mouse

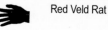

Red Veld Rat

117

Distribution: Grant's Rock Mouse is restricted to the central Karoo of the Northern Cape province and may be found together with the Namaqua Rock Mouse. The latter is widely distributed in southern Africa. Red Veld Rat is also widespread, as is Tete Veld Rat, *A. ineptus*, (see map) in north-east South Africa, but is absent from southern and western areas.

Habitat: Namaqua and Grant's Rock Mice largely restricted to rocky habitats. Red Veld Rats are found in a wide range of habitats, from grassland to savanna woodland and including rocky outcrops.

Behaviour: Nothing is known about the behaviour of Grant's Rock Mouse. The other two species are nocturnal. The Namaqua Rock Mouse lives in small colonies and a characteristic of its communal shelters are the large accumulations of dry grass and other plant material dragged into the entrances. It is also known to dig burrows at the base of bushes.

Food: All species eat grass- and other seeds.

Reproduction: Red Veld Rat breeds throughout the year; Namaqua Rock Mouse gives birth in warmer months. Both species usually have 3–5 young per litter.

■ African Marsh Rat *Dasymys incomtus*

Recent revision of the species indicates that as many as 5 distinct species may occur in the subregion, for example, Cape Marsh Rat *Dasymys capensis* in the south-west; Roberts's Marsh Rat in eastern South Africa and adjacent Zimbabwe. This could explain the disjunct nature of its range as shown on the map. All very similar in appearance.

Dasymys incomtus

Total length 30–35 cm; tail 14–18 cm; mass 100–220 g.

Identification pointers: Similar to Vlei Rat (page 130) but longer tail; dark, long, shaggy fur and white claw bases, which contrast with the dark feet. Flat, disc-like face with small eyes. Incisors not grooved.

Description: Similar in appearance to vlei rat but has longer tail. Hair is relatively long and shaggy and dark grey-black in colour with brown flecks. Underparts are paler. Ears are large and rounded and the dark feet contrast with the white bases of the claws.

Distribution: African Marsh Rat occurs along the southern coastal belt and in the east and north-eastern areas of southern Africa.

Habitat: Well-vegetated and wet habitats.

Behaviour: As with the vlei rats, the African Marsh Rat uses distinct runways and in fact probably shares them with those species. It swims well and takes readily to water. Most activity takes place during the day.

Food: A variety of reeds, grasses and other plants but also insects.

Reproduction: As many as 9 young have been recorded in a litter, although the usual number is about 5. Young are born in the summer months.

■ Four-striped Grass Mouse *Rhabdomys pumilio*

This widespread mouse may consist of a complex of as yet undescribed species but all woud be easily recognisable as belonging to this group and separation would depend largely on genetic analyses.

Total length 18–21 cm; tail 8–11 cm; mass 30–85 g.

Rhabdomys pumilio

Identification pointers: Four dark stripes down the back. Cannot be confused with any other species.

Description: This mouse is easily distinguished from all other species as it has four distinct longitudinal stripes running down the back. General colour is variable and ranges from dark russet-brown to almost grey-white. Similarly, the underparts

The Cape Marsh Rat, probably a distinct species within the African Marsh Rat complex.

Striped Grass Mouse skins (l. to r.): Four-striped Grass Mouse, Single-striped Grass Mouse.

Four-striped Grass Mouse. Inset: Note the reddish-brown ears.

Four-striped Grass Mouse

African Marsh Rat

vary from off-white to pale grey-brown. The backs of the ears (and often the snout) are russet to yellowish-brown.

Distribution: Four-striped Grass Mouse occurs widely in South Africa and Namibia but only patchily in Zimbabwe, Mozambique and Botswana.

Habitat: Wide-ranging, from desert fringe to high-rainfall montane areas. The only consistent requirement is the presence of grass. From sea-level to 2 700 m.

Behaviour: Principally diurnal but also often active at night. Makes own burrows from which radiate numerous runways. Often around houses.

Food: Mainly seeds, but also other plant parts; insects.

Reproduction: Litters of 2–9 (usually 5–6) young are born after a gestation period of about 25 days, usually in summer.

Lemniscomys rosalia

■ Single-striped Grass Mouse *Lemniscomys rosalia*

Total length 27 cm; tail 15 cm; mass 60 g.

Identification pointers: Single dark stripe runs down centre of back; the climbing mice also have single dark dorsal stripes but they are much smaller than this species.

Description: The upperparts vary in colour from pale grey-brown to orange-brown and a single dark-brown or black stripe runs down the middle of the back. The underparts are white, often russet-tinged.

Distribution: Restricted to the far northern and eastern areas of southern Africa, but outside the subregion occur widely south of the Sahara Desert.

Habitat: Grass cover is essential but in associations varying from dry scrub to savanna woodland or even around agricultural land.

Behaviour: A diurnal species that excavates its own burrows. Runways lead out from the burrows to the feeding-grounds.

Food: Grass- and other seeds, green plant material, some insects.

Reproduction: Litters of 2–11 (average 5); between September and March.

Pygmy Mice   Genus *Mus*

Six species of pygmy mice are recorded as occurring in southern Africa.

■ *Mus setzeri*
■ *Mus triton*

■ Setzer's Pygmy Mouse *Mus setzeri*
Total length 9 cm; tail 4 cm; mass 7 g.
■ Grey-bellied Pygmy Mouse *Mus triton*
Total length 10 cm; tail 4.5 cm; mass 10 g.
■ Desert Pygmy Mouse *Mus indutus*
Total length 10 cm; tail 4 cm; mass 6 g.
■ Pygmy Mouse *Mus minutoides*
Total length 10 cm; tail 4 cm; mass 6 g.
■ Neave's Pygmy Mouse *Mus neavei*
Total length 10 cm; tail 4.0 cm.
■ Free State Pygmy Mouse *Mus orangiae*

■ *Mus indutus*
■ *Mus neavei*

Identification pointers: Very small; tail shorter than head-and-body length; only Grey-bellied does not have white underparts; Desert Pygmy Mouse has patch of white hair at base of each ear. Pygmy mice can be distinguished from the climbing mice (*Dendromus* spp.), see page 112, by their much shorter tails and lack of dark dorsal stripe.

Single-striped Grass Mouse.

Desert Pygmy Mouse has white underparts.

The tiny Pygmy Mouse has a tail that is shorter than its body length.

Single-Striped
Grass Mouse

Grey-Bellied
Pygmy Mouse

Pygmy Mouse

Mus minutoides

Description: Small, with tails shorter than length of head and body. All but Grey-bellied Pygmy Mouse have white underparts. Upperparts range from greyish-brown to reddish-brown. Tail of Desert Pygmy Mouse is white below while in Pygmy Mouse it is pale brown; the former also has a small patch of white hair at the base of the ear.

Distribution: See maps. Pygmy Mouse most widespread. Desert Pygmy Mouse is found in Botswana and north-eastern Namibia. Free State Pygmy Mouse known only from a limited area of Free State (Viljoensdrift) and adjacent Lesotho.

Habitat: Pygmy Mouse from Cape fynbos to savanna grassland and woodland. Desert Pygmy Mouse in arid scrub savanna but also Okavango.

Behaviour: Nocturnal and terrestrial, and usually occur solitarily, in pairs or in family parties. Although they will dig their own burrows in soft soils, they usually make use of burrows dug by other species, or shelter under dead vegetation, rocks and the debris of human occupation.

Food: Seeds, but they also feed on green plant food and insects.

Reproduction: Pygmy Mouse has a gestation period of 19 days and births take place in summer; a typical litter consists of 4 young (1–7), each weighing less than a gram at birth. Desert Pygmy Mouse probably has young throughout the year with peaks in summer. Five young is the usual litter size.

Mus musculus

■ House Mouse *Mus musculus* (Introduced)

Total length 16 cm; tail 9 cm; mass 18 g.

Identification pointers: Nondescript; associated with human dwellings. Larger than the pygmy mice and has light-brown, not white, underparts. Could be confused with Mastomys group (page 126), but smaller and lighter.

Description: The upperparts are grey-brown with the underparts being slightly lighter in colour. The tail is lighter brown below than above.

Distribution: This introduced species with worldwide distribution is strongly tied to human settlement and therefore has a patchy but wide distribution. It is widely distributed in South Africa but is also known to occur in most other southern African countries.

Habitat: Human settlements.

Behaviour: Nocturnal and lives in pairs or family parties. Untidy nests are constructed from a wide range of man-made and natural materials.

Food: Omnivorous. It can be extremely destructive in food stores.

Reproduction: Breeds throughout year, giving birth to 1–13 (usually 6) young per litter; gestation about 19 days; first litters at the age of 6 weeks.

Thallomys paedulcus
Thallomys nigricaudatus

■ Acacia Rat *Thallomys paedulcus*
■ Black-tailed Tree Rat *Thallomys nigricaudatus*

These two rats are very similar in appearance and occur over much of the same range, but have been shown to be genetically distinct.

Total length 30 cm; tail 17 cm; mass 100 g.

Identification pointers: Arboreal habits; tail longer than head and body; dark ring around eye and extending onto muzzle; prominent ears.

Description: Both species characterized by having a tail longer than the head-and-body length, prominent ears and a dark ring around the eyes. Upperparts usually pale grey tinged with fawnish-yellow; underparts white; tail usually dark.

Distribution: Widely distributed in northern parts of the subregion, largely absent in Lesotho and areas south of Gariep (Orange) River.

Habitat: Savanna woodland – particularly areas dominated by acacias.

The common, widespread House Mouse.

Black-tailed Tree Rats inhabit acacia woodland.

The Acacia Rat has a tail longer than the head and body, and a dark ring around the eyes. Inset: It is arboreal and nocturnal.

House Mouse

Black-tailed Tree Rat
Acacia Rat

Behaviour: Nocturnal and arboreal. Lives in holes in trees but may also make use of large birds' nests to which it adds finer plant material. Nests may be occupied by a family group or several adults.
Food: Green leaves, fresh seeds and seed-pods but also insects.
Reproduction: 2–5 young per litter are born during the summer.

Grammomys dolichurus

Grammomys cometes

■ **Woodland Thicket Rat** *Grammomys dolichurus*
Total length 27 cm; tail 17 cm; mass 30 g.
■ **Mozambique Woodland Thicket Rat** *Grammomys cometes*
Total length 30 cm; tail 18 cm.
Identification pointers: Long, thin tail; white underparts clearly separated from grey-brown or reddish-brown upperparts. Forest and woodland habitat. A third species, Macmillan's Thicket Rat *Grammomys macmillani*, is believed to occur in eastern Zimbabwe and adjacent Mozambique.
Description: Both species of woodland mice have long tails well over half their total length. Colour of the upperparts may be reddish-brown with a grey tinge or much more grey-brown; underparts white. Ears are large and prominent. Mozambique Woodland Thicket Rat sometimes has white patch at base of ear.
Distribution: Both found in woodland habitats along eastern coastal plain.
Habitat: Forest and dense woodland; Woodland Thicket Rat sometimes found in more open woodland.
Behaviour: Nocturnal and arboreal. The Woodland Thicket Rat constructs nests of grass and other fine plant material in vegetation tangles up to 2 m from the ground. It will also make use of holes in trees and even weaver-bird nests.
Food: Green plant material, wild fruits and seeds.
Reproduction: The young of the Woodland Thicket Rat are born throughout the year, with a possible peak in summer. Litter size varies from 2–4.

Pelomys fallax

■ **Creek Grooved-toothed Rat** *Pelomys fallax*
Total length 22–36 cm; tail 12–18 cm; mass 100–170 g.
Identification pointers: Similar in appearance to the vlei rats (page 130), but distinguished by much longer tail; tail dark above, lighter below. Face not as blunted as vlei rats. Usually indistinct dark band down back. Strong association with wet habitats.
Description: The upperparts vary from reddish-brown to yellow-brown and the rump may be more reddish than the rest of the body. An indistinct dark band is usually present down the mid-back. The tail is dark above and pale below. An interesting feature of the fur on the back is that in certain light conditions it has a distinct greenish-blue sheen.
Distribution: Restricted to eastern Zimbabwe and Mozambique but also found in well-watered parts of northern Botswana.
Habitat: The fringes of vleis, swamps, reed-beds and river-banks.
Behaviour: Mainly nocturnal and excavates its own burrows.
Food: Green plant food such as young reed shoots; seeds.
Reproduction: Litters are born in summer.

Note: Rudd's Mouse (*Uranomys ruddi*) is mainly associated with wet grassland and floodplains. Digs own burrows and seems to be mainly insectivorous.

The Woodland Thicket Rat (also called Woodland Mouse) inhabits forests and woodlands along the eastern coastal plain.

Creek Grooved-toothed Rat.

Rudd's Mouse. Only three skins from Zimbabwe's Eastern Highlands exist. Total length ±20 cm.

Woodland Thicket Rat eats green plant material, fruits and seeds.

Woodland
Thicket Rat

Mozambique Woodland
Thicket Rat

Creek Grooved-toothed Rat

125

Mastomys Group Genera *Mastomys* and *Myomyscus*

Four species fall within this group, two of which, the Multimammate Mouse and the Natal Multimammate Mouse, are impossible to tell apart in the field.

Mastomys natalensis and *M. coucha*; ranges are not clearly defined.

■ **Natal Multimammate Mouse** *Mastomys natalensis*
Total length 24 cm; tail 11 cm; mass 60 g.
■ **Southern Multimammate Mouse** *Mastomys coucha*
Total length 20 cm; tail 11 cm; mass 50 g.
■ **Shortridge's Mouse** *Mastomys shortridgei*
Total length 22 cm; tail 10 cm; mass 45 g.
■ **Verreaux's Mouse** *Myomyscus verreauxii*
Total length 25 cm; tail 14 cm; mass 40 g.

■ *Mastomys shortridgei*
■ *Myomyscus verreauxii*

Identification pointers: Typical mouse-like appearance; underparts paler than upperparts; females of Natal Multimammate Mouse and Southern Multimammate Mouse have up to 12 pairs of nipples; Verreaux's Mouse has darker facial markings, white upper-surfaces to feet. Shortridge's Mouse is very dark above with greyish-white underparts.

Description: Range in colour from pale grey through grey-brown to almost black, with paler sides and grey underparts. Tail is finely scaled, with sparse hair covering. All species have soft, silky hair. Southern Multimammate mice females unique with 8–12 pairs of nipples. Shortridge's Mouse has much darker fur and greyish-white underparts; females have five pairs of nipples. Verreaux's Mouse has a dark band running between the ears and onto the muzzle, with dark hair around the eyes; upper-surfaces of its feet are white, as is under-surface of tail.

Distribution: See maps; the two multimammate mice are liable to be confused.
Habitat: Multimammate mice have wide habitat tolerance. The other two species favour wet habitats and relatively dense vegetation.
Behaviour: Nocturnal and terrestrial. Often around houses.
Food: Seeds and fruit but also insects.
Reproduction: Southern Multimammate Mouse most fecund of all southern African mammals, 22 foetuses having been recorded in a single female; 6–12 is more usual litter size. Gestation 23 days; newborn young weigh only 2 g.

Rattus rattus

Rattus norvegicus

■ **House Rat** *Rattus rattus* (Introduced)
Total length 37 cm; tail 20 cm; mass 150 g.
■ **Brown Rat** *Rattus norvegicus* (Introduced)
Total length 40 cm; tail 19 cm; mass 300 g.

Identification pointers: Brown Rat – large size; heavy tail, slightly shorter than head and body; restricted to coastal towns. House Rat – large size; tail longer than head and body; large, naked ears; associated with human settlements.

Description: House Rat more slender than Brown Rat. Large feet; tail prominently scaled and longer than head and body. Ears large, thin and naked. Upperparts grey-brown to black; underparts white to grey. Brown Rat is bulkier, with shorter tail and smaller ears; usually greyish-brown.

Distribution: Brown Rat restricted to coastal settlements and adjacent areas; House Rat is widespread but patchy. Both occur worldwide.
Habitat: Around human settlements, but House Rat less so.
Behaviour: Nocturnal. Active diggers; swim well. House Rat adept at climbing. Live in family groups and build large, untidy nests from a wide range of materials.
Food: Omnivores, taking a wide range of foodstuffs. Destructive to stored food.
Reproduction: Several litters of 5–10 per year. Gestation three weeks.

Southern Multimammate Mouse and Natal Multimammate Mouse are identical in appearance.

Verreaux's Mouse has dark facial markings and white feet.

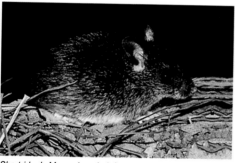

Shortridge's Mouse has dark fur.

The alien Brown Rat is large, with a heavy tail.

The alien Black, or House, Rat is widespread around the world.

Shortridge's Mouse

Verreaux's Mouse

House Rat

Brown Rat

127

Parotomys and Otomys Groups

These are all fairly large, short, stocky rats with blunt faces and rounded ears. The fur is quite long and shaggy and the tail length is usually less than the head-and-body measurement. With the exception of Littledale's Whistling Rat, all species have grooved upper incisors. The cheek-teeth are laminated.

Whistling Rats Genus *Parotomys*

Two species of whistling rat occur in southern Africa.

Parotomys brantsii

Parotomys littledalei

■ **Brants's Whistling Rat** *Parotomys brantsii*
Total length 23 cm; tail 10 cm; mass 120 g.
■ **Littledale's Whistling Rat** *Parotomys littledalei*
Total length 25 cm; tail 10 cm; mass 120 g.
Identification pointers: See description. Both species, as their name implies, give a sharp whistling call and this is diagnostic for *Parotomys*. Open sandy country is favoured. See 'Behaviour' below.
Description: Like other members of this group, the whistling rats are stockily built, with tails shorter than the length of head and body. Body colour is very variable and ranges from pale reddish-yellow with white underparts to a brownish or greyish yellow with grey underparts. The tail may be similar in colour to the upperparts or dark above and pale below. Littledale's Whistling Rat tends to be somewhat darker on the back. The only sure way to differentiate between the two species is to examine the upper incisors. Those of Littledale's Whistling Rat are not grooved, but the upper incisors of Brants's Whistling Rat are grooved.
Distribution: The whistling rats are restricted to the arid western areas and are only found in southern Africa. Large, loosely tied colonies of Brants's Whistling Rat can be observed in the Kgalagadi Transfrontier Park.
Habitat: Arid, sandy environments. Brants's occurs mainly in areas receiving less than 300 mm of rain per annum, whereas Littledale's favours even drier areas with under 200 mm of rain. Littledale's Whistling Rat occurs along the extremely arid Namib Desert coastline, from which Brants's is absent.
Behaviour: Largely diurnal and completely terrestrial. Brants's Whistling Rat may live solitarily in burrows but more commonly in colonies, whereas Littledale's is apparently often solitary. When alarmed they stand on their hindlegs, in close proximity to the burrow, and then give shrill whistling calls before disappearing down the burrow. When feeding, they occasionally feed at the food site, but more commmonly they bite off pieces of vegetation and carry them back to the burrow entrance, into which they can rapidly retreat if danger threatens.
Food: They are vegetarian, eating the leaves of succulents and other green plant food, as well as seeds and flowers.
Reproduction: Littledale's Whistling Rat has up to 4 litters, with 1–3 young each, in a good wet season. Brants's Whistling Rat gives birth to 1–4 young, mainly during late summer. The young cling to the female's nipples, and are dragged along when she goes out to feed.

Above and inset: *Brants's Whistling Rat: the colour can vary from pale reddish-yellow to brownish or greyish yellow.*

Littledale's Whistling Rat often tends to be darker on the back than Brants's.

Littledale's Whistling Rat

Brants's Whistling Rat

129

Vlei Rats Genus *Otomys*

Six species of *Otomys* are recognized as occurring in southern Africa.

■ *Otomys laminatus*
■ *Otomys sloggetti*

■ *Otomys angoniensis*
■ *Otomys unisulcatus*

Ootomys saundersiae

Otomys irroratus

■ **Laminate Vlei Rat** *Otomys laminatus*
Total length 30 cm; tail 10 cm; mass 190 g.
■ **Angoni Vlei Rat** *Otomys angoniensis*
Total length 30 cm; tail 8 cm; mass 100–250 g.
■ **Saunders's Vlei Rat** *Otomys saundersiae*
Total length 25 cm; tail 9 cm; mass 100 g.
■ **Vlei Rat** *Otomys irroratus*
Total length 24 cm; tail 9 cm; mass 120 g.
■ **Sloggett's Rat** *Otomys sloggetti*
Total length 20 cm; tail 6 cm; mass 130 g.
■ **Bush Karoo Rat** *Otomys unisulcatus*
Total length 24 cm; tail 9 cm; mass 125 g.

Identification pointers: All species have robust, stocky appearance, short tails, blunt muzzles, rounded ears and grooved upper incisors. Use distribution maps and habitat preferences to assist identification, but only examination of teeth and skull can give positive identification. Confusion could arise with African Marsh Rat (page 118) but it has tail more or less equal in length to that of head and body, and no grooves on upper incisors.

Description: Measurements above subject to variation. Coloration can also vary and there is a degree of colour overlap between the different species. Only certain way to distinguish between different species is to examine skull and cheek-teeth. Distribution maps can be used to eliminate species that should not be present in given area. All species are densely furred and usually grizzled grey-brown, although Vlei Rat and Angoni Vlei Rat may be almost black. Sloggett's and the Bush Karoo Rats both tend to be brown to grey-brown, but former has particularly short tail.

Distribution: Vlei Rat and Angoni Vlei Rat are the most widespread but only former occurs widely south of the Gariep (Orange) River. Bush Karoo Rat only found in south-west. Sloggett's Rat is found in east-central parts of South Africa and in Lesotho, even on the summits of the Drakensberg Mountains. Large Vlei Rat is now considered to be a subspecies of Angoni Vlei Rat.

Habitat: Despite the common name 'vlei rat', only the Vlei Rat and Angoni Vlei Rat are commonly associated with moist, marshy habitats, but even they can also be found in drier habitats – grassy hillsides in the case of the former and open savanna for the latter. Sloggett's Rat is the only species that is associated with rocky habitats at high altitudes, although Saunders's Vlei Rat is recorded as occurring in the mountains in close association with sedge meadows in heathland. Only the Bush Karoo Rat is found in arid areas.

Behaviour: Predominantly diurnal, live singly, in pairs or small family parties. Several species construct nests of grass and other vegetation in dense grass tussocks and vegetation tangles. Sloggett's Rat lives in rock crevices and among boulders. Runs are marked by small piles of discarded grass, reed and leaf segments and small cylindrical droppings. Bush Karoo Rat constructs large stick lodges.

Food: Shoots and stems of grass, sedges, reeds and other plants.

Reproduction: No reproduction information is available for most species. Angoni Vlei Rat gives birth to its 2–5 young between August and March. Only the Vlei Rat has been studied in detail; its litters of 1–4 young are born, usually in summer, after a gestation period of about 40 days. A female may have as many as 7 litters in one season. Bush Karoo Rat breeds throughout the year in the Karoo.

Angoni Vlei Rat may sometimes be almost black in colour.

Bush Karoo Rat occurs mainly in arid western areas.

Vlei Rat and Whistling Rat skins (top row l. to r.): Brants's Whistling Rat, Littledale's Whistling Rat, Saunders's Vlei Rat; (bottom row l. to r.): Bush Karoo Rat, Sloggett's Rat, Angoni Vlei Rat, Vlei Rat, Large Vlei Rat.

Bush Karoo Rat constructs lodges from twigs and sticks.

Sloggett's Rat has thick grey-brown fur.

Laminate Vlei Rat

Sloggett's Rat

131

Pygmy Rock Mice Genus *Petromyscus*

Petromyscus collinus

Petromyscus barbouri

Petromyscus monticularis

Petromyscus shortridgei

■ **Pygmy Rock Mouse** *Petromyscus collinus*
Total length 19 cm; tail 10 cm; mass 20 g.
■ **Barbour's Pygmy Rock Mouse** *Petromyscus barbouri*
Total length 16 cm; tail 8 cm; mass 15 g.
■ **Brukkaros Pygmy Rock Mouse** *Petromyscus monticularis*
Total length 15 cm; tail 7 cm.
■ **Shortridge's Pygmy Rock Mouse** *Petromyscus shortridgei*
Total length 18 cm; tail 9 cm.

Identification pointers: Small size; well-scaled tail; prominent ears and facial whiskers; rocky habitat.

Description: Pygmy Rock Mouse: this small mouse is grey-yellow to brownish-yellow above; the underparts and upper surface of the feet are greyish-white. The tail is heavily scaled and sparsely haired. Prominent ears; long facial whiskers. Barbour's Pygmy Rock Mouse has dull-grey upperparts with indistinct brownish grizzling. Underparts pale-grey to off-white, with upper foot surfaces dirty white. Tail scales much smaller than those of Pygmy Rock Mouse. Coarse hairs sparse on tail but more numerous towards tip. Brukkaros Pygmy Rock Mouse is, on average, slightly smaller than other species, and the ears are shorter. Fur brownish-yellow above, underparts are grey. Upper surfaces of the feet are white. Shortridge's Pygmy Rock Mouse has dark greyish upperparts and an overall grizzled appearance. Underparts and throat are both grey.

Distribution: Consult the distribution maps, but all are restricted to the arid west of southern Africa. Range limits are not exactly known.

Habitat: All species are associated with rocky habitats, as their collective name implies. These range from continuous mountain ranges to broken hill country and isolated rock outcrops. In the Namib Desert, the Pygmy Rock Mouse reaches quite high densities on rocky inselbergs (island mountains) that are completely isolated from other outcrops.

Behaviour: As far as is known, all four species are nocturnal. Only the Pygmy Rock Mouse has been studied in the wild. During the hottest summer period in the Namib Desert, it is known to aestivate (pass the time in a dormant condition). They are solitary foragers but several individuals may occupy the same rock crevices. These crevices are also often occupied by Namaqua Rock Mice, Rock Dormice and the rock-dwelling Sengis within their range. Their tiny size presumably allows them to occupy the deepest areas of such crevices. Barn Owls and Spotted Eagle-Owls are known to prey on them.

Food: They are predominantly seed eaters, but Barbour's collected on the western escarpment of South Africa included some green plant material in their diet. They are also known to forage on rock hyrax (dassie) dung middens (crevices often shared), possibly for undigested seeds and other material. Pygmy Rock Mouse eats some insects and this may well apply to other species as well.

Reproduction: Pygmy Rock Mouse in the Namib breeds in the summer months, producing litters of 2–3 young weighing just over 2 g at birth. Unusually for small rodents, they only produce one litter per season. Shortridge's is recorded as producing 2–3 young per litter. Pregnant females have only been collected in May, but the season is likely to be longer. Nothing is known for the other two species.

The Pygmy Rock Mouse is grey-yellow to brownish-yellow above, with greyish-white underparts.

Barbour's Rock Mouse, like the Pygmy Rock Mouse, occurs in the arid west of the subregion.

Pygmy Rock Mouse

CARNIVORES | Order Carnivora

FOXES, JACKALS & WILD DOG | Family Canidae

Vulpes chama

■ **Cape Fox** *Vulpes chama*
Total length 86–97 cm; tail 29–39 cm; shoulder height 30 cm; mass 2.5–4.0 kg.
Identification pointers: Typically fox-like appearance; long, bushy tail; greyish-grizzled back and sides; light-coloured legs; muzzle generally light in colour; ears 'normal' in size. Compare with Bat-eared Fox, which has black legs and muzzle and disproportionately long ears. Cape Fox normally seen singly or in pairs; Bat-eared Fox usually in pairs or small groups.
Description: Only 'true' fox in subregion. Back and sides grizzled silvery-grey and neck, chest and forelegs pale tawny-brown to almost white. Throat usually white. Tail long and bushy and usually darker than rest of body. Ears long and pointed, brown at back and fringed with white hair at front.
Distribution: Restricted to subregion and south-western Angola.
Habitat: Open areas, such as grassland and arid scrub. Also wheatlands and Cape fynbos vegetation zone in the Western Cape, South Africa.
Behaviour: Mainly nocturnal. Usually alone or in pairs. During the day it lies up in holes or dense thickets. Hunting ranges extend up to 5 km².
Food: Mainly insects, other invertebrates and rodents; also reptiles, birds, carrion and wild fruit. Rarely newborn lambs.
Reproduction: 1–4 (usually 3) pups born in spring. Gestation 50 days.

Otocyon megalotis

■ **Bat-eared Fox** *Otocyon megalotis*
Total length 75–90 cm; tail 23–34 cm; shoulder height 35 cm; mass 3–5 kg.
Identification pointers: Jackal-like appearance; disproportionately large ears; bushy, silvery-grey coat; black legs; bushy tail – black above and at tip; face black below eyes, paler above eyes.
Description: This small jackal-like carnivore has slender legs, a sharp-pointed, fairly long muzzle and disproportionately large ears. The ears may reach a length of 14 cm and are dark at the back, particularly at the tip; the insides of the ears are white or light in colour. The body is covered in fairly long, silvery-grey hair with a distinctly grizzled appearance and the legs are black. The tail is bushy and black above and at the tip. Although the front of the face is generally black, a light or white band runs across the forehead to the base of the ears.
Distribution: Widespread in central and western areas of subregion.
Habitat: Open country, such as short scrub and grassveld and sparsely wooded areas. Absent from mountains, dense woodland and forest.
Behaviour: Both diurnal and nocturnal activity is recorded but it lies up during the hotter hours of the day. It is an active digger but although it will excavate its own burrows, it frequently modifies those dug by other species. Normally seen in groups numbering from 2–6 individuals. As pairs mate for life, groups usually comprise a pair and their offspring. Occasionally more may be seen but such groupings are temporary, perhaps associated with an abundant, localized food source. When foraging, it appears to wander aimlessly, stopping periodically with ears turned to the ground; when food is located, it digs shallow holes with the forepaws.
Food: Mostly insects (particularly Harvester termites) and a variety of beetle species; also reptiles, rodents and wild fruits.
Reproduction: 4–6 pups born in burrow, Sep–Nov, gestation 60 days. Pale-grey at birth, with eyes closed. Populations rise and fall in poorly understood cycles.

Adult Cape Fox in the central Namib.

Cape Fox is the only true fox in southern Africa.

Bat-eared Fox has very large ears and contrasting black-and-white facial markings. Inset: *Pairs mate for life.*

Cape Fox

38 mm

Front   Back

35 mm

Front   Back

Bat-eared Fox

135

Canis mesomelas

■ Black-backed Jackal *Canis mesomelas*

Total length 96–110 cm; tail 28–37 cm; shoulder height 38 cm; mass 6–10 kg.
Identification pointers: Dog-like appearance; dark, white-flecked 'saddle' on back; black tail; fairly large, pointed, reddish-backed ears. See Side-striped Jackal where distributions overlap.

Description: Medium-sized, dog-like carnivore with characteristic black saddle, which is broad at neck and shoulders, narrowing to base of tail. Saddle liberally sprinkled with white hair. Face, flanks and legs reddish-brown; underparts usually paler. Lips, throat and chest are white. Fairly large pointed ears, reddish on back surface and lined with white hair on inside. Black bushy tail.

Distribution: Very widely distributed in subregion but absent from parts of north-east and eradicated by farmers in other areas. In recent years this jackal has reoccupied most areas from which it was eliminated up to the 1980s.

Habitat: Wide habitat tolerance, from coastal Namib Desert to moist Drakensberg. Unlike Side-striped Jackal, however, it prefers drier areas.

Behaviour: Mainly nocturnal when in conflict with man, but in protected reserves is frequently seen during day. Normally solitary or in pairs but also occurs in family parties. Pairs form long-term pair-bonds, with both the male and the female marking and defending a territory, which varies considerably in size, depending on the availability of food and competition with other jackals. It is well known for its wariness and cunning and is generally able to avoid all but the most sophisticated of traps. When resting, it may lie up in a burrow dug by other species, or under a bush or other vegetation. Its call is characteristic and has been described as a screaming yell, finished off with three or four short yaps. Calling is more frequent during the winter months when mating takes place.

Food: It takes an extremely wide range of food items, from young antelope, rodents, hares, birds, reptiles and insects to wild fruits and berries. It also feeds on carrion; in fact, there is little that it has not been recorded eating. Unfortunately, it has proved to be a problem in sheep- and goat-farming areas, but only certain individuals take to stock-killing, not all.

Reproduction: Seasonal breeder with 1–6 (usually 3) pups being born between July and October. Gestation approximately 60 days. Newborn dark-brown pups are helpless and are born in burrows dug by other species. Both male and female bring food to young, as do 'helpers', subadults from the previous breeding season. Pups start to forage with the parents when they are about 14 weeks old.

Note: The Black-backed Jackal is one of three carnivore species that occur in two widely separated populations, one in southern Africa and the other in East Africa. The other members of this 'club' are the Bat-eared Fox and the Aardwolf.

Canis adustus

■ Side-striped Jackal *Canis adustus*

Total length 96–120 cm; tail 30–40 cm; shoulder height 40 cm; mass 7.5–12 kg.
Identification pointers: Overall grey appearance with a light-and-dark stripe along each side; lacks dark, silver-mottled saddle of the Black-backed Jackal; tail usually with white tip; ears fairly large but smaller and less pointed than those of Black-backed Jackal. Habitat can be a useful aid to identification. Also see distribution maps of the two jackals.

Description: From a distance this jackal has a uniform grey appearance but at close quarters a light-coloured band, liberally fringed with black, can be seen along each flank. These side-stripes give the jackal its name. The underparts and throat are paler than the upperparts. The tail is quite bushy, mostly black and usually has a white tip.

The Black-backed Jackal is easily identified by its dark 'saddle' flecked with white hair.
Inset: Facial colour varies from pale to rich reddish-brown, while the throat, lips and chest are white.

The Side-striped Jackal has a light-and-dark stripe along each side and a white-tipped tail.

Black-backed
Jackal

54 mm

Front   Back

Side-striped
Jackal

52 mm

Front   Back

Distribution: Only found in the far northern and eastern areas of southern African subregion, but has a wide distribution elsewhere in sub-Saharan Africa, excluding the equatorial forest zone.

Habitat: It shows a preference for well-watered wooded areas, but not forest.

Behaviour: Although it is mainly nocturnal, it may be seen in the early morning and late afternoon. Most sightings are of single animals, although pairs and family parties are often encountered. Call has been likened to owl hoot, quite unlike long, drawn-out howl of the Black-backed Jackal.

Food: It is an omnivorous species taking a wide variety of food items ranging from small mammals, birds, reptiles, insects and carrion to wild fruits.

Reproduction: 4–6 pups born between August and January, in the abandoned burrows of other species.

■ Wild Dog *Lycaon pictus*

Lycaon pictus
■ Historical distribution
Wild Dog packs occasionally move outside those areas marked on the map; but then they are usually in transit or are killed by stock farmers.

Total length 105–150 cm; tail 30–40 cm; shoulder height 65–80 cm; mass 20–30 kg.

Identification pointers: Heavily blotched black, white and yellow-brown; slender body, long legs; normally white-tipped tail; large, dark, rounded ears; black muzzle and stripe from between eyes over top of head.

Description: Unmistakable; similar in size to a domestic German Shepherd dog. It has large, rounded ears, long legs and a bushy, white-tipped tail. Body irregularly blotched with black, white, brown and yellowish-brown. Muzzle is black, with black continuing as line from muzzle to between the ears. Forehead on either side of the black line is pale-fawn to white.

Distribution: In South Africa, the Wild Dog occurs permanently only in the Kruger National Park (±320 individuals) but a number of animals have been introduced to the Hluhluwe/Imfolozi complex in KwaZulu-Natal, also Madikwe and Pilansberg game reserves in the north-west of South Africa. In the other southern African countries it only survives in the larger reserves and uninhabited areas. Wild Dogs previously occurred widely in Africa outside the equatorial forests, but have been greatly reduced in numbers by man. Rarest large carnivore in subregion.

Habitat: As it hunts by sight it is usually associated with open country. It avoids dense woodland, forest and extensive areas of tall grass.

Behaviour: It is a highly specialized hunter, living in packs usually numbering from 10–15 animals, although smaller and larger groups have been observed. It is predominantly diurnal, most of its hunting taking place in the cooler morning and late afternoon hours. Hunting is undertaken by the pack, which moves slowly towards the intended prey at first, increasing the pace as the quarry starts to move away. Once an individual has been singled out, the pack rarely deviates from its goal and a chase may continue for several kilometres. Smaller prey may be pulled down immediately but larger prey is bitten and torn while on the move until it weakens from shock or loss of blood and can be overpowered. Despite its reputation as a wanton killer, the Wild Dog kills only for its immediate needs. During hunts it is able to reach speeds of over 50 km/h. When pups begin to eat solids, the adults regurgitate meat at the den for the pups, as well as for the adults that remained to guard the young and any sick animals unable to take part in the hunts.

Wild Dogs do not establish territories but have very large home ranges. The average home range size in Kruger National Park has been estimated at 450 km², but in arid areas home ranges are considerably larger. It is a very vocal species with a wide range of calls. Normally, only a single female comes into breeding condition (oestrus) at any one time and she is mated by the dominant male.

Once found throughout sub-Saharan Africa, Wild Dogs are extinct as a viable breeding species in many countries, with most populations restricted to conservation areas. The total population estimates for Africa range from 3 000 to 5 750 animals.

The endangered Wild Dog, Africa's largest canid, is characterized by its patterned coloration and rounded ears.

Wild Dog

76 mm

Front

Back

Food: Wild Dogs hunt a wide range of mammals, ranging in size from Steenbok to Buffalo. They also take rodents, hares and birds. Impala is the most important prey species in the Kruger National Park, with Springbok being very important throughout much of the Wild Dogs' range in Botswana.

Reproduction: Young are born during the dry winter months (March to July) when grass is short and hunting conditions are at their best. Between 2 and 10 pups are born after a gestation period of 69–73 days. The young are born in the abandoned burrows of other species; for the first three months of their life they remain in close proximity to the den.

OTTERS, BADGER, WEASEL & POLECAT | Family Mustelidae

Aonyx capensis

■ Cape Clawless Otter *Aonyx capensis*
Total length 110–160 cm; tail 50 cm; mass 10–21 kg.

Identification pointers: Quite large size; dark-brown coat (appears black when wet) with white lips, chin, throat and upper chest. Finger-like digits. On land, ambles along with back arched. Larger than Spotted-necked Otter and lacks neck spots. Unlike the latter, Cape Clawless Otter may be found away from permanent water. Occasionally confused with Water Mongoose (page 152).

Description: Larger of two otter species occurring in subregion. Soft dark-brown coat, with lips, chin and throat being silvery-white; white coloration sometimes extends to upper part of chest. Legs short and stout and tail long, heavy at base and tapering towards tip. On land it walks with back arched. Toes distinctively finger-like, but lack claws, although there are small, flat, rudimentary nails on some digits of hindfeet.

Distribution: Absent from most of the dry interior of subregion.

Habitat: Rivers, marshes, dams and lakes; also dry stream-beds in most terrain if pools of water exist. May wander several kilometres from water. Also utilizes the coastal intertidal zone.

Behaviour: Active during early morning and late afternoon but may hunt at any time of day or night. Lies up in cover or shade during hotter hours. Occurs singly, in pairs, or small family parties. 'Latrine' areas with numerous droppings made up largely of crushed crab-shell are useful indication of its presence. Otters crush and eat the entire crab; Water Mongoose usually leaves carapace, pincers and legs of larger crabs. Cape Clawless Otter will hunt by sight, but much prey is found by feeling with fingers, and it therefore thrives in water with poor visibility. (Compare Spotted-necked Otter, below.)

Food: Freshwater crabs, but also fish and frogs. Takes molluscs, small mammals, birds and insects. Freshwater mussels are dug out with the fingers and smashed against a rock or hard object to break the shell, and the meat eaten.

Reproduction: Usually 2–3 cubs per litter; gestation 60–65 days.

Lutra maculicollis

■ Spotted-necked Otter *Lutra maculicollis*
Total length 100 cm; tail 30–50 cm; mass 3–6.2 kg.

Identification pointers: Upperparts uniform brown to dark brown; underparts lighter with pale blotching on throat and upper chest and occasionally between hindlegs. Considerably smaller than Cape Clawless Otter; closer in size to Water Mongoose (page 152) but lacks the long hair of the latter. Closely associated with water and rarely seen far from it.

Description: Smaller of two otter species occurring in subregion. Body slender and long, with somewhat flattened tail. Feet fully webbed and toes clawed. Coat

Cape Clawless Ottter inhabits rivers, marshes and dams.

Spotted-necked Otter has well-developed claws.

The Cape Clawless Otter has finger-like digits.

Cape Clawless Otters sometimes utilize coastal habitats. Like all otters, they appear much darker when wet.

Cape
Clawless
Otter

100 mm

Front   *Back*

Spotted-necked Otter

58 mm

Front   *Back*

uniform dark brown to reddish-brown, with throat and upper chest mottled or blotched with creamy-white. Appears black when wet.

Distribution: Patchy distribution in subregion. Declining in numbers perhaps because of soil erosion, consequent muddy rivers and poor visibility for otter.

Habitat: Larger rivers, or those with large permanent pools, as well as lakes, dams and well-watered swamps. More closely tied to water than Cape Clawless Otter; not associated with estuaries or coastal environment.

Behaviour: Diurnal. Normally in groups of 2–6, but sometimes larger groups or single. Prey usually taken to bank to eat but also eaten in water. It is quite vocal, with whistles being most frequently heard, probably as a means of maintaining group contact. Uses latrine sites close to water's edge. Droppings are smaller than those of Cape Clawless Otter and similar in size to those of Water Mongoose. Those of latter species, however, usually contain greater quantity of mammal hair and are rarely so white.

Food: Mostly fish but also crabs, frogs, birds and insects.

Reproduction: 2–3 cubs probably born in summer. Gestation 60 days.

Mellivora capensis

■ Honey Badger (Ratel) *Mellivora capensis*

Total length 90–100 cm; tail 18–25 cm; shoulder height 30 cm; mass 8–14 kg.

Identification pointers: Stocky build and short legs; silver-grey upperparts including top of head; black underparts and legs; short, bushy black tail – often held erect when walking. Cannot be confused with any other species.

Description: Unmistakable animal, with its thickset form, silver-grey upperparts and black underparts and legs. Top of head and upper neck usually paler than rest of upperparts. Tail short, bushy and black and often held erect when walking. Ears are small and barely noticeable. Spoor distinctive with clear impressions in prints left by long, heavy claws of forefeet (see opposite).

Distribution: Widespread in subregion, but apparently absent from much of the Free State and Lesotho.

Habitat: Found in most major habitats, but absent from coastal Namib Desert.

Behaviour: Tough and aggressive; records of attacks on Elephant and Buffalo and also humans when threatened. Usually seen singly, but pairs and family groups may also be observed. Mainly nocturnal, but where not disturbed is active in early morning and late afternoon. Largely terrestrial but can climb well.

Food: Wide range of food items but insects, other invertebrates and rodents are the most important. Reptiles, birds, other small mammals, wild fruit and carrion are also eaten. Common name is derived from their tendency to break into beehives (both natural and man-made) to eat honey and larvae. 'Rogue' individuals may take to killing poultry, sheep and goats.

Reproduction: Young may be born at any time of year, with 1–4 (usually 1 or 2) born after a gestation period of about 180 days, in a grass- and leaf-lined burrow. They stay with the mother for up to 20 months.

Poecilogale albinucha

■ African Striped Weasel *Poecilogale albinucha*

Total length 40–50 cm; tail 12–16 cm; shoulder height 50 cm; mass 220–350 g.

Identification pointers: Long, thin body; fairly long, bushy white tail and very short legs; overall colour black with white cap on head and 4 white to yellowish stripes running from neck to base of the tail. Often confused with Striped Polecat (page 144), but latter has much longer hair and white patches on face.

Description: This is a long, slender carnivore, with short legs. The overall colour is black with 4 off-white to yellowish stripes running from the neck to the base of

The Honey Badger is extremely tough and shows little fear; they are mainly nocturnal and, to a lesser extent, crepuscular. Inset: The ears are barely noticeable.

The African Striped Weasel has a long, thin body and a long, bushy white tail.

Honey Badger

54 mm

Front   Back

21 mm

Front   Back

African Striped Weasel

143

the tail, combining into a white cap on the top of the head. The tail is quite bushy and white but the body hair is coarse and short.

Distribution: The Striped Weasel has a wide distribution in the eastern areas of southern Africa, with a few records from Namibia, Botswana and Mozambique.

Habitat: It has a wide habitat tolerance but most of the records are from grassland areas. Recent records in fynbos/farmland mosaics in south-west.

Behaviour: Occasionally sighted during the day but predominantly nocturnal. Although usually solitary, pairs and family parties may be observed. When it walks or runs, the back has an arched appearance. It is an efficient digger in soft soil but probably uses rodent-burrows as well as its own for shelter.

Food: It hunts small, warm-blooded prey, particularly rodents. Food may be hoarded or carried to the shelter to be eaten. Its build is well adapted for the pursuit of rodents in their burrows.

Reproduction: Most records of births are in the summer months, from November to March. Litters consist of 1–3 young, each with a mass of about 4 g; the gestation period is about 32 days. At birth the young are almost hairless and their eyes are closed; they open after about 2 weeks.

Ictonyx striatus

■ Striped Polecat *Ictonyx striatus*

Total length 57–67 cm; tail 26 cm; shoulder height 10–15 cm; mass 0.5–1.4 kg.
Identification pointers: Small size and long white and black hair; white hair in 4 stripes down back; white patch between eyes and one at base of each ear. (See African Striped Weasel, above.)

Description: Conspicuous black-and-white markings warn would-be predators that they can expect a squirt of foul-smelling liquid from its anal glands. Long body hair is shiny black with 4 distinct white stripes extending from top of head to base of tail along back and flanks. White patch on forehead between eyes and larger white patch at base of ear. The tail is predominantly white but black shows through.

Distribution: Throughout subregion except for Namib Desert coast.

Habitat: Found in all the major habitat types, including agricultural lands.

Behaviour: Strictly nocturnal; usually solitary, but also in pairs and family parties. Shelter is sought in other species' burrows, on rocky outcrops, among matted vegetation and even under the floors of buildings; can dig own burrow. If threatened it adopts threat posture, with rump towards aggressor, back arched and tail held erect. If threat persists, it squirts foul-smelling fluid at aggressor.

Food: Mostly insects, rodents and other small animals.

Reproduction: After gestation of 36 days, litter of 1–3 young (up to 5) born in summer, each weighing 10–15 g.

MONGOOSES | Family Herpestidae

Mungos mungo

■ Banded Mongoose *Mungos mungo*

Total length 50–65 cm; tail 18–25 cm; mass 1.0–1.6 kg.
Identification pointers: Small size; usually have 10–12 dark-brown to black transverse stripes on grey to grey-brown back. Superficially similar to Suricate but the banding is much more distinct and tail bushier. Also occurs in groups. Compare the distribution maps and habitat preferences.

Description: This small, very distinctive mongoose has 10–12 dark-brown to black transverse bands on back, from behind shoulders to base of tail. Colour varies from grizzled grey to grey-brown. Tail bushy and usually darker in colour towards tip. Head relatively long and pointed.

144

The Striped Polecat has four distinct white stripes on the back and a bushy black-and-white tail.
Inset: *These skins show the difference in size between the Striped (African) Weasel (top) and Striped Polecat (below).*

The Banded Mongoose has a number of dark-brown to black stripes across the back.

Striped
Polecat

22 mm

Front   *Back*

26 mm

Front   *Back*

Banded
Mongoose

Distribution: It is restricted to eastern and northern areas of southern Africa and mainly absent from the drier central and western regions. In recent years there have been sightings of small bands of this mongoose in the Kgalagadi Transfrontier Park, including two observations by the authors. It is unlikely that this is an isolated population, but originates with animals that have followed dry watercourses from either the northern or eastern ranges.

Habitat: Wide habitat tolerance but absent from desert, semi-desert and rain-forest. Preference for woodland with adequate ground cover.

Behaviour: Highly gregarious and social species; troops number 5–30 or more. When foraging, they maintain contact with constant soft calls. Troop's home range will include several shelters, usually in termitaria. Size of home range depends on number of pack members and availability of food, from 80 ha to over 4 km². Frequent marking with anal gland secretions is performed on rocks and logs. Encounters between different troops may result in conflict but apparently they do not defend territories.

Food: Insects and other invertebrates are the most important food items but they also take reptiles, amphibians, birds, carrion and probably small rodents. When feeding on birds' eggs they use the front feet to throw the eggs between the hindlegs against a rock or other hard object.

Reproduction: Usually 2–6 (up to 8) young, each weighing about 20 g, are born after a gestation period of approximately 60 days. The young suckle from any lactating female, not just the mother, and all the adults perform guard duty over the young animals. Juveniles begin following the troop about 5 weeks after birth.

■ Meller's Mongoose *Rhynchogale melleri*

Total length 60–90 cm; tail 30–38 cm; mass 1.7–3 kg.

Rhynchogale melleri

Identification pointers: May have black, brown or white tail; individuals with white tails may be confused with White-tailed Mongoose (page 154) but are smaller with a blacker overall appearance than latter. May also be confused with Selous's Mongoose (page 148). The crest-like parting on the neck, although difficult to see, is a useful identification aid. The distribution ranges of White-tailed, Meller's and Selous's Mongooses overlap in the far north-eastern areas of the subregion.

Description: Hair shaggy. Colour above varies from light to dark brown; underparts lighter. Mongoose tail colour often aids identification but in this species is variable. Although near base it is usually brown, towards the tip it may be black, brown or white; dark brown to black, however, is the most usual. At close quarters upperparts have grizzled appearance. Legs are black. Useful distinguishing characteristic is a distinct crest-like parting in the hair on either side of the neck. Head quite short; muzzle swollen.

Distribution: Patchy distribution in north-eastern parts of southern Africa.

Habitat: Open woodlands but extends marginally into grassland savanna, nearly always in the vicinity of dense ground cover and water.

Behaviour: Nocturnal and usually solitary.

Food: Mainly termites. Also other invertebrates, reptiles, amphibians and wild fruit.

Reproduction: 2–3 young born in summer in burrows or rock crevices.

Banded Mongoose. Inset: *Banded Mongooses readily dig for invertebrates and other prey.*

Meller's Mongoose varies in colour from light to dark brown. Inset: *Meller's Mongoose skin.*

Meller's Mongoose

25 mm

Front   Back

Bdeogale crassicauda

■ Bushy-tailed Mongoose *Bdeogale crassicauda*

Total length 65–72 cm; tail 23–30 cm; mass 1.5–2.1 kg.

Identification pointers: Overall black appearance; should not be confused with any other mongoose species occurring in southern Africa.

Description: Overall body and tail colour appears black, but at close quarters appears grizzled. Legs and long-haired bushy tail are jet-black.

Distribution: Apparently very rare in subregion and seldom seen. Restricted to extreme northern and eastern Zimbabwe and central Mozambique.

Habitat: Open woodland with grass, often in rocky outcrops.

Behaviour: Apparently solitary and nocturnal, although day-time sightings have been made. Little is known of the way of life of this mongoose.

Food: Insects, other invertebrates, but also rodents, reptiles and amphibians.

Reproduction: Nothing known.

Paracynictus selousi

■ Selous's Mongoose *Paracynictis selousi*

Total length 63–90 cm; tail 28–43 cm; mass 1.4–2.0 kg.

Identification pointers: Smaller and more slender than White-tailed Mongoose (page 154). Tail only white towards the tip, whereas in White-tailed Mongoose it is white for three-quarters of its length.

Description: The overall body colour of this mongoose is pale speckled grey to tawny-grey; the legs are brown to black. The fairly long-haired tail is usually light-coloured but only white towards the tip.

Distribution: Restricted to north-east and far north of subregion.

Habitat: Savanna grassland and woodland.

Behaviour: Nocturnal and usually solitary, but pairs and females with young are not uncommon. It digs its own burrows. This mongoose is probably overlooked because of its relatively small size and its nocturnal habits.

Food: It feeds mainly on invertebrates but also takes a wide range of small rodents, amphibians, reptiles and birds.

Reproduction: Litters of 2–4 born from August to March.

Galerella pulverulenta

Galerella flavescens

■ Small Grey Mongoose *Galerella pulverulenta*

Also known as Cape Grey Mongoose. The northern Nambian population is now recognized as a separate species, Kaokoland Slender Mongoose, *Galerella flavescens*. Unlike Small Grey Mongoose, which until recently was considered a subspecies, Kaokoland Slender Mongoose shows no grizzling of the coat and appears black when observed in the field.

Total length 55–69 cm; tail 20–34 cm; mass 0.5–1.0 kg.

Identification pointers: Small size; uniform grey colouring; only marginally overlaps distribution range of Slender Mongoose (page 150). It lacks the latter's black tail-tip and holds tail horizontally when running, whereas Slender Mongoose holds tail vertically or curved slightly over the body. Much smaller than Large Grey Mongoose which, in any case, has black tail-tip.

Description: Uniform light- to dark-grey above, appearing grizzled at close quarters. In north-west some animals may appear more brown. Legs darker than rest of body. Head quite long and muzzle pointed. Tail long, bushy and uniformly grizzled grey.

Distribution: Small Grey Mongoose occurs widely south of the Gariep (Orange) River and extends through the southern Free State, Lesotho and marginally into KwaZulu-Natal and southern Namibia.

Habitat: It has a very wide habitat tolerance, from forest to open scrub. Particularly common in the southern coastal areas and adjacent interior.

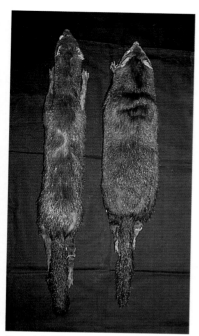

Bushy-tailed Mongoose skins.

Selous's Mongoose is nocturnal and usually solitary. It is small in size with uniformly grey colouring.

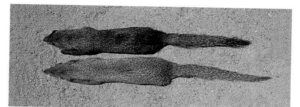

Skins showing colour variants of Small Grey Mongoose.

Small Grey Mongoose is common throughout southern South Africa. Inset (left): The rare Bushy-tailed Mongoose is solitary and nocturnal; (right): Kaokoland Slender Mongoose appears black.

Bushy-tailed
Mongoose

Selous's Mongoose

25 mm

Front   Back

28 mm

Front   Back

Small Grey
Mongoose

Behaviour: Active by day, although tends to lie up during the hottest part of the day in summer. Usually solitary but pairs and family parties are occasionally seen. It makes use of regular pathways within home range. Home ranges overlap considerably and although this species marks with glandular secretions, it is not known whether it is territorial.

Food: Invertebrates (mainly insects) and small rodents; also carrion, birds, reptiles, amphibians and wild fruits.

Reproduction: From 1–3 young are born in holes, among rocks or in dense vegetation, from about August to December in the south.

■ Large Grey Mongoose *Herpestes ichneumon*

Total length 100–110 cm; tail 45–58 cm; mass 2.5–4.0 kg.

Identification pointers: Large size; long grey-grizzled body hair; black tail-tip and black lower legs. Much larger than Small Grey Mongoose, which has a completely grey tail and no black at tip.

Herpestes ichneumon

Description: As its name indicates, this is a large grey mongoose. The tail is prominently black-tipped and the lower parts of the legs are black. The body hair is very long. Tail hair is long, becoming shorter towards the black tip.

Distribution: Occurs in a narrow belt along the southern coast from close to Cape Town, then northwards into KwaZulu-Natal. It is fairly widely distributed in the eastern areas of southern Africa and marginally in the far north. Records from the 1950s indicated that it occurred only as far as Knysna, but by the 1970s it had spread to the Caledon and Bredasdorp districts. Since then, it has steadily expanded its range westwards up the West Coast to Lambert's Bay and, in 2006, was observed at Kleinsee, just 120 km south of the Gariep (Orange) River estuary. It is also widespread in other parts of Africa, although absent from much of the equatorial forest zone and from the desert regions.

Habitat: Riverine vegetation and around lakes, dams and marshes. When foraging, however, it may wander several kilometres from its usual habitat.

Behaviour: Mainly diurnal, although nocturnal activity has been recorded. It is usually seen solitarily or in pairs, but family parties are not uncommon. Such parties may walk in a line, nose to anus, giving the group a snake-like appearance. It frequently stands on its hind legs to view the surrounding area. Droppings are deposited at regular latrine sites and it also marks objects within its home range with anal gland secretions.

Food: Small rodents are very important in its diet but it also eats other small mammals, reptiles, birds, amphibians and a wide range of invertebrates, as well as wild fruits. It is known to eat snakes, including fairly large puff-adders.

Reproduction: Young are probably born in the summer months but there is no information available for southern Africa. Litter size has been recorded as 2–4, born after a gestation period of about 75 days.

■ Slender Mongoose *Galerella sanguinea*

Total length 50–65 cm; tail 23–30 cm; mass (male) 500–800 g, (female) 370–560 g.

Identification pointers: Small size and slender body; colour grey, brown or chestnut-orange; short legs and fairly bushy tail with black tip – raised or vertical but with forward curve when running; compare with Small Grey Mongoose (page 148) where range overlaps, but latter lacks black-tipped tail. (According to some taxonomists, more than one species is involved.)

Galerella sanguinea

Description: Body colour of this slender species varies from grizzled yellow-brown to rich red-brown; with the latter colour most frequently encountered in the

Large Grey Mongoose. Note the grizzled grey coat and relatively long hair.

Slender Mongoose. Inset: *Two colour forms of the Slender Mongoose: the chestnut-red colour form (top) is found in the Kalahari thornveld of the Northern Cape and southern Botswana.*

Large Grey Mongoose

42 mm

Front   Back

Slender Mongoose

26 mm

Front   Back

151

north-western areas of the subregion. Species in central and northern Namibia are usually dark brown but reddish-brown specimens also occur. Tail bushy and black-tipped. When the animal runs, tail typically held well clear of ground and often vertical, but curving forward over back and not rigidly upright as is the case with the Suricate (page 156).

Distribution: Widespread in subregion north of Gariep (Orange) River.

Habitat: It is found in areas of high and low rainfall, and from forest to open savanna, as long as there is adequate cover.

Behaviour: Terrestrial but climbs well. Usually solitary. One of most commonly seen small carnivores within its range, particularly along roads.

Food: Insects and other invertebrates; also takes reptiles, small rodents, birds and amphibians as well as wild fruits.

Reproduction: Litter size 1–2, sometimes 3, born in summer. Gestation period approximately 45 days.

Atilax paludinosus

■ Water (Marsh) Mongoose *Atilax paludinosus*

Total length 80–100 cm; tail 30–40 cm; shoulder height 22 cm; mass 2.5–5.5 kg.
Identification pointers: Large; generally uniform dark-brown in colour; associated with water. Sometimes confused with the two otter species, but much smaller than Cape Clawless Otter, and lacks the pale markings found on throat and neck of the Spotted-necked Otter (both page 140). The head is long and pointed and typically mongoose-like.

Description: Large, usually uniformly dark-brown, shaggy-haired animal. Short hair on feet and face. Some are reddish-brown or almost black.

Distribution: Widespread in subregion but absent from arid interior. It penetrates the Karoo along the length of the Gariep (Orange) River to the west coast.

Habitat: The Water Mongoose is usually associated with well-watered areas, along rivers and streams, and around dams, lakes, estuaries and swamps wherever there is cover. It utilizes temporary stream-beds where there are pools and may wander some distance from water.

Behaviour: This mongoose is active mainly at night but is also crepuscular (active at dusk and dawn). It is probably territorial and sightings are mostly of single animals, although pairs and females with young are occasionally seen. The home ranges tend to be linear, in that they follow rivers and streams or the perimeters of other bodies of water. Droppings accumulate at latrine sites, which are usually situated near the water's edge; these latrines are not, however, as dispersed as those of otters and the droppings are usually darker in colour. When foraging, it follows regular pathways. It swims readily.

Food: Mainly crabs and amphibians but also small rodents, birds, fish, insects, reptiles and occasionally wild fruits. Aquatic food hunted in shallows where feet are used to dig in the mud and explore under rocks. It smashes freshwater mussels by throwing them against rocks with front feet between hindlegs. It forages along beaches and in rock-pools in coastal areas.

Reproduction: Most of the young probably born from August to December. There are usually 1–3 young, each weighing about 120 g at birth, and they are born in burrows, rock crevices or among dense vegetation.

The Water, or Marsh, Mongoose is usually associated with marshes, lakes, estuaries, dams and other bodies of water.

Water Mongoose; note the shaggy coat and naked toes.

Water Mongoose cubs weigh about 120 g at birth.

Water Mongoose

46 mm

Front   Back

153

Helogale parvula

■ Dwarf Mongoose *Helogale parvula*
Total length 35–40 cm; tail 14–20 cm; shoulder height 7 cm; mass 220–350 g.
Identification pointers: Very small size; uniform dark brown, glossy coat; always in troops.
Description: Dwarf Mongoose is the smallest carnivore occurring in southern Africa. Its body is a uniform dark brown and from a distance appears to be almost black. The fur is glossy and has a slightly grizzled appearance at close quarters.
Distribution: Dwarf Mongoose is restricted to the northern and eastern regions of the southern African subregion. Elsewhere in Africa it extends through central and East Africa to as far north as Somalia.
Habitat: Open woodland and grassland savanna. It is absent from very dry areas and forest but is often associated with rocky areas.
Behaviour: A strictly diurnal mongoose usually living in troops of up to 10 individuals, although as many as 30 have been recorded. They have a fixed home, frequently in termitaria, but will use burrows dug by other species or excavated by themselves. Dwarf Mongoose troops have a rigid social system with a dominant male and female, the rest of the members falling into a 'pecking order'. Usually only the dominant female breeds, and apart from suckling the young, she leaves their care to the other troop members. When disturbed, Dwarf Mongooses will dive for cover but they are inquisitive and will soon re-emerge, standing on their hindlegs to look around.
Food: Insects and other invertebrates are by far the most important prey items but they will also eat reptiles, birds and birds' eggs. Several troop members may co-operate to overpower larger prey.
Reproduction: 2–4 young are born in the summer months after a gestation period of some 50–54 days. The young are covered with hair at birth and the eyes are closed.

Ichneumia albicauda

■ White-tailed Mongoose *Ichneumia albicauda*
Total length 90–150 cm; tail 35–48 cm; mass 3.5–5.2 kg.
Identification pointers: Large size; white tail, dark body and legs. The superficially similar Selous's Mongoose (page 148) is smaller and its tail is only white towards the tip. When walking, the head is held lower than the rest of the body.
Description: This very large mongoose has a coarse shaggy coat and distinctively long, white tail. The body and the long legs are brown-grey to almost black but the head is usually somewhat lighter in colour. When it walks, its hindquarters appear to be higher than the shoulder region.
Distribution: Found in the eastern parts of the southern African subregion. Further north, it occurs widely in central and East Africa, extending as far north as Egypt, and also occurs through the savannas of West Africa to Senegal. Also present in southern Arabia.
Habitat: Woodland savanna but marginally in forest. Largely absent from equatorial forest and desert.
Behaviour: Nocturnal and usually solitary but occasionally pairs or family parties may be seen. It lies up in burrows dug by other species, or in rock crevices and among dense vegetation. Little is known about the biology of this mongoose.
Food: Insects and other invertebrates are by far the most important food but it also takes rodents, amphibians, reptiles, birds and wild fruits. It is recorded as catching mammals up to the size of hares and cane-rats.
Reproduction: The young are probably born in spring and early summer. There are between 1 and 4 young per litter.

The social Dwarf Mongoose often lives in large termite mounds. Inset: Dwarf Mongoose.

The large White-tailed Mongoose has a coarse shaggy coat and a long white tail.

Dwarf Mongoose

16 mm

Front   *Back*

White-tailed Mongoose

45 mm

Front   *Back*

Cynictis penicillata

■ Yellow Mongoose *Cynictis penicillata*

Total length 40–60 cm; tail 18–25 cm; mass 450–900 g.

Identification pointers: Small size; yellowish body and tail; white tail-tip; in parts of northern range, specimens are greyer, lacking white tail tip; pointed face.

Description: Usually reddish-yellow to tawny-yellow with prominent white tip to tail. However, in northern parts of range, particularly Botswana, it is more grey and usually lacks white tip to tail. Tail quite bushy. Chin, throat and upper chest paler than rest of body and eyes are orange-brown.

Distribution: Western and central areas of subregion, extending as far east as north-western KwaZulu-Natal and Limpopo Province, South Africa.

Habitat: This is a mongoose of open habitats, such as short grassland and semi-desert scrub, but it also occurs in the more open areas along the coast. It is absent from forest, dense vegetation and the coastal Namib Desert.

Behaviour: Diurnal species and, although usually seen alone, it lives communally in warrens of 5–10 (sometimes as many as 20) individuals. It may dig its own burrows but will readily occupy those dug by Suricate or Ground Squirrels, sometimes with all three species living in the same burrow systems. Each morning the Yellow Mongoose colony disperses along regularly used pathways to forage. The droppings are deposited in latrines in close proximity to the entrances to the burrows.

Food: Mostly insects and invertebrates, but also takes small rodents, amphibians and reptiles and occasionally carrion.

Reproduction: In the southern parts of its distribution range, litters of 2–5 young are born between October and January, but in the north this extends through to March. It is possible that births also occur at other times of the year as well.

Suricata suricatta

■ Suricate (Meerkat) *Suricata suricatta*

Total length 45–55 cm; tail 20–24 cm; mass 620–960 g.

Identification pointers: Small size; pale body colour with several irregular transverse bands on the back; thinly haired tail, usually with darker tip, and often used as a fifth 'leg' when standing on hindlegs and held rigidly vertical when running. Occurs in groups. Could be confused with Banded Mongoose (page 144) but ranges only overlap marginally (see maps) and banding much more distinct in that species. Habitat preferences also differ.

Description: The body is fawn to silvery-grey with a number of darker, irregular transverse bars running from behind the shoulders to the base of the tail. The tail is thin, tapering and short-haired. The head is broad at the back and the muzzle is pointed. Frequently stands on hindlegs and the tail is used for support. When running, tail held vertically (see Slender Mongoose, page 150). The front claws are very long and are used when digging for prey.

Distribution: Widely distributed in the central and western parts of the subregion, extending marginally eastwards.

Habitat: Open, arid, lightly vegetated country.

Behaviour: Completely diurnal in habit, and lives in groups numbering from 5–40 individuals. It will dig its own burrow complexes (warrens) but also makes use of those dug by Ground Squirrels and Yellow Mongooses, often living in harmony with both species. When foraging or on the move, it maintains communication with a constant soft grunting.

Food: Predominantly insects and other invertebrates, but will also eat reptiles and birds. Much of the food is obtained by digging with the long claws of the forefeet.

Reproduction: 2–5 young mainly born in summer, but records throughout the year. Gestation period 73 days. All troop members care for the young.

The Yellow Mongoose has a white-tipped tail. Inset: *The reddish-yellow form is the most widespread.*

Suricates frequently stand on their hindlegs, using the tail as a 'fifth leg' for balance.
Inset: *Skins of Banded Mongoose (top) and Suricate (bottom), showing the variations in banding on the back.*

Yellow Mongoose

26 mm

Front

Back

25 mm

Front

Back

Suricate

GENETS & CIVETS | Family Viverridae

Recent thinking identifies four species of genet found in southern Africa: the Small-spotted (*Genetta genetta/G. felina*) with a wide range; South African Large-spotted (*Genetta tigrina*), found along the coastal plain of South Africa; Common Large-spotted (*Genetta maculata*), found widely to the north-east of this; and the Angolan (*Genetta angolensis*) from northern Zimbabwe and Botswana. However, there is no finality on the range limits of the different species, nor on their taxonomic standing. We suspect these problems will be revisited many more times in the future.

Genetta genetta

Genetta maculata

Genetta tigrina

■ **Small-spotted Genet** *Genetta genetta*
Total length 86–100 cm; tail 40–50 cm; mass 1.5–2.6 kg.
■ **Common Large-spotted Genet** *Genetta maculata*
Total length 85–110 cm; tail 40–50 cm; mass 1.5–3.2 kg.
■ **South African Large-spotted Genet** *Genetta tigrina*
Total length 85–110 cm; tail 40–50 cm; mass 1.5–3.2 kg.
Identification pointers: All genets have long, slender bodies and tails; Small-spotted Genet has a white tail-tip, smaller dark to black spots, and a crest of longish hair that is only raised when alarmed. Large-spotted Genets usually have a black tail-tip, larger, rusty-brown spots, and no crest along the back. Compare distribution maps and habitat requirements. Sometimes confused with African Civet (page 160), but very much smaller.

Description: Genet species have long, slender bodies and tails, and short legs. The ears are long, rounded and thin. Small-spotted Genet is usually off-white to greyish-white, spotted with dark-brown to almost black spots and bars. The tail is black-ringed and usually has a white tip. A crest of fairly long, black-tipped hair runs along the back and is raised when the animal is frightened or angry. In the Large-spotted Genets, the spots are generally larger and rusty-brown in colour and the legs are usually paler. There is no prominent crest down the back and the hair is shorter and softer. The tail-tip is usually dark-brown to black. The black-and-white facial markings are usually more prominent in Small-spotted than in Large-spotted Genets; the chin of the former is dark and the latter usually white.

It should be noted that the systematics of the various species of African genet, including the southern African species, have not yet been fully clarified. There are enormous variations in colour and patterning and all grades of intermediate between the two may be encountered.

Distribution: Small-spotted Genet is widespread in southern Africa but absent from much of Mozambique, northern and eastern Zimbabwe; occurring marginally in KwaZulu-Natal. Also occurs widely in southern Angola and the extreme west of Zambia. It is absent from central Africa but a separate population extends from Tanzania northwards to Sudan and through the Sahel to West Africa, North Africa, the Middle East and parts of Europe (sometimes referred to as *G. felina*). Common Large-spotted Genet is chiefly restricted to the eastern areas of southern Africa, but extends in a narrow belt along the south coast, west to Cape Town, where it is recognized as the South African Large-spotted Genet. Common Large-spotted Genet also occurs widely in the rest of Africa.

Habitat: Small-spotted Genet has a very wide habitat tolerance, ranging from desert margins to areas with high rainfall. This includes woodland, riverine margins and even isolated rocky outcrops on open plains. Large-spotted genet is more associated with well-watered areas and fairly dense vegetation. Both species occur together in some areas of southern Africa.

Small-spotted Genet has prominent black-and-white facial markings. Inset: *Close-up of coat.*

South African Large-spotted Genet has large spots, usually rusty brown in colour, and a dark-brown or black-tipped tail.
Inset: *Common Large-spotted Genet is found mainly in the eastern areas of southern Africa.*

Genets

20 mm

Front   Back

159

Behaviour: Genets are mainly nocturnal, lying up under cover during the day. They are excellent climbers although much of their foraging is done on the ground. Normally solitary, pairs are occasionally seen. Droppings are deposited at latrine sites and these are usually in open or conspicuous places.

Food: Genet species have a similar diet. Invertebrates, particularly insects, are very important sources of food, as are small rodents. Reptiles, amphibians, birds and other small mammals are taken, as well as wild fruits. Genets can be a problem to poultry-owners; if they gain access to a poultry-run or hen-house, they will often kill far more than they require.

Reproduction: Young are born in the summer months in holes, rock crevices or among dense vegetation. Between 2 and 4 young (up to 5 have been recorded for the Large-spotted Genet) are born after a gestation period of about 70 days. The eyes are closed at birth.

■ **African Civet** *Civettictis civetta*

Total length 120–140 cm; tail 40–50 cm; shoulder height 40 cm; mass 9–15 kg.

Civettictis civetta

Identification pointers: Large size; white, black and grey facial markings; grey body heavily marked with black spots, blotches and irregular stripes; black legs; black-and-white neck bands; bushy tail with white bands below and black tip; walks with back arched and head held low. Sometimes confused with genets but is much larger, with shorter tail. See the genets (page 158).

Description: Long-bodied, heavily built and long-legged – about the size of a medium-sized dog. When moving, it holds its back in an arched position and its head low. Hair long and coarse. Forehead light-grey, muzzle white, and broad black band runs horizontally between forehead and muzzle and extends round head on to throat. Distinct light band extends from ear base towards chest. Greyish to grey-brown overall with many black spots, blotches and bands covering the body. Spotting is less distinct on, or may be absent from the shoulder and neck. Legs black. Ridge of dark hair along spine to tail is erected when African Civet is threatened or under stress. Ears small with black tip. Bushy tail banded white and black below; upperside and tip black.

Distribution: Restricted to the northern and eastern parts of subregion. Recent records outside the African Civet's natural normal distribution range have been noted in parts of the southern Free State, and south-eastern Namibia. At this stage, we have no explanation why this expansion is taking place, but it may have something to do with changing agricultural or farming practices.

Habitat: Fairly wide habitat tolerance but preference for more densely vegetated areas, for example, open woodland; near permanent water.

Behaviour: Mainly nocturnal but often active in early morning and late afternoon. Solitary or in pairs. Regular latrine sites known as 'civetries'. Marks points within its range with secretions from anal glands.

Food: Insects, other invertebrates, wild fruits, small rodents, reptiles, birds and carrion. Largest prey recorded are hares and guinea-fowl.

Reproduction: Litter 2–4 usually born in summer, in burrows excavated by other species, in rock crevices, or in dense vegetation. Gestation period 60–65 days.

The heavily built African Civet is strictly terrestrial. This photograph clearly shows the distinctive facial markings.

An African Civet photographed in the early morning hours. Inset: The coarse hair and spots in close-up.

African Civet

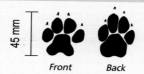

45 mm

Front   Back

PALM CIVET | Family Nandiniidae

Nandinia binotata

■ **African Palm Civet** *Nandinia binotata*
Total length 87–97 cm; tail 45–50 cm; mass 1.5–3.0 kg.
Identification pointers: Previously called Tree Civet. Long, fairly slender body and tail; generally dark appearance in the field, but at close quarters seen to be lighter brown with numerous darker, irregular spots. Forest habitat. Compared with the genet species (page 158), African Palm Civets have a very limited distribution in southern Africa. See distribution map.
Description: Similar to but stouter than genets. Head rounder with short ears. At a distance appear uniformly dark brown but at close quarters, upperparts noticeably spotted with small, irregularly shaped, dark-brown, almost black spots, on a lighter-brown background. More or less visible white or yellowish spot above shoulder-blade. Sides and lower parts of limbs not spotted. Hair soft and woolly on body and quite long on the long tail.
Distribution: In the subregion, occurs only in eastern Zimbabwe and adjacent areas of Mozambique. Widespread in the equatorial forest zone.
Habitat: Found in areas of high forest or Afro-montane rain-forest with an annual rainfall of 1 000 mm or more.
Behaviour: It is nocturnal, solitary and largely arboreal. Usually moves in the taller trees but does descend to the ground.
Food: Its principal food is wild fruit, although it also feeds on birds, rodents and insects. It has also been recorded as catching and eating fruit-bats. Carrion is eaten and they may take to raiding poultry-runs.
Reproduction: Virtually nothing is known about its biology in southern Africa but it seems likely that it may breed at any time of the year. Usually 2, but up to 4, young are born in tree-holes after a gestation period of about 64 days.

HYAENAS | Family Hyaenidae

Crocuta crocuta
■ Historical distribution

■ **Spotted Hyaena** *Crocuta crocuta*
Total length 120–180 cm; tail 25 cm; shoulder height 85 cm; mass 60–80 kg.
Identification pointers: Large size; shoulders higher than rump; short-haired, fawn-yellow coat with numerous dark-brown spots or blotches; lacks the long hair and pointed ears of Brown Hyaena (page 164). Characteristic repertoire of whooping, giggling and cackling calls.
Description: Unmistakable. Heavily built forequarters stand higher than rump. Large head with prominent rounded ears; black muzzle. Body usually fawn-yellow to grey-fawn with scattering of dark-brown spots and blotches, less distinct in old animals. Head, throat and chest not spotted. Short tail has coarse hair covering. Short erect mane along neck and shoulders.
Distribution: Formerly occurred as far south as Cape Town. Now only found in the northern and eastern parts of subregion.
Habitat: Open country but also rocky areas and in open woodland. Absent from forest and the Namib coastal belt. Requires access to drinking water.
Behaviour: Usually live in family groups or 'clans' led by a female. Clan members share the same range and dens and may number from 3 or 4, to 15 or more individuals. Territories are defended against other clans and are marked with anal gland secretions, urine and the distinctive bright white droppings – usually deposited in latrine sites. Mainly nocturnal but frequently seen during day. Very vocal with whoops, groans, grunts, whines, yells and giggles.

The African Palm Civet is a tree-dweller.

Young Spotted Hyaena develop spots in the fourth month.

Spotted Hyaena, the best-known of Africa's three hyaena species, has an extensive range south of the Sahara.

African Palm Civet

33 mm

Front

Back

Spotted Hyaena

96 mm

Front

Back

Food: In the past regarded as a cowardly scavenger, now known to be an efficient and regular hunter. Hunts singly, in small groups or in packs, depending on type of food taken. Diet ranges from insects to large game such as zebra, wildebeest and giraffe. Scavenges and will chase other predators from their kills. Raids dustbins and rubbish-heaps at campsites.

Reproduction: 1 or 2 cubs is usual, very rarely more; largely a non-seasonal breeder although seasonal peaks can be discerned in some regions. Two or more females may keep young in same burrow for several months. Uniform dark brown at birth with lighter heads.

Parahyaena brunnea

■ Historical distribution

■ Brown Hyaena *Parahyaena brunnea*

Total length 130–160 cm; tail 17–30 cm; shoulder height 80 cm; mass 47 kg (male), 42 kg (female).

Identification pointers: Large size with shoulders higher than the rump; long dark-brown hair, lighter in colour on neck and shoulders; large head with long pointed ears; long-haired tail. Spotted Hyaena has shorter hair, a spotted coat to lesser or greater extent, and has shorter, more rounded ears.

Description: Brown Hyaena is higher at the shoulder than at the hindquarters; shoulders and chest are heavily built. The body is covered in a long, shaggy coat, with a dense mantle of hair on the back and shoulders. The mantle is lighter in colour than the rest of the body. Body colour varies from light to dark-brown and the legs are striped black and light-brown. The tail is short, bushy and dark. Ears are long, erect and pointed.

Distribution: Brown Hyaena used to occur widely in southern Africa but today are only seen occasionally south of the Gariep (Orange) River. It is most frequently encountered in the Kalahari and along the coastline of southern Namibia, but wanderers may turn up far outside their main range.

Habitat: Although it is now found mainly in the drier parts of southern Africa, even occurring along the arid Namib Desert coastal belt, its past distribution shows that it has a potentially wide habitat tolerance.

Behaviour: Brown Hyaenas are mainly nocturnal and solitary, usually seen singly. However, several animals may share a territory, although foraging tends to be an individual activity. Territory size varies considerably, from about 19 km² in one study to between 235 and 480 km² in the southern Kalahari. Animals sharing a territory are apparently an extended family unit consisting of 4–6 individuals, all of whom assist in raising cubs. Territories are marked with droppings and secretions of the anal glands. Unlike the Spotted Hyaena, the Brown Hyaena is not particularly vocal.

Food: Brown Hyaenas are mainly scavengers but they also eat a wide variety of small vertebrates, insects and fruits. Hunting and killing of large prey is rare, although on occasion it has been recorded as killing sheep and goats in farming areas. Surplus food may be hidden in holes or under vegetation.

Reproduction: Nomadic males overlap the territories of several groups and mate with receptive females, while males resident within the groups do not mate. 2–3 cubs are born after a gestation of 90 days. The eyes are closed at birth and open after 2 weeks. Young are born from August to January.

Note: The coastline of the Namib Desert offers a reasonable chance of observing this hyaena. Good locations are the vicinity of Lüderitz, especially Grosse Bucht, the campgrounds north of Swakopmund and Cape Cross. The latter site is home to a big South African Fur Seal colony and Brown Hyaenas are especially attracted during the seal pupping season, from November to early December.

The Brown Hyaena is most likely to be seen in the Kalahari, or in the coastal Namib Desert.

The Brown Hyaena is distinguished by its long shaggy coat and pointed ears.

Brown Hyaena

Front

Back

85 mm

AARDWOLF | Family Protelidae

Proteles cristatus

■ **Aardwolf** *Proteles cristatus*
Total length 84–100 cm; tail 20–28 cm; shoulder height 50 cm; mass 6–11 kg.
Identification pointers: Hyaena-like appearance; prominent mane of long hair down neck and back; pale-buff background colour with dark vertical body stripes, with black bands on upper part of legs; feet, muzzle and much of distal part of tail black; long, pointed ears. Much smaller than the two hyaena species. Sometimes included in Family Hyaenidae.

Description: The Aardwolf is a medium-sized carnivore that is higher at the shoulders than at the rump. The hair is quite long and coarse, with a long mane of erectile hair down the neck and back, raised only when the animal is frightened or threatened. The general background colour varies from pale tawny to yellow-white and there are several vertical black stripes on the body and black bands on the upper parts of the legs. The muzzle and feet are black. At its base the bushy tail is yellow-fawn but the remainder is black. The ears are large and pointed.

Distribution: Aardwolf is very widely distributed in the subregion and extends into southern Angola and marginally into Zambia. It is largely absent from central Africa but there is a population in East Africa that extends north along the Red Sea to southern Egypt.

Habitat: This carnivore has a very wide habitat tolerance, occurring in regions of both low- and high-rainfall. It shows a marked preference for open habitats and avoids wooded or forested areas. Its distribution is dictated by the availability of termites, its principal food.

Behaviour: Although mainly active at night, it may be seen during the early morning and late afternoon, as well as on overcast days. It occurs singly, in pairs or in family parties. A home range may be occupied by two or more animals and several females may drop their pups in the same den. Although it often digs its own burrows, it will also use burrows dug by other species. Droppings are usually deposited at a number of latrine sites within the home range and grass-stalks are marked with a secretion from the anal glands.

Food: Mostly termites, but it will occasionally take other insects. Despite the frequent claim that it kills and eats sheep, there is no evidence of this. Although the canine teeth are well developed, the cheek-teeth (page 289) are greatly reduced in size and are not capable of dealing with flesh. Aardwolf feed almost exclusively on harvester termites of the genus *Trinervitermes*. In a single night, an individual Aardwolf can consume up to 300 000 termites, with a combined weight of about 1.2 kg. In one study, it was estimated that a single Aardwolf may consume an astounding 105 million termites in one year, which would amount to 420 kg. A farmer's friend indeed!

Reproduction: 1–4 young are born in a burrow after a gestation period of about 90 days. Although most young are dropped between October and February, they have also been recorded at other times of the year. Pups remain in the den for their first month, and at 9 to 12 weeks of age they accompany an adult on foraging expeditions up to 100 m from the den. From 7 months they will forage alone and at 12 months they are independent of their parents.

Note: There is controversy as to whether the Aardwolf belongs to the Hyaena family (three species), or its own, single species, family. There are characteristics that indicate that the Aardwolf is, in fact, a highly specialized Hyaena, both anatomically and behaviour-wise.

The Aardwolf is the smallest of the hyaenas. Inset: *The footpads are similar to those of the hyaenas, but smaller.*

The Aardwolf is distinguished by its dark, vertical body stripes and long, pointed ears.

Aardwolf

44 mm

Front   Back

167

CATS | Family Felidae

Felis silvestris lybica

■ African Wild Cat *Felis silvestris lybica*
Total length 85–100 cm; tail 25–37 cm; shoulder height 35 cm; mass 2.5–6.0 kg.
Identification pointers: Very similar in appearance to domestic cat but distinguishable from it by the rich reddish-brown colour of back of ears, over belly and on back of hindlegs. Vertical body stripes are present but range from very distinct to very faint.

Description: Similar in appearance to domestic cat but larger with proportionately longer legs. Colour ranges from pale sandy-brown in drier areas to light or dark grey in wetter parts of subregion. Body marked with more or less distinct dark vertical stripes. Relatively long tail dark-ringed with black tip. Chin and throat white and chest usually paler than rest of body. Belly usually reddish. Back of each ear coloured rich reddish-brown. Interbreeds readily with domestic cats and resulting hybrids can cause confusion.

Distribution: Throughout subregion, but absent from Namib Desert coastal belt.

Habitat: Wide habitat tolerance but requires cover.

Behaviour: Solitary, except when mating or when female is tending kittens. Droppings usually buried in the same way as domestic cat but they also establish small latrines where droppings accumulate.

Food: Mainly small rodents but they also eat other small mammals, birds, reptiles, amphibians, insects and other invertebrates. The largest recorded prey items are hares, springhares and birds up to the size of guinea-fowl.

Reproduction: 2–5 kittens are born in summer among dense vegetation cover, rocks or in burrows dug by other species; gestation period 65 days.

■ Small Spotted Cat *Felis nigripes*

Felis nigripes

Total length 50–63 cm; tail 16 cm; shoulder height 25 cm; mass 1.0– 2.0 kg.
Identification pointers: Small size; pale body colour well covered with smallish dark-brown to black spots; white chin and throat; back of ears same colour as body. Smaller and more distinctly marked than African Wild Cat, also lacks reddish-ginger colour at back of ears; can be distinguished from genets (page 158) by short tail and typical short, cat-like face.

Description: Also called Black-footed Cat. This is the smallest cat species occurring in the subregion. Colour ranges from reddish-fawn in southern parts of range to much paler in north. Numerous black (red-brown in north) spots and bars on body, legs, head and tail. Tail is short, black-ringed and -tipped. Chin and throat are white but there are two or three distinct dark bands on the throat. Back of ear is usually same colour as rest of body but lacks markings.

Distribution: Small Spotted Cat is restricted to the more arid southern and central parts of southern Africa. Only recently found to occur on the west coast and south-western interior of the Western Cape province.

Habitat: Open, dry habitats with some vegetation cover.

Behaviour: Small Spotted Cat is nocturnal and rarely seen. It is nowhere common and little is known about its behaviour. Most sightings are of solitary animals and it lies up in burrows dug by other species and in hollow termite mounds. For this reason, it is sometimes called the 'Anthill Tiger'.

Food: Mostly small rodents, but also takes reptiles, birds and insects. The largest recorded prey item is a Ground Squirrel, but there are also records of Cape Hare.

Reproduction: A litter of 1–3 kittens is born in the summer months after a gestation period of about 68 days. Mean birth mass 78 g.

Domestic cats are significant predators of small vertebrates.

African Wild Cat can be distinguished by its red-brown ears.

African Wild Cat: note pale-reddish belly.

The Small Spotted Cat, the smallest in the subregion, has numerous spots and bars on the body, legs, head and tail.

African
Wild Cat

36 mm

Front   Back

24 mm

Front   Back

Small Spotted Cat

Leptailurus serval
■ Historical distribution

■ **Serval** *Leptailurus serval*
Total length 96–120 cm; tail 25–38 cm; shoulder height 60 cm; mass 8.0–13.0 kg.
Identification pointers: Pale, usually yellowish-fawn coat, black-spotted and black-barred; large, rounded ears each with two black bands separated by white patch at back; short, black-banded and-tipped tail, Much smaller than either the Cheetah (page 172) or Leopard (page 176), with a proportionately shorter tail and large ears.
Description: Slender, long-legged, spotted cat with short tail and large, rounded ears. Body colour very variable but usually yellowish-fawn with scattered black spots and bars. Black bars and spots on neck; black bands extend down legs. Underparts paler but usually also spotted. Back surface of ear has black band, separated from black tip by white patch. Tail banded with black and has black tip.
Distribution: North and east of subregion; formerly along south coast. Widespread elsewhere in Africa.
Habitat: Usually environments with water, adjacent tall grassland, reed-beds or rank vegetation fringing forest.
Behaviour: Usually nocturnal but sometimes active in early morning and late afternoon. Usually solitary but also in pairs and family groups. Mainly terrestrial but a good climber.
Food: Small mammals (particularly vlei rats, but up to hares and cane-rats), birds, reptiles and insects. Perhaps young of smaller antelope species.
Reproduction: Most young are born in summer after a gestation of 68–72 days. Usually 1–3 (up to 5) kittens, each weighing about 200 g, are born in burrows dug by other species or in dense vegetation.

Caracal caracal

■ **Caracal** *Caracal caracal*
Total length 70–110 cm; tail 18–34 cm; shoulder height 40–45 cm; mass 7–19 kg.
Identification pointers: Hindquarters slightly higher than shoulders; general reddish-fawn coloration; short tail; pointed ears with tuft of black hair at tip and black at back sprinkled with white hairs.
Description: A robustly built cat, its hindquarters slightly higher than its shoulders. Coat thick but short and soft; colour varies from pale reddish-fawn to a rich brick-red. Underparts off-white with faint spotting or blotching. Long, pointed ears with tuft of longish black hair at the tip are characteristic. Backs of ears are black, liberally sprinkled with white hairs. Face prominently marked with black-and-white patches, notably around eyes and mouth. Short reddish tail.
Distribution: Widespread in subregion but absent from much of KwaZulu-Natal and the Namib coastal strip. Occurs widely in the rest of Africa, but absent from equatorial forest, and extends into Middle East and as far east as India.
Habitat: Semi-desert to savanna woodland; hilly country to coastal forests.
Behaviour: Mainly nocturnal, but partly diurnal if undisturbed. Solitary, except when mating or females accompanied by kittens. Stalks its prey as close as possible and then relies on a direct pounce or short, fast run.
Food: The Caracal hunts mainly small- to medium-sized mammals, ranging from mice to antelope (up to the size of Bushbuck ewes). It also catches birds and reptiles. In some small-stock farming areas it is considered to be a major problem because of its depredations on sheep and goats.
Reproduction: Litters of 1–3 kittens may be born at any time of the year, although there is a summer peak. The gestation period is about 79 days and the birth mass is around 250 g. Kittens may be born in burrows excavated by other species, in rock crevices or among dense vegetation.

The Serval has distinct black-and-white markings on the backs of the ears. Inset: A Serval sub-adult.

The Caracal has long pointed ears with a black tuft on the tips. Inset: A two-month-old Caracal kitten.

Serval

47 mm

Front

Back

47 mm

Front

Back

Caracal

Acinonyx jubatus
■ Historical distribution

■ Cheetah *Acinonyx jubatus*

Total length 18–22 m; tail 60–80 cm; shoulder height 80 cm; mass 40–60 kg.

Identification pointers: Large size; slender, greyhound-like build; long, spotted white-tipped tail, black-ringed towards tip; spotted coat – single, rounded, black spots; rounded face with a black line from inner corner of eye to corner of mouth ('tear-mark'). Leopard (page 176) has a heavier build; its spots form rosettes, it has no black lines on the face and it usually frequents different habitats. Serval (page 170) is much smaller, with a disproportionately short tail.

Description: The Cheetah, sometimes referred to as the 'greyhound of cats', is probably the most elegant member of the cat family. It is tall and slender, with long legs and a short muzzle with a rounded head. The body colour is off-white to pale-fawn and is liberally dotted with black, rounded, spots more or less uniform in size. A clear black line (the 'tear-mark') runs from the inner corner of each eye to the corner of the mouth. Numerous small black spots are present on the forehead and top of the head. The tips of the ears are white. The long tail is black-ringed with a white tip. A short, erectile crest is situated on the back and sides. The Cheetah is the only cat that does not have fully retractile claws and the impressions of the claws can be seen in their tracks. The well-publicized 'King Cheetah' is merely an aberrant colour form, albeit an attractive one.

Distribution: Although formerly widespread in southern Africa, it is estimated that between 4 000 and 6 000 survive here. It is still widespread in Botswana and Namibia and has been reintroduced to KwaZulu-Natal but is nowhere common. It is difficult to establish accurate Cheetah numbers; South Africa has just 350 in major reserves, of which some 200 are found in Kruger and Kgalagadi national parks. A further 300 are sparsely distributed in the northern reaches of Limpopo, North-West and Northern Cape. Cheetah still occur widely but patchily throughout much of Africa, except in the equatorial forest regions, although in greatly reduced numbers. Previously it occurred as far east as India, where it is now extinct, but small numbers survive in parts of Iran and possibly western Pakistan.

Habitat: Open savanna and light woodland, but also hilly country on occasion. The availability of drinking water is not essential.

Behaviour: Normally seen singly, in pairs or small family parties consisting of female and cubs. It is principally diurnal, but tends to hunt in the cooler hours. Adult males move singly or in bachelor groups and females establish territories from which they will drive other females. Males are apparently not territorial and may move over areas held by several females. Favoured lying-up spots are usually raised above the surrounding area and are urine-marked by both males and females. When hunting, Cheetah stalk to within a short distance of their intended prey and then sprint in for the kill. Although they may top speeds of more than 70 km per hour, this can only be sustained for a few hundred metres.

Food: Normally Cheetah hunt medium-sized mammals up to a mass of ±60 kg, although if two or more cheetah hunt together, larger prey may be overpowered. Antelope are the principal prey items. In Kruger National Park, Impala is the most important prey. It also catches birds up to the size of Ostrich.

Reproduction: Cheetah have a long, drawn-out courtship. The litters of 1–5 (usually 3) young may be born at any time of the year. The cubs are blind and helpless and weigh between 250 g and 300 g at birth. For the first 6 weeks they are usually hidden in dense plant cover, thereafter following the mother.

General: Cheetah used to be tamed and used for hunting, particularly in Asia. The 16th century Indian Mogul emperor, Akbar the Great, was said to have kept a 'stable' of 1 000 Cheetahs.

The sleek, long-legged Cheetah is built for speed. Inset: The black tear-mark running from the eye the mouth is distinctive.

The so-called 'King Cheetah' is merely an aberrant colour form, albeit an attractive one.

Cheetah

85 mm

Front   Back

Panthera leo
■ Historical distribution

■ Lion *Panthera leo*

Male: total length 2.5–3.3 m; tail 1.0 m; shoulder height 1.2 m; mass 150–225 kg.
Female: length 2.3–2.7 m; tail 1.0 m; shoulder height 1.0 m; mass 110–152 kg.
Identification pointers: Large size; usually uniform tawny colour; males with long mane; dark-tipped tail. Cannot be confused with any other species.

Description: Largest of the African cats and adult males and females are easy to tell apart. Body colour ranges from reddish-grey to pale tawny with lighter underparts. Although faint spots are present on the sides of cubs, these are usually lost by adulthood. Tail is short-haired and same colour as rest of body but has a dark tip. Only the adult male carries a mane of long hair, extending from the sides of the face onto the neck, shoulders and chest. Mane colour ranges from pale tawny to black. 'White' lions from the South African Lowveld are not true albinos but are genetic variants with strongly reduced pigmentation.

Distribution: In the recent past, Lion occurred throughout the subregion but are now found only in the northern and eastern areas, largely restricted to the major conservation areas. Of the ±2 500 Lions occuring in the wild in South Africa, some 2 000 are found in the Kruger National Park, while the Kgalagadi Transfrontier Park has ±450 Lions; both naturally occurring populations. Reintroduced to the Hluhluwe/Imfolozi complex in KwaZulu-Natal, Madikwe and Pilanesberg in North-West Province. Lions once occurred widely in parts of Europe, Asia, the Middle East and throughout most of Africa. They now have a patchy distribution in Africa and are only found south of the Sahara, excluding the equatorial forest regions.

Habitat: The Lion has a very wide habitat tolerance, from desert fringe to woodland or open savanna, but is absent from equatorial forest.

Behaviour: It is the most sociable member of the cat family, living in prides of 3–30 individuals. Pride size varies according to the area and prey availability. In Botswana prides usually 6 or fewer individuals, whereas average pride size in Kruger National Park is about 12. Prides normally consist of from 1–4 adult males, several adult females (one of which is dominant) and a number of subadults and cubs. A pride area or territory is defended against strange Lions by both the males and females but some prides and solitary males are nomadic. Territories are marked by urine, droppings and by earth-scratching. The mighty roars of the Lion, audible over several kilometres, also serve to indicate that an area is occupied. Most of their activity takes place at night and during the cooler daylight hours. The females undertake most of the hunting, and despite the fact that the males play little part in most kills, they feed before the females. Cubs compete for what remains once the adults have finished their meal.

Food: Although Lion mainly hunts medium- to large-sized mammals, particularly ungulates, it will take anything from mice to young Elephants as well as a wide range of non-mammalian prey. It also scavenges, and often chases other predators from their kills.

Reproduction: No fixed breeding season; 1–4 (occasionally 6) cubs each weighing about 1.5 kg are born after gestation of 110 days. Lioness gives birth under cover, soon returning to the pride. Any lactating lioness allows any pride cub to suckle. Pride females often conceive at approximately the same time, ensuring that maximum food and maternal care are available to cubs. Cubs may remain with their mother for 2 years or longer.

General: Unless provoked, Lions will rarely attack humans, but it is useful to know the warning signs: an angry Lion will drop into a crouch, flatten its ears and give vent to growls and grunts, meanwhile flicking its tail-tip rapidly from side to side. Just prior to a charge the tail is usually jerked up and down.

The Lioness does not carry a mane. Inset: *Cubs have brown spots, which become less distinct, or disappear, with age.*

Main picture and inset: *The extent and coloration of the male Lion's mane is variable.*

Lion

128 mm

Front   Back

Panthera pardus
■ Historical distribution

■ **Leopard** *Panthera pardus*
Total length 1.6–2.1 m; tail 68–110 cm; shoulder height 70–80 cm; mass 20–90 kg (male), 17–60 kg (female).

Note: Leopards from the mountain ranges of the Western Cape are generally much smaller than those from further north; however, in all areas, the males are considerably larger than the females.

Identification pointers: Large size; rosette spots on body, solid black spots on legs, head, sides and hindquarters; lacks the black facial-lines of Cheetah and is more heavily spotted (see Cheetah, page 172). Size, long tail and different form of spots make easy differentiation from Serval.

Description: An elegant, powerfully built cat, with a beautifully spotted coat. The basic body colour varies from almost white to orange-russet, with black spots on the legs, flanks, hindquarters and head. The spots on the rest of the body consist of rosettes or broken circles of irregular black spots. The tail is about half of the total length, with rosette spots above and a white tip. The ears are rounded and white-tipped. The underparts are usually white to off-white. Cubs have dark, woolly hair and less-distinct spots.

Distribution: Extremely widely distributed in southern Africa, but now absent from the sheep-farming areas of central South Africa. Widely distributed in the rest of sub-Saharan Africa, the Middle East and through Asia into China. By far the most successful of the large cats.

Habitat: It has an extremely wide habitat tolerance, from high mountains to coastal plain, from low- to high-rainfall areas. South of the Gariep (Orange) River it has been eradicated from all but the more mountainous and rugged areas. Although drinking water is not essential, cover is an essential requirement.

Behaviour: Normally solitary except when a pair comes together to mate or when a female is accompanied by cubs. Although it is mainly active at night, in areas where it is not disturbed it can be seen moving during the cooler daylight hours. Although it is mainly terrestrial, it is a good climber and swimmer. Males mark and defend a territory against other males, and a male's territory may overlap that of several females. Territories are marked with urine, droppings and tree-scratching points. Home ranges may be as small as 10 km² or cover areas of several hundred square kilometres; the size being largely dependent on the availability of food. Normally silent, the Leopard does have a characteristic call that has been likened to the sound of a coarse saw cutting wood. Leopards stalk and pounce on their prey and do not rely on running at high speed like the Cheetah.

Food: A broad diet, ranging from insects, rodents and birds to medium-sized and occasionally large antelope. In some rocky and mountainous areas dassies make up an important part of the diet. It will on occasion kill more than its immediate needs, the surplus being stored for later use. Kills may be dragged under dense bush, among rocks or, in some areas, into trees out of reach of other predators. Leopard readily feed from rotten carcasses.

Reproduction: Litters of 2–3 cubs, each weighing around 500 g, are born in dense cover, rock crevices or caves after a gestation of about 100 days. There is no fixed breeding season.

General: Although Leopards may take to man-eating, this has not apparently been recorded for southern Africa. Trapped, wounded or threatened, the Leopard can be extremely dangerous, but under normal circumstances it is shy and withdraws from disturbance.

Leopards are masters of camouflage.

Leopards are agile climbers, readily taking to trees to rest or observe.

The Leopard's spots take the form of rosettes. Inset: The face is heavy and, unlike the Cheetah, there is no 'tear-mark'.

Leopard

92 mm

Front

Back

AARDVARK | Order Tubulidentata | Family Orycteropodidae

Orycteropus afer

Aardvark *Orycteropus afer*
Total length 1.4–1.8 m; tail 45–60 cm; mass 40–70 kg.
Identification pointers: Unmistakable; large size; elongated, pig-like snout; tubular ears; generally heavy build; walks with back arched.

Description: The Aardvark resembles no other mammal occurring in southern Africa, with its long, pig-like snout, elongated tubular ears, heavily muscled kangaroo-like tail and very powerful, stout legs, which terminate in spade-like nails. It has only a sparse covering of hair and the skin is grey-yellow to fawn-grey. The hair at the base of the tail and on the legs tends to be quite dark. Normally, however, an Aardvark will be of a colour similar to the soil in the area in which it lives. The back is distinctly arched.

Distribution: This strange mammal is found throughout southern Africa with the exception of the coastal Namib Desert. It is widespread in Africa south of the Sahara but is absent from the equatorial forest region.

Habitat: The Aardvark is found in a wide range of habitats and the limiting factor is probably the availability of suitable food. It shows a preference for open woodland, sparse scrub and grassland. This is one of the few species that has benefited from man's overstocking of areas with domestic stock. As they trample the grass, domestic stock make it more accessible to the termites on which the Aardvark feeds.

Behaviour: It is rarely seen during the day, most of its activity taking place at night. During the winter months, activity and foraging may begin early in the afternoon. This may well be because their termite prey moves deeper underground during the coldest night hours. Periods of drought, and hence shortage of their prey, cause Aardvark to become active during daylight hours. During one severe drought in north-western Namibia in the late 1980s, Aardvark were commonly seen foraging throughout the daylight hours; many Aardvark and Ground Pangolin died of starvation at that time. Although normally solitary, females may be accompanied by a single young; they excavate extensive burrow-systems. Males usually dig quite shallow burrows to lie up in during the day and are greater wanderers than the females. Occupied burrows are often characterized by numerous small flies in the entrance-way. Aardvarks may walk several kilometres to feeding grounds each night, where they appear to wander aimlessly, nose close to the ground. When they locate an ant or termite colony they rip into it with the massive claws on the front feet. In areas where the Aardvark is present, numerous termite mounds have holes excavated at their bases. It is generally unpopular with farmers because it excavates holes in roads and dam-walls.

Food: Mainly ants and termites. Termites dominate the diet in the rainy season and ants during the dry season. Once a colony has been opened up, the long sticky tongue probes for the small insects, their larvae and eggs. It occasionally eats other insects and the fruit of the wild cucumber.

Reproduction: There are very few records of births but it is probable that it single young is born during the rainy season; it has a mass of almost 2 kg and the gestation period is about 7 months. A baby Aardvark will start following its mother in its third week.

Note: Although they are, in the main, protected, Aardvark are persecuted by farmers because their excavations undermine dam walls and burrow under jackal-proof fences. This level of hunting has little impact on their numbers and although seldom seen, they remain relatively common.

Above: *With its long, pig-like snout and elongated ears, the Aardvark cannot be mistaken for any other animal.*
Inset (left): *A termite mound opened up by an Aardvark in search of its preferred food;* (right): *In profile, the characteristic humped back and kangaroo-like tail can be clearly seen.*

Aardvark

90 mm

Front   Back

ELEPHANT | Order Proboscidea | Family Elephantidae

Loxodonta africana
■ Historical distribution

■ **African Elephant** *Loxodonta africana*
Male: tail 1.5 m; shoulder height 3.2–4.0 m; mass 5 000–6 300 kg.
Female: tail 1.5 m; shoulder height 2.5–3.4 m; mass 2 800–3 500 kg.
Identification pointers: Massive size; long trunk; usually carries tusks; large ears. Cannot be mistaken for any other species.
Description: Apart from its vast size, the elephant is characterized by its long trunk, large ears and the (normal) presence of tusks. The trunk is extremely mobile and is almost as efficient as the human hand. The large ears serve a display function but also assist in cooling the body. The backs of the ears are well supplied with blood vessels and, as the ears are flapped, the blood is cooled. Elephants may also squirt water behind the ears to cool the blood. Tusks are characteristic of most elephants, although some individuals and even populations may be tuskless. The heaviest pair of tusks on record, weighing 102.3 kg and 97 kg, came from a Kenyan elephant. Tusks continue to grow throughout life but, because of continuous wear and breakages, they never reach their full potential length.
Distribution: Once occurring virtually throughout southern Africa but now restricted to the extreme northern and north-eastern areas. An isolated, natural population is present in the Greater Addo National Park in the Eastern Cape, while 2 or 3 individuals may survive in the forests near Knysna in the southwestern Cape. It still occurs widely in Africa south of the Sahara but the populations are becoming increasingly isolated and numbers are being reduced by poaching.
Habitat: African Elephants have an extremely wide habitat tolerance as long as sufficient food, water and shade are available.
Behaviour: Live in small family groups, each led by an older cow, the matriarch, together with her offspring, and may include related cows with their young. A number of family groups may come together to form larger herds, not infrequently numbering several hundreds. The family group retains its identity during these gatherings and normally the smaller groups move off on their own. These large congregations gather at water sources or when food is abundant, but there are no reproductive or social benefits. If left uncontrolled, large herds may destroy their habitat, not only for themselves but for other species as well, making culling inevitable. Adult bulls usually join the family herds when cows are in breeding condition, leaving for bachelor groups afterwards. A cow may mate with several bulls during oestrus. Although Elephants are active by both night and day, they usually rest in shade during the heat of the day. Elephants are normally peaceful but can be dangerous when wounded, sick, or defending a small calf.
Food: A very wide variety of plants. Although not specialized feeders they do show a marked preference for certain species, for which they will travel long distances. During the rains, green grass forms a large percentage of their diet. An adult Elephant may eat as much as 300 kg per day.
Reproduction: A single calf, weighing approximately 120 kg, is dropped after a 22-month gestation period. Calves may be born at any time of the year but in some areas there is a peak in births that coincides with the rainy season. The calf is pinkish-grey and hairier than the adults. Cows are very protective of calves and, should anything happen to a nursing mother, another lactating female will usually take over the nursing of the orphan.
General: Elephants are threatened by ivory poaching and human encroachment on their traditional areas. When confined to limited areas, they can inflict considerable damage on vegetation, making control programmes essential.

Elephants frequently use their trunks to touch each other.

African Elephant bull. Elephants feed on a wide range of plant food, from grass to tree bark.

Elephant cows providing shelter for a resting calf.

Access to water is vital, as an adult elephant requires an average of 160 litres of water daily.

Elephant

500 mm

Front

Back

DASSIES (HYRAX) | Order Hyracoidea | Family Procaviidae

Although, at first sight, dassies appear rodent-like, their evolutionary relationships lie with the Elephant and the Dugong. Three species occur in southern Africa: two of which are associated predominantly with rocky habitats, while the third, the Tree Dassie (page 186), lives in forested areas.

There is considerable scientific debate over the taxonomy of the Rock Dassie, or Hyrax (*Procavia capensis*). It has a vast range that extends over large areas of suitable habitat across Africa, extending into the Arabian Peninsula. Many subspecies have been described, as well as a number of species, not all of which can be separated in the field. Identification of many of these has therefore been based on pelage coloration, which is a dubious character at best. Recent genetic work is starting to identify the possibility that at least two species are located in South Africa, with several more across the continent. However, the average observer will be unable to distinguish these 'potential' species, as identity relies primarily on genetic differentiation.

Procavia capensis

Heterohyrax brucei

■ **Rock Dassie (Hyrax)** *Procavia capensis*
Total length 45–60 cm; mass 2.5–4.6 kg.
■ **Kaokoveld Rock Dassie (Hyrax)** *Procavia capensis welwitschii*
Total length 36–50 cm.
■ **Yellow-spotted Rock Dassie (Hyrax)** *Heterohyrax brucei*
Total length 45–55 cm; mass 2.5–3.5 kg.

Identification pointers: Small, but stocky build; no tail; small rounded ears; rocky habitat; where the Rock Dassie overlaps with the other species, the colour of the erectile hair in the middle of the back is the most certain character – black for the Rock Dassie; white to off-white or yellowish in the other species and one subspecies.

Description: The two species of Rock Dassie, or Hyrax, are small, stoutly built, tail-less animals with short legs and small, rounded ears. Hair colour varies considerably in both species. Both species have a patch of erectile hair overlying a glandular area in the centre of the back, the colour of which is a very important characteristic for distinguishing the different species and subspecies, as indicated in the table below.

	Rock Dassie	Kaokoveld Rock Dassie	Yellow-spotted Rock Dassie
General colour	Yellow-fawn to dark-brown	Yellow-fawn to dark-brown	Grey to dark-brown
Dorsal gland	Black	White or yellowish	White or yellowish
Underparts	Slightly pale; never white	White to off-white	White to off-white
Other	Inconspicuous fawn-buff patch above eye and at ear-base	Off-white patch at ear base	Conspicuous white patch above eye

Three Rock Dassies (right) *and a single Yellow-spotted Rock Dassie* (subspecies H.b. ruddi)*, photographed in the Tuli region of south-eastern Botswana.*

Above and top: *Yellow-spotted Rock Dassies (note distinctive pale dorsal spot); in some areas they are darker and in South Africa this form is represented by* H.b. granti.

Dassie urine leaves characteristic white and brown streaks on rocks and overhangs.

Rock Dassie

32 mm

Front   Back

Distribution: The Rock Dassie is the most widespread of the two rock-dwelling dassies occurring in southern Africa. However, it is absent from the north-central areas, the Namib Desert coastal belt and most of Mozambique. The Kaokoveld subspecies is restricted to north-western Namibia but extends into south-western Angola. Yellow-spotted Rock Dassies only occur in the north-eastern parts of southern Africa but thence as far north as northern Egypt.

Habitat: Rocky areas, from mountain ranges to isolated rock outcrops. Rock Dassie and Yellow-spotted Rock Dassie frequently occur together where ranges overlap. Rock Dassies generally favour dry areas but are also found in higher rainfall areas. They may be found living in holes in erosion gulleys (dongas), or among the roots and leaves of sisal, prickly pear and spekboom.

Behaviour: The behaviour of all the rock-dwelling dassie species is similar. They are predominantly diurnal but on warm, moonlit nights they may emerge to feed. Normally they only become active after sunrise when they lie for some time on the rocks in the sun to warm up before moving off to feed. While the group basks in the sun, an adult male or female keeps watch for predators. If disturbed, the 'guard' gives a sharp cry and the dassies scuttle for cover among the rocks. Groups usually number from 4–8, but larger groups may live together, depending on the available habitat. Each group or colony has a dominant male and female and the other animals fit into a hierarchy or pecking order. During the mating period, males may fight fiercely.

Most feeding is done in the morning and late afternoon and they retreat to the shelter of rocks during the hotter hours. They usually feed close to the shelter although they will move up to several hundred metres to feeding areas. If a food shortage develops, a dassie colony will migrate to a more favourable area. Rock Dassies readily climb into trees and bushes to feed and, because of this, are often thought to be Tree Dassies.

Dassies deposit their droppings at fixed latrine sites and accumulations of their pellets may become very large. Dassie urine leaves white and brown streaks on rocks and often serves as an indication of their presence.

Food: Grazers and browsers, with quantities of each varying according to the season. Feeding usually takes place on ground but they will climb trees to feed on leaves, bark and fruits. They eat a very wide range of plants.

Reproduction: Both give birth to precocious young: fully haired, with eyes open and able to move about soon after birth. They are perfectly proportioned miniatures of the adults. There is a distinct birth season in the Rock Dassie but the timing varies considerably in different regions. In south-western South Africa, births normally occur in September and October, and in Zimbabwe in March and April. In the lower Gariep (Orange) River area of the north-west, with its extremely hot summer temperatures, the young are dropped in the cooler months of June and July. 1–4 young may be born but 2–3 is usual. Birth weight varies according to the size of the litter and may range between 150 and 300 g. The Kaokoveld subspecies gives birth during February and March to 2 or 3 young, rarely 4. Yellow-spotted Rock Dassies apparently give birth at any time of the year to litters with an average of 2 offspring, each weighing approximately 200 g.

Note: Rock Dassies comprise the main diet of Verreaux's (Black) Eagle, between 70 and 90 per cent in most areas. Crowned Eagles also take substantial numbers of both Rock and Tree Hyraxes. In many mountain and hill ranges, such as the Cedarberg and Soutpansberg, as well as Zimbabwe's Matobos, Leopards are important predators of hyraxes. In the Karoo hills, the Caracal is a significant Hyrax predator, with African Wild Cat taking substantial numbers of young.

Young Rock Dassies suckling. They are perfectly proportioned miniatures of the adults and able to move about soon after birth. Gestation averages about 210 days, but the timing of the birth season varies from region to region.

A Yellow-spotted Rock Dassie (H.b. ruddi) from Tuli, Botswana.

Dendrohyrax arboreus

■ Tree Dassie (Hyrax) *Dendrohyrax arboreus*

Total length 42–52 cm; mass 2.0–3.5 kg.

Identification pointers: Similar in size to Rock Dassie species; hair quite long and woolly in appearance; upperparts grey, flecked with white or brown; white to creamy underparts and dorsal gland; forest or dense bush habitat; distinctive, nocturnal screaming call.

Description: Similar in size to the Rock Dassies but body hair is much longer and has a woolly appearance. Upperparts vary from grey flecked with white to grey-brown. Underparts are white to creamy white, as is the long hair around the dorsal gland in the centre of the back. No external tail.

Distribution: Their distribution is limited to suitable habitat. They occur along the coastal plain in the Eastern Cape and extend into KwaZulu-Natal. Another isolated population occurs in south-central Mozambique. Elsewhere, they are found in Zambia, eastern Congo and throughout the western parts of East Africa. Its forest and densely bushed habitats are generally in decline in South Africa, but substantial populations probably survive in Amatole, Pirie and Alexandria forests in the Eastern Cape, as well as Oribi Gorge and Vernon Crookes nature reserves in KwaZulu-Natal. The status of populations in Mozambique is unknown, but it is common in parts of Zambia, Tanzania, Kenya and Uganda. However, habitat destruction could greatly reduce these populations in future.

Habitat: Tree Dassies inhabit suitable forest and bush areas, including coastal dune forest. Fairly dense cover is an essential habitat requirement.

Behaviour: Solitary, arboreal and nocturnal, but may bask in the sun, particularly in the early morning. Although a solitary hyrax, in some areas they occur at quite high densities. Based on call rates, the authors once estimated more than 30 individuals in a relatively small forest pocket on the lower slopes of Mount Kenya. Tree Dassies are largely arboreal, but they descend to the ground when moving between trees and it is not unusual for them to forage on the ground. Like their Rock Dassie relatives, they will also dust bathe if the substrate is suitable. Although they are rarely seen, their hair-raising screaming call at night is characteristic. For those unfamiliar with this bloodcurdling shriek, it can be a disturbing experience. Droppings accumulate on lower branch forks and particularly at base of trees.

Food: Mainly a browser but will feed on grasses and herbaceous plants. They are generally selective feeders, with favoured species varying from location to location. For example, in Pirie Forest in the Eastern Cape, Yellowwood foliage is important, and in Alexandria Forest to the west of Port Alfred, Bush Boerbean makes up a significant part of the Tree Dassie's diet.

Reproduction: It probably breeds throughout the year, with 1–3 young being born after a gestation period of 7–8 months.

Note: Apart from *Dendrohyrax arboreus*, there are two other species of Tree Hyrax. *Dendrohyrax dorsalis* occurs from Uganda westwards to Senegal, while the much more localized *D. validus* is restricted to a few montane areas in East Africa and the islands of Unguja and Pemba (Zanzibar). However, not all are tree dwellers; a population of Tree Hyrax (*D. a. ruwenzorii*) found in the upper reaches of the Ruwenzori Mountains (straddling the Uganda/DRC border) lives in colonies among rocks, and is partly diurnal. In the lower forested areas, however, the Tree Hyrax reverts to type and is arboreal, solitary and nocturnal.

A young Tree Dassie; these nocturnal animals inhabit suitable forest and bush areas, seeking dense cover.

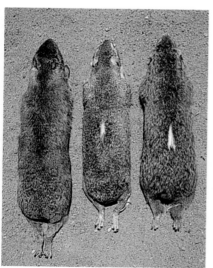

Dassie skins (l.t.r.): Rock Dassie, Kaokoveld Rock Dassie, Tree Dassie.

The Tree Dassie has white underparts.

Tree Dassie

ODD-TOED UNGULATES | Order Perissodactyla

ZEBRAS | Family Equidae

■ *Equus zebra zebra*
■ *E.z. hartmannae*

■ **Cape Mountain Zebra** *Equus zebra zebra*
■ **Hartmann's Mountain Zebra** *Equus zebra hartmannae*
Cape subsp.: shoulder height 1.3 m; tail 40 cm; mass 250–260 kg.
Hartmann's subsp.: shoulder height 1.5 m; tail 40 cm; mass 250–350 kg.
Identification pointers: Black-and-white stripes without shadow stripes; legs striped to the hoofs; grid-iron pattern on rump; throat with dewlap. Range of Hartmann's overlaps marginally with that of Plains Zebra in north-western Namibia. Hartmann's introduced to farms and reserves outside normal range.
Description: Both subspecies of mountain zebra are similar in appearance but Hartmann's is slightly larger, with some variations in striping on the hindquarters. Both, however, are white with black stripes, the legs being striped to the hoofs; underparts are white. No shadow stripes (see opposite page) and over the top of rump above the tail there is a series of transverse black stripes forming a grid-iron pattern characteristic of the species. Tip of muzzle is black with orange-brown hair extending a short way towards eyes. An erect mane runs from top of the head to the shoulders. A dewlap is present on the throat; this feature is diagnostic of the species and does not occur in other zebras.
Distribution: Cape Mountain Zebra was once widespread in the mountains south of the Gariep (Orange) River, but is now restricted to a small group of nature reserves. Hartmann's is restricted to the montane escarpment of Namibia but occurs marginally in south-western Angola, and a population has crossed the Gariep into the Richtersveld in recent times. Hartmann's has also been introduced onto several game farms and nature reserves outside its natural range.
Habitat: Mountainous areas and adjacent flats.
Behaviour: Breeding herds consist of an adult stallion with mares and their foals and usually number 4 or 5 but occasionally more. In the dry season, however, Hartmann's may congregate in loose associations of up to 40.
Food: Predominantly grazers but also browse occasionally.
Reproduction: A single foal (±25 kg) is born after gestation of about 360 days.

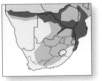

Equus quagga
■ Historical distribution

■ **Plains Zebra** *Equus quagga*
Shoulder height 1.3 m; tail 45 cm; mass 290–340 kg.
Identification pointers: Stocky and horse-like; black-and-white stripes with shadow stripes superimposed on white stripes; stripes extend onto underparts; lacks dewlap on throat.
Plains Zebra is now classified as *Equus quagga* in southern Africa and Burchell's Zebra *Equus burchellii* in central and East Africa. Throughout much of southern Africa, Plains Zebra has 'shadow' stripes over the white stripes, whereas shadow stripes are not present in the Central and East African forms.
Description: Plains Zebra shows considerable variation in coloration and patterning but is usually striped in black and white with a fainter 'shadow' stripe superimposed on the white stripe, particularly on the hindquarters. No grid-iron pattern on rump and striping extends onto underparts. Long, erect mane extends from top of head to shoulders. Striping may or may not extend to the hoofs.
Distribution: North and east of subregion but widely reintroduced.
Habitat: Grassland plains and open grassed woodland.

Cape Mountain Zebras have no shadow stripes and striping does not extend onto the belly.
Inset (top): *Skin showing the grid-iron pattern on the rump of Mountain Zebra;* (bottom): *Hartmann's Mountain Zebra.*

Plains Zebra from northern Namibia, showing the shadow stripes characteristic of the southern races, with striping that extends onto the belly. Inset: *Plains Zebra without the shadow stripes.*

Mountain Zebra

100 mm

Front

Plains Zebra

90 mm

Front

Behaviour: Plains Zebras associate in family herds consisting of an adult stallion, plus a number of mares and their foals; other stallions form bachelor herds or run alone. Family units normally number 4–6. Larger herds usually consist of numerous smaller herds coming together temporarily. Most populations are seasonal migrants, such as those in Etosha and over their Botswana range. Their characteristic call has been likened to a bark, 'kwa-ha-ha'; it was also the call of the extinct Quagga, hence the name.

Food: Grazers but they do occasionally browse.

Reproduction: Single foal with mass of 30–35 kg born usually in summer; gestation period 375 days.

RHINOCEROSES | Family Rhinocerotidae

Diceros bicornis
■ Historical distribution

■ Hook-lipped Rhinoceros *Diceros bicornis*
Shoulder height 1.6 m; tail 70 cm; mass 800–1 100kg.
Record front horn length 1.359 m (East Africa), 1.05 m (KwaZulu-Natal).
Identification pointers: Large size but smaller than Square-lipped Rhinoceros; lacks neck hump present in Square-lipped; characteristic pointed upper lip; shorter head than Square-lipped (see page 192); two horns on face.

Description: Frequently called the Black Rhinoceros, this species is more appropriately known as the Hook-lipped Rhinoceros, as the triangular-shaped prehensile upper lip is characteristic. Dark grey with slightly lighter underparts. Body colour influenced by its habit of wallowing in dust and mud. Sparse scattering of body hair. No raised hump on neck, unlike the Square-lipped Rhinoceros. Two horns on face, one behind other, the front horn usually being the longer. Rhino horn is composed of numerous, matted, hair-like filaments, which are attached to the skin, not to the bone; it is not a sheath-like covering to a bony core as is the case with antelope horns. The spoor (footprint) is rounded at the back, whereas that of the Square-lipped Rhinoceros is sharply indented.

Distribution: Once widely distributed throughout subregion, but now occurs naturally only in some Maputaland reserves, north-western Namibia, the Zambezi Valley, and possibly in parts of southern Mozambique. Reintroduced to Greater Addo National Park and the Great Fish River Conservation Area in Eastern Cape and Augrabies National Park in the Northern Cape. There are more than 2 000 Hook-lipped Rhinoceroses in southern Africa, making up a large percentage of the world total for the species. Previously common throughout central and East Africa, extending into West Africa, but has been brought to the verge of extinction over much of its former range through relentless poaching.

Habitat: The Hook-lipped Rhinoceros requires areas with shrubs and trees reaching to a height of about 4 m, with dense thickets for resting. Although it requires water for drinking and wallowing, it may go several days between visits to water in arid areas. It occupies a wide range of habitats where these basic requirements are met, from the arid plains of Kaokoland to the rich savanna woodland of the KwaZulu-Natal game reserves.

Behaviour: Hook-lipped Rhinoceroses are solitary animals although groups may come together temporarily at water. Bulls and cows only come together for mating and cows are often accompanied by calves. Serious fighting may take place when bulls compete for a receptive cow. During the heat of the day they usually lie up in dense thickets, feeding in the early morning and late afternoon but also after dark. The dung may be dropped in latrine or midden areas or at random through the home range. Bulls kick the dung vigorously with the hindfeet at the

The Hook-lipped Rhinoceros occupies a wide variety of habitats, from the dry areas of Kaokoland to dense riverine bush and the savanna woodland of KwaZulu-Natal.

The triangular prehensile upper lip of the Hook-lipped Rhinoceros is ideally suited for browsing selected shoots.

Hook-lipped Rhinoceros

200 mm

Front

Back

191

latrine sites leaving distinct grooves in the ground. Apart from being smaller, the dung balls can be distinguished from those of the Square-lipped Rhinoceros by their content of light-coloured, coarse woody material. The Square-lipped Rhinoceros, being a grazer, has much finer, darker material in the dung. Hook-lipped Rhinoceroses are notoriously bad-tempered, this being particularly true of bulls associating with receptive cows, and of cows with calves. Despite their cumbersome appearance they are surprisingly fast and agile; they rely on their hearing and sense of smell to locate a threat as their eyesight is poor.

Food: The Hook-lipped Rhinoceros uses its pointed, mobile upper lip to grasp twigs and shoots, which are either snapped off or cut through by the cheek-teeth. It is a selective feeder and tends to reject dry plant material. During the rains it will on occasion take grass.

Reproduction: There is no fixed breeding season and a single calf, weighing about 40 kg, is born after a gestation period of about 450 days. It is able to walk and suckle within 3 hours of birth. The calf either walks alongside or behind the mother, the reverse of the situation with the Square-lipped Rhinoceros.

General: The rapid decline in numbers of both African rhinoceros species is a result of the demand for their horns. Until recently most of the horns found their way to Yemen, where they were carved into dagger handles for tribesmen, and to the Far East where they are used in the production of traditional medicines. The best chance for the survival of both species at present appears to lie in southern Africa, and particularly in South Africa.

Ceratotherium simum
■ Historical distribution

■ Square-lipped Rhinoceros *Ceratotherium simum*

Shoulder height 1.8 m; tail 1.0 m; mass (bull) 2 000–2 300 kg, (cow) 1 400–1 600 kg. Record front horn length (southern Africa) 1.58 m.

More than 7 000 Square-lipped Rhinoceroses are dispersed across national parks, nature reserves and private game farms in southern Africa. The largest national southern African 'herd' is located in Kruger National Park, followed by that of the Hluhluwe/Imfolozi complex in KwaZulu-Natal.

Identification pointers: Large size; broad, square muzzle; hump on neck; large, pointed ears; two horns on face. See Hook-lipped Rhinoceros (page 190).

Description: The Square-lipped Rhinoceros, also known as the White Rhinoceros, is much larger than the Hook-lipped Rhinoceros. The skin colour is grey but this is often influenced by the colour of the mud and dust in which it rolls. A large, distinctive hump is present on the neck. The head is long and carried low, frequently only a few centimetres above the ground, and terminates in a broad, square muzzle – hence the common name. There are two horns on the face, the front one usually being the longer. The ears are large and pointed.

Distribution: Restricted by the beginning of the 20th century to the Imfolozi Game Reserve in KwaZulu-Natal, the southern subspecies of the Square-lipped Rhinoceros was strictly protected and, over time, spread naturally into the adjacent Hluhluwe Game Reserve; it has since been widely reintroduced and introduced to other reserves and game-farms throughout the subregion.

The Square-lipped Rhinoceros once had a very wide distribution, with the northern subspecies occurring in Sudan, Chad, Uganda and the DRC, and the separate southern subspecies in South Africa, Mozambique, Zimbabwe, Botswana, Namibia and Angola. Tiny population pockets of the endangered northern subspecies may still survive in southern Sudan and the DRC (less than 10), although it is possible they may still be exterminated in the latter country, as happened with those animals that were present in Uganda into the 1970s.

The head of the Hook-lipped (or Black) Rhinoceros is noticeably smaller than that of the Square-lipped.

Coarse plant remains in Hook-lipped Rhino dung.

Fine plant remains in Square-lipped Rhino dung.

A substantial population of Square-lipped Rhinoceros, like this cow and her large calf, can be found in the Hluhluwe-Imfolozi Game Reserve in northern KwaZulu-Natal, where they have been protected since early in the 20th century.

Square-lipped Rhinoceros

250 mm

Front

Back

Habitat: This species shows a preference for short-grassed areas, with thick bush cover and water. Where adequate food and water is available, it will occupy a wide range of open woodland associations.

Behaviour: The Square-lipped Rhinoceros is much more sociable than the Hook-lipped Rhinoceros. Territorial bulls occupy clearly defined territories, which they will defend against neighbouring bulls; subordinate bulls may be allowed to remain within a territory if they remain submissive. The home range of cows may overlap with the territories of several territorial bulls but when a cow is receptive for mating, the bull will attempt to keep her within his area. Family groups usually number between 2 and 5 individuals, although larger numbers may come together for short periods. The home ranges and territories are only left when water is not readily available. When they move to watering points they follow the same paths each time. Feeding takes place during the cooler morning and afternoon hours but they are also active at night. Bulls usually have a number of fixed latrine sites within their territories.

Food: Square-lipped Rhinoceroses are grazers, with a preference for short grass. A reliable source of drinking water is an essential requirement.

Reproduction: Calves, weighing about 40 kg, are dropped at any time of the year after a gestation period of approximately 480 days. The cow moves away from the rhinoceros group to give birth and remains separated with her newborn calf for several days. In contrast to the Hook-lipped Rhinoceros, the calf of the Square-lipped Rhinoceros walks in front of the mother.

EVEN-TOED UNGULATES

PIGS & HOGS | Order Suiformes | Family Suidae

Phacochoerus africanus

■ **Common Warthog** *Phacochoerus africanus*
Male: shoulder height 70 cm; tail 45 cm; mass 60–105 kg.
Female: shoulder height 60 cm; tail 45 cm; mass 45–70 kg.
Identification pointers: Pig-like appearance; grey, sparsely haired body; wart-like lumps on face; thin tail with dark tufted tip, held erect when running; curved, upward-pointing tusks in adults.

Description: Often described as ugly and grotesque but not without appeal. Grey with sparse, dark, bristle-like hairs scattered over body, and mane of long erectile hair along back, which lies flat except when Warthog is under stress; mane may be yellowish-brown to black in colour. Tufts of pale-coloured whiskers lie along side of face. Snout is typically pig-like and prominent wart-like protuberances are present on face – two pairs in male, one less-conspicuous pair in female. Canine teeth of adults develop into long curved tusks; those of the boar may reach considerable lengths and make effective defensive weapons. Thin tail with its tuft of black hair is held erect when Warthog runs, unlike that of Bushpig.

Distribution: Northern and eastern areas of subregion. There is an expanding, introduced, population in the western sector of the Eastern Cape.

Habitat: Open country but also lightly wooded areas; savanna.

Behaviour: Predominantly diurnal but sometimes nocturnal. Groups, or sounders, of Common Warthogs usually consist of sows and their young, or bachelor groups. Sexually active boars usually move freely and alone except when with a sow. Can dig their own burrows, but usually take over Aardvark or Porcupine holes.

The male Warthog has two pairs of warts on its face.

A Warthog family with young piglets.

Common Warthog sow with piglets. Although the Warthog is not as water dependent as other African pigs, it will drink and wallow regularly when water is available. Inset: The white facial whiskers are more distinct in younger animals.

Common Warthog

45 mm

Front

Food: Mostly short grasses and grass roots. When grazing they usually kneel. Browse occasionally and rarely feed on animal matter.

Reproduction: Sow separates from sounder to give birth to litter of 2–3 (up to 8) piglets in burrow, after a gestation period 170 days. Newborn piglets weigh from 480–850 g. Emerge from burrow about 2 weeks after birth. Seasonal breeders, with most births taking place early summer.

Potamochoerus larvatus

■ Bushpig *Potamochoerus larvatus*

Shoulder height 55–88 cm; tail 38 cm; mass 60 kg (up to 115 kg).

Identification pointers: Pig-like appearance; well-haired body; tufts of hair on ear tips; long head; tail held down when running – unlike the Warthog whose tail is held vertically upwards; facial hair much lighter in colour than rest of body.

Description: More typically pig-like than Common Warthog. Boar slightly larger than sow. Body is well covered with long bristle-like hair which, although variable, is usually reddish-brown to grey-brown. Mane of longer and paler hair extends from the back of neck to shoulders and facial hair is usually grey-white. Head is long and ears are pointed with tuft of longish hair at the tip. Older boars may develop a pair of warts on the muzzle, but not as large as those of Warthog. Thin tail has tassel of black hair at tip. Piglets dark brown with several longitudinal pale stripes along body.

Distribution: Northern and eastern areas of subregion south to Mossel Bay.

Habitat: Forest, dense bush and riverine woodland, reed-beds and stands of long grass where there is water. Can be a problem in farming areas.

Behaviour: Mainly nocturnal, but in areas where they are not disturbed, they may be seen during the day. Live in sounders of 4–10 individuals but larger groups have been recorded. A sounder consists of a dominant boar, a dominant sow, other sows and young. Solitary animals also occur, as well as bachelor groups. If wounded or cornered, Bushpigs can be dangerous. They are territorial, but their ways of marking territory are not well known. This may involve middens of droppings, urine and scent deposits from male facial glands. It has been suggested that secretions from these glands may also play a part in tree-bark tusking. In the latter, pieces of bark on the favoured trees are cut away by the tusks. In the Soutpansberg, Waterberry trees are frequently used for claw-scratching by Leopards and tusking by Bushpigs, often on the same trees.

Food: Bushpigs use their hard snouts to root for rhizomes, bulbs and tubers; areas where they have been active look like small ploughed plots. In some areas they do considerable damage to crops. They also browse. Animal matter may feature quite prominently in their diet and may include insects, other invertebrates, frogs and carrion; rarely sheep and goats. Bushpigs can detect the presence of carrion by scent from several kilometres distance. A cow carcass that had been dead for a week was visited by a sounder of Bushpigs from riverine thicket two kilometres away. The intervening vegetation comprised short grassland covering rocky hill slopes that were not normally frequented by the Bushpig.

Reproduction: Most births occur in summer. Sow constructs a 'haystack' of grass, up to 3 m in diameter and 1 m in height, in bush cover. A litter consists of 2–4 piglets, up to eight, each weighing approximately 750 g. The young are born in the centre of the stack.

The Bushpig uses its hard snout to search for food, such as tubers, bulbs and rhizomes.

Bushpigs vary in colour, and some develop extremely hairy coats, with a mane of paler hair that extends from the back of the neck to the shoulders. Inset: Bushpig piglets are striped, whereas those of the Warthog are unstriped.

Bushpig

55 mm

Front

HIPPOPOTAMUS | Order Whippomorpha |
Suborder Ancodonta

HIPPOPOTAMUSES | Family Hippopotamidae

Hippopotamus amphibius
■ Historical distribution

■ **Hippopotamus** *Hippopotamus amphibius*
Shoulder height 1.5 m; tail length 40 cm; mass from 1 000–2 000 kg (bull), 1 000–1 700 kg (cow).
Identification pointers: Large size; barrel-shaped body and short legs; massive head with broad muzzle; most often found in water by day.
Description: Large, rotund animal with smooth, naked skin, short, stocky legs and a massive, broad-muzzled head. Mouth is equipped with an impressive set of tusk-like canines and incisors. Short, flattened tail is tipped with a tuft of black hair. Body colour greyish-black with pink tinge at the skin folds, around eyes and ears, while underparts are pinkish-grey. Four-toed feet leave a characteristic track.
Distribution: The Hippopotamus is restricted to the extreme northern and eastern parts of southern Africa. At the present time, the most southerly natural population is in northern KwaZulu-Natal but they previously occured in the vicinity of Cape Town, along the southern coastal belt and along the entire length of the Gariep (Orange) River, until hunted out by colonial settlers. It has a patchy distribution over the rest of sub-Saharan Africa but is widespread.
Habitat: The Hippopotamus requires sufficient water in which to submerge and shows a preference for permanent waters with a sandy substrate. This includes rivers, dams and lakes.
Behaviour: This semi-aquatic mammal spends much of the day lying in water, emerging at night to move to feeding-grounds. It also lies up on sand- or mud-banks in the sun, particularly during the winter months. Although it normally occurs in herds or schools of 10–15 animals, larger groups and solitary bulls are not uncommon. Schools are usually composed of cows and young of various ages with a dominant bull in overall control. Territories are narrow in the water but broaden out towards the feeding-grounds. Dominant bulls mark their territories by scattering their dung, with a vigorous sideways flicking of the tail, onto rocks, bushes and other objects. Territoriality is apparently strongest closer to the water but virtually absent in the feeding-grounds. Fixed pathways are used and these are characterized by a 'double' trail – each one made by the feet of one side. Exceptionally, they may travel up to 30 km to reach feeding areas, depending on the availability of food.
An adult Hippopotamus can remain under water for up to 6 minutes. Skin glands secrete a reddish fluid which is frequently mistaken for blood but probably acts as a skin lubricant and moisturizer. The Hippopotamus is extremely vocal and its deep roaring grunts and snorts constitute one of the typical sounds of Africa. Provoked, it can be extremely dangerous, particularly solitary bulls or cows with calves.
Food: The Hippopotamus is a selective grazer. In areas with high populations, considerable damage can be done to grazing areas near water.
Reproduction: Mating takes place in the water; after a gestation period of between 225 and 257 days a single calf is born weighing between 25 and 55 kg (usually about 30 kg). The cow gives birth on land in dense cover and she and the calf remain separated from the school for about 2 weeks. Calves may be produced at any time of the year but there is some evidence of seasonal peaks.

A herd of cows and calves; reddish secretions often look like blood, but serve to lubricate and protect the skin.

Hippopotamuses spend much of the day submerged. Inset: A Hippopotamus displaying the tusk-like canines.

Hippopotamus

250 mm

Front

Back

RUMINANTS | Order Ruminantia

GIRAFFE | Family Giraffidae

Giraffa camelopardalis
■ Historical distribution

■ **Giraffe** *Giraffa camelopardalis*
Male: height (top of head) 3.9–5.2 m; height (shoulder) 2.5–3.5 m;
tail 95–150 cm; mass 970–1 400 kg.
Female: height (top of head) 3.7–4.7 m; height (shoulder) 2.0–3.0 m;
tail 75–90 cm; mass 700–950 kg.
Identification pointers: Large size; long legs and neck; patchwork patterning. Cannot be mistaken for any other species.

Description: The Giraffe apparently gets its name from the Arabic *xirapha*, which means 'one who walks swiftly', and anyone who has observed Giraffe on the move would agree that this is entirely appropriate. The Giraffe is the tallest animal in the world and with its long neck and legs is unmistakable. A beautiful lattice pattern consisting of large, irregularly shaded patches separated by networks of light-coloured bands covers the body. The colouring of the patches is very variable, ranging from light fawn to almost black. Old bulls are often very dark. Knob-like horns are present on the top of the head and these are well developed in adult bulls.

Distribution: In southern Africa, the population that occurs in Mpumalanga and Limpopo provinces and adjacent areas of Mozambique and Zimbabwe is isolated. Giraffe also occur in western Zimbabwe and northern Namibia, extending from there into Angola and Zambia. Once occurring widely and continuously in savanna country south of the Sahara, they are now broken up into numerous isolated populations scattered throughout West and East Africa. Widely reintroduced in their original habitat, and introduced in the south to nature reserves and privately owned game farms, often well outside the traditional natural range.

Habitat: Dry savanna woodland; in some areas, penetrating into the desert along wooded river courses.

Behaviour: Active during the day and at night, resting during the hot midday hours. They occupy large home ranges of between 20 km² and 85 km², but do not establish defended territories. Usually seen in herds of 4–30 individuals, although these groups are unstable and much wandering takes place. Bulls only associate with cows temporarily. Although Giraffes are generally believed to be silent, they do have a range of grunting and snorting calls.

Food: Giraffes are browsers, only rarely eating grass. Their long necks and legs give them access to a food supply beyond the reach of all other browsers. Although they feed from a fairly wide range of trees and bushes, they are selective in what they eat. Twigs are pulled into the mouth by the lips and the long prehensile tongue, which may reach 45 cm in length, and the leaves are shredded off into the mouth. Between 15 and 20 hours of each day may be spent feeding.

Reproduction: Calves weighing about 100 kg may be born at any time of the year after a gestation period of about 450 days, the longest of any of the ungulates. The newly born calf can stand and walk within an hour of birth but remains isolated from the herd for up to 3 weeks. There is a very high mortality of calves in their first year, up to 70 per cent in some range areas.

Note: Up to 70 per cent of South Africa's giraffe population, <5 500 animals, is located in Kruger National Park, with an estimated 3 000 Giraffe in reserves and game farms in eastern Limpopo and Mpumalanga; KZN's population totals some 800, although Giraffes probably never occurred naturally in that province.

Giraffe are usually found in herds numbering from 4–30 animals; coloration and markings vary in different regions.

Giraffes adopt an ungainly stance when drinking, and they are particularly vulnerable to predators at this time.
Inset: The tips of the knob-like 'horns' are ringed with black hair.

Giraffe

180 mm

Front

BUFFALO & ANTELOPES | Family Bovidae

Syncerus caffer
■ Historical distribution

■ **African Buffalo** *Syncerus caffer*
Shoulder height 1.4 m; tail 70 cm; mass 550 kg (cow), 700 kg (bull).
Average horn length: 100 cm along curve from centre of boss to tip.
Record horn length for southern Africa: 124.8 cm (Zimbabwe).
Identification pointers: Cattle-like appearance: large size; uniform dark-brown or black colouring; heavily built; characteristically massive horns.
Description: African Buffalo are massive, heavily built, cattle-like animals. Adult bulls are dark-brown to black in colour but the cows are usually not so dark and calves are reddish-brown. They have stocky, relatively short legs, with large hoofs, those on the forefoot being larger than those on the hindfoot. The horns are heavy and massive, and the central horn base or 'boss' is particularly well developed in the bulls. The horns first curve down and outwards and then upwards and inwards, narrowing towards the tips. When viewed from the front the horns form a shallow 'W'. The horn boss of the cow is much less pronounced, and is absent in younger animals. Ears are large and hang below the horns. The tail is cow-like with a tip of long brown or black hair.
Distribution: Once widely distributed in southern Africa, the African Buffalo is now restricted to the northern and eastern parts of the region. The largest populations are in Kruger National Park (±30 000), Hwange and the Zambezi floodplain in Zimbabwe, and the Okavango complex in northern Botswana. Buffalo in the Hluhluwe/Imfolozi complex and other KwaZulu-Natal parks probably number fewer than 3 000 animals. Bovine TB is present in these populations, but the naturally occuring herds in Greater Addo National Park are classified disease-free and can be translocated to other reserves to form satellite populations. Despite its wide distribution south of the Sahara, many African Buffalo populations have been fragmented by human expansion and the species now has a markedly discontinuous distribution. It has, however, been reintroduced to several nature reserves and game-farms, for example, the Great Fish River Conservation Area in the Eastern Cape.
Habitat: The African Buffalo has a fairly wide habitat tolerance but requires areas with abundant grass, water and cover. It shows a preference for open woodland savanna and will utilize open grassland as long as it has access to cover.
Behaviour: African Buffalo are gregarious animals, occurring in herds that may number several thousands. Smaller groups may break away from the main concentration only to rejoin it later. Bachelor groups may form away from the main herd and solitary bulls are quite commonly encountered. Adult bulls within the mixed herd maintain a dominance hierarchy, the complexity of which is influenced by the size of the herd. The cows also establish a pecking order among themselves. The dominant bull or bulls will mate with the cows that are receptive or in breeding condition. Buffalo herds have clearly defined home ranges and herd areas rarely overlap. They come to water in the early morning and late afternoon and seek out shade during the heat of the day. Most feeding takes place at night.
Food: Predominantly grazers but also occasionally browse.
Reproduction: Buffalo are seasonal breeders with the majority of calves being dropped in the wet and warm summer months. A single calf, weighing between 30 kg and 40 kg, is born after a gestation period of about 340 days. Calves are born within the herd and are able to keep up within a few hours of birth.

The African Buffalo bull has massive horns, which form a heavy boss where they meet. Although Buffalo are gregarious herd animals, solitary bulls are often encountered, and bachelor groups may break away from the main herd.

African Buffalo are principally grazers.

There is a notable difference in the horn boss of an African Buffalo bull (left) when compared with the cow (right).

African Buffalo

120 mm

Front

Tragelaphus oryx
▦ Historical distribution

■ Common Eland *Tragelaphus oryx*

Male: shoulder height 1.7 m; tail 60 cm; mass 700 kg (but up to 900 kg).
Female: shoulder height 1.5 m; tail 60 cm; mass 450 kg.
Average horn length (both sexes) 60 cm; record horn length (Namibia) 118.4 cm.
Identification pointers: Massive size; fawn-tawny with some grey on fore-quarters; both sexes with straight horns, each with a slight twist or spiral.

Description: The largest living antelope, the Eland has a cow-like appearance. Its general colour is usually fawn or tawny, turning blue-grey with age, particularly on the neck and shoulders. Adult bulls develop a patch of fairly long, dark, coarse hair on the forehead. A short, dark mane runs down the back of the neck. The tail is fairly long with a tuft of black hair at the tip. Older bulls typically develop a large dewlap on the throat. Both sexes have horns but those of the bull are thicker and the shallow spiral is marked by a prominent ridge.

Distribution: Once occurred widely in southern Africa but now restricted to the northern parts, except for a natural population in the Drakensberg and numerous localities where it has been reintroduced to farms and reserves. Occurs widely in central and East Africa but is absent from the forested areas of equatorial Africa. The Eland population in Kruger National Park has been in decline since the 1980s and may number fewer than 500 today. There may be more than 2 000 Eland in the Kgalagadi Transfrontier Park, but these herds move freely in and out of the park on the Botswana side and so may be absent at times.

Habitat: The Common Eland occupies a wide range of habitats from desert scrub to montane areas but shows a preference for open scrub-covered plains and woodland savanna.

Behaviour: Normally occurs in herds of 25–60 individuals but temporary associations of over 1 000 are occasionally seen. The larger gatherings usually occur during the rainy season. In some areas, Eland tend to be more or less sedentary, whereas in others, such as the Kalahari, they may move considerable distances in search of suitable sources of food. Although a hierarchy exists within Eland herds, there appears to be no defence of territories. Eland are predominantly diurnal but also feed at night, particularly during the summer months.

Food: Predominantly browsers, Common Eland do occasionally eat grass. They dig for roots and bulbs with their front hoofs and also use their horns to knock down foliage. They are independent of water but will drink when it is available.

Reproduction: The dominant bulls mate with the receptive cows and a single calf, weighing 22–36 kg, is born after a gestation period of approximately 270 days. The calf remains hidden for the first 2 weeks after birth. Calves may be dropped in any month of the year but there is a peak in summer. They grow rapidly and can achieve a mass of 450 kg by the end of their first year.

General: Despite their massive size the Eland is an excellent jumper and can easily clear a 2-m fence. When moving, the animals make a distinct clicking noise, which is believed to be caused by the two halves of each hoof striking together. This sound carries quite well and is sometimes the first indication of the species' presence. Eland feature frequently in Bushman paintings.

Eland have been successfully domesticated in Zimbabwe and Russia. Although the Zimbabwe programme, begun in 1954, has since collapsed, the Russian farming venture is still underway. Eland produce good quality meat and the milk has a very high fat content and is said to have great nutritional value.

The Eland cow has no forehead tuft.

A herd of Common Eland in the Drakensberg, KwaZulu-Natal.

Eland bull, showing the large dewlap on the lower neck and the tuft of fairly long, coarse dark hair on the forehead. Despite their size, Eland are excellent jumpers, easily clearing fences of up to 2 m from a standing position.

Common Eland

100 mm

Front

Tragelaphus strepsiceros

Horn development

9 months

14–17 months

17–21 months

24 months

30⁺ months

Bull in prime

(after C.D. Simpson, 1966)

■ **Greater Kudu** *Tragelaphus strepsiceros*
Shoulder height 1.4–1.55 m; tail 43 cm; mass 250 kg (bull), 165 kg (cow).
Average horn length 120 cm; record horn length (along the curve) 187.6 cm.
Identification pointers: Large size; long legs; 6–10 vertical white stripes on grey-brown sides; large rounded ears; bushy tail, blackish or brownish above, white underneath; characteristic long, spiral horns of bull.

Description: This large and handsome antelope is grey-brown to rufous in colour, with the bulls being more grey than the cows and calves. The sides are clearly marked with 6–10 vertical white stripes. There is a distinct white band across the face, with white spots on the cheeks. The bull has a prominent mane from the neck to beyond the shoulders and a fringe of longer hair on the throat and lower neck. The blackish or brown bushy tail is white underneath with a black tip. The ears are very large, showing pink on the inside. Only the male has the long, spiral horns.

Distribution: Kudu occur principally in the northern and eastern parts of southern Africa with apparently isolated populations in the south, where it has spread westwards from the Eastern Cape into the northern Western Cape and Northern Cape provinces over the past 20 years. Kudu can now be found in the Nuweveld range near Beaufort West, the dry water courses in the vicinity of Williston, Carnarvon and Van Wyksvlei, with individuals being recorded as far west as Niewoudtville on the western escarpment. Sightings are now regular to the north of the Swartberg range which separates the Little and Great Karoo. Elsewhere, Kudu occur widely in central Africa south of the equatorial forests, and through East Africa to Ethiopia, Sudan and Chad.

Habitat: The Greater Kudu is an antelope of wooded savanna. It may occur in arid areas but only where there are stands of bush that provide cover and food. It does not occur in open grassland or forest. It has, however, been able to penetrate the Karoo and the Namib Desert along wooded watercourses. In many areas it shows a preference for acacia woodland and rocky hill country.

Behaviour: Although it normally occurs in small herds, from 3–10 animals, larger groups are occasionally seen. Outside the midwinter rutting period the adult bulls are either solitary or join small bachelor herds. At the time of the rut an adult bull will run with a group of cows and their young. Although usually active in early mornings and late afternoons, in areas where they are disturbed or hunted they have taken to nocturnal activity. They are well known for their jumping ability, having no difficulty in clearing fences of up to 2 m.

Food: Although predominantly a browser, it does occasionally graze. It eats a wider variety of browse species than any other of our local antelopes. It is considered a pest in some areas because it feeds on crops such as lucerne, mealies (maize) and vegetables.

Reproduction: Calves are born throughout the year but most births take place in the summer months, the main rutting period being in midwinter. As in the case with the Sable and Roan antelopes, the Greater Kudu cow moves away from the herd to drop a single calf, which weighs about 16 kg. The gestation period is around 270 days. The calves remain hidden for at least 2 months after birth, with the cows visiting them just once a day to suckle. After this time, calves move with their mothers and join the nursery herds.

A Greater Kudu cow stands about 1.5 m high at the shoulder.

The Greater Kudu bull has massive, spiralled horns.

Greater Kudu cows lack horns and are generally smaller and weigh less than the bulls.

Greater Kudu

68 mm

Front

Back

207

Tragelaphus angasii

Horn development

9 months

12 months

18 months

30 months

54 months

(after J.L. Anderson, 1986)

■ Nyala *Tragelaphus angasii*
Male: shoulder height 1.15 m; tail 43 cm; mass 108 kg.
Female: shoulder height 97 cm; tail 36 cm; mass 62 kg.
Average horn length 60 cm; record horn length 83.5 cm.
Identification pointers: Ram slate-grey overall with long mane along entire length of back, and long fringe hanging below underbelly from throat to between hindlegs; lower part of legs rufous or yellow-brown; 8–14 vertical white stripes on sides; tail quite bushy and white below; horns spiralled but much shorter, lighter and less spiralled than those of Greater Kudu (page 206). Ewe is smaller, has no horns and is yellow-brown to chestnut in colour with up to 18 vertical white stripes on sides.

Description: Falls between Greater Kudu and Bushbuck in size. Like other members of genus *Tragelaphus*, only the male Nyala has horns, but the sexes are also markedly different in other aspects. Ram has fringe of long hair hanging from underparts, from just behind chin to between hindlegs, and a mane of hair from back of head to rump. Mane normally lies flat but is raised during certain behavioural interactions, such as on encountering another ram. Buttocks and upperparts of hindlegs are also lined with long hair. From 8–14 vertical white stripes are present on the sides but these disappear or become less distinct in older rams. Ground colour is slate-grey to dark-brown. Lower parts of legs are rufous to yellow-brown. There are 2–3 white cheek spots, and chin and upper lip are also white. Shallow V-shaped white line runs between eyes. Ewe differs from ram, being much smaller and lacking the long shaggy hair. In addition, ewes and lambs have yellow-brown to chestnut ground colour and up to 18 vertical white lines on sides of body. Ram's slightly spiralled horns curve outward after the first turn. Horn tips are whitish-yellow.

Distribution: Occurs patchily in the north-eastern parts of southern Africa, with a marginal occurrence north of the Zambezi in Mozambique and southern Malawi. In South Africa there are two major centres of distribution: northern KwaZulu-Natal and the lowveld of Mpumalanga and Limpopo provinces. Although some populations have disappeared in recent years, others have expanded and increased in numbers. Nyala have also been introduced to game farms well outside of their traditional range, including the Eastern Cape and Namibia and, in many cases, thrive in these areas. Probably the best location to observe this antelope is Mkuzi Game Reserve in KwaZulu-Natal.

Habitat: Restricted to dry savanna woodland and along watercourses. It may be seen grazing in open areas adjacent to bush or tree cover.

Behaviour: Nyala rams are not territorial and seldom fight, but display by raising the dorsal crest and 'slow-walking' in what is called the 'lateral presentation'. The biggest ram wins and the competitor withdraws. However, when fighting does take place it can be very intensive. Commonly seen in small groups, either ewes and lambs, or all rams together. Solitary rams are often seen. Group composition changes constantly, although ewe-and-lamb groups are the most stable. Larger groups may be observed, but these are usually associated with a waterhole or a localized abundance of food.

Food: Principally a browser, eating from wide variety of plants. Fresh grass taken during rains. As with Bushbuck and Impala, Nyala will feed on fallen tree flowers and fruits knocked down by foraging Baboons and Vervet Monkeys.

Reproduction: Single lamb, weighing 4.2–5.5 kg, born at any time of year. Gestation period 220 days. Remains hidden for first 2 weeks.

The Nyala ram has a mane along the length of the back and a fringe of hair from below the chin to between the hindlegs.

Nyala ewes suckle their young for up to seven months.

Nyala ewes and fawns, showing the distinct vertical stripes.

Nyala

57 mm

Front   Back

Tragelaphus spekei

■ **Sitatunga** *Tragelaphus spekei*

Shoulder height 90 cm; tail 22 cm; mass 115 kg (ram).

Average horn length 60 cm; record horn length 92.4 cm.

Identification pointers: Semi-aquatic habitat requirements totally different from those of Nyala (page 208); Sitatunga considerably larger than Bushbuck. Hindquarters higher than front; fairly long, shaggy hair. Spoor unmistakable.

Description: Adult rams larger than ewes; shaggy-haired, drab, dark brown with no body stripes – sometimes lighter marks on back. Ewes also dark-brown or reddish-brown but have black band down centre of back, four vertical stripes on side, white lateral band and white spots on haunches. Both sexes have an incomplete white band between eyes and white spots on cheeks. White patch above chest and another below chin. Dark-brown tail is white below; not very bushy. Hoofs are extremely widely splayed and up to 18 cm long – an adaptation to marshy habitat. Only rams have horns; quite long and similar in form to Nyala.

Distribution: In subregion, occurs only in Botswana's Okavango Delta and adjacent areas in Caprivi Strip. Patchy distribution northwards to Lake Chad.

Habitat: Semi-aquatic and spends most of its time in dense reed-beds, with water to a depth of one metre. Swims in deeper water to escape danger.

Behaviour: Common grouping is adult ram with ewes and juveniles, but solitary animals and groups of subadults are also seen. Active throughout day, but lies up during hottest hours on trampled mats of reeds or other vegetation. Will also feed at night. If alarmed will swim to safety.

Food: Papyrus and other reeds; also grass and occasional browse.

Reproduction: Single calf born after 220-day gestation, usually in midwinter.

Tragelaphus scriptus

■ **Bushbuck** *Tragelaphus scriptus*

Male: shoulder height 80 cm; tail 20 cm; mass 45 kg.

Female: shoulder height 70 cm; tail 20 cm; mass 30 kg.

Average horn length 26 cm; record horn length 52.07 cm.

Identification pointers: Presence of vertical white stripes and spots on sides of the body to a greater or lesser extent, more so in north; broad ears; short bushy tail, dark above and white below; ram has short, almost straight horns with slight spiral and ridge. Much smaller than Nyala (page 208).

Description: Small bright-chestnut to dark-brown antelope; those in north of subregion more brightly coloured and clearly marked than those from south, but considerable variation in colour and markings exist within populations. Patterns of white lines and spots are present on the flanks to a greater or lesser extent, more so in the north. No white band between the eyes as in Sitatunga, Nyala and Kudu, but there are two white patches on throat. Crest of longish hair down back of ram is raised when it displays or threatens. Bushy tail white below and dark-brown above. Only ram has horns which project backwards in a single spiral with a prominent ridge along edge. Can be extremely sharp-pointed in young rams.

Distribution: Southern coastal belt and eastern and northern parts of subregion.

Habitat: Riverine woodland and bush associated with water, from coastal dune bush to montane forest, and from sea level to an altitude of 1 800 m in South Africa.

Behaviour: Usually single but occasionally in pairs or small groups of ewes and lambs. Mainly nocturnal but also active during day in cooler or overcast weather.

Food: Predominantly browsers but will take grass. May damage young trees in forestry plantations or agricultural crops.

Reproduction: Single young weighing 3.5–4.5 kg born after gestation period of 180 days. Follows mother regularly after 4 months of remaining hidden.

A young Sitatunga ram.

Sitatunga ram: the southern race has very few white markings and is greyish-brown in colour.

A Sitatunga ram swimming through water.

Bushbuck ewe, Zambezi Valley. Note the white patches on the throat and the overall bright colour.

Bushbuck ram, Riversdale, Western Cape. Bushbuck are very variable in colour.

Sitatunga

80 mm

Front

44 mm

Front

Bushbuck

Hippotragus equinus
■ Historical distribution

■ Roan Antelope *Hippotragus equinus*

Shoulder height 1.1–1.5 m (average 1.4 m); tail 54 cm; mass 220–300 kg (average 270 kg).

Average horn length (bull) 75 cm; record horn length (Zimbabwe) 99.06 cm.

Identification pointers: Large size; greyish-brown colour with lighter underparts; black-and-white facial pattern; heavily ridged, swept-back, curving horns; long, narrow, tufted ears. See Sable Antelope (page 214).

Description: After the Common Eland, the Roan Antelope is the second-largest antelope species occurring in southern Africa. It has a somewhat horse-like appearance with a general colouring of greyish-brown, often with a reddish tinge ('roan' coloration). The underparts are lighter. The face is distinctly marked with black and white, giving it a slightly clown-like appearance and the long, narrow ears have prominent tassels of hair at the tip. The tail is long and tufted. A distinct, light-coloured, dark-tipped mane runs from between the ears to just beyond the shoulders. Both sexes carry the back-curved horns, but the cow's are lighter and shorter than the bull's.

Distribution: Restricted to the northern and north-eastern areas of southern Africa where it is considered to be rare. The total Roan population in South Africa is estimated to be about 1 500 animals, of which only a small number are in national parks. For example, they used to occur throughout Kruger National Park but by 2003 their numbers had dwindled to fewer than 50 individuals. Beyond the southern African subregion it occurs widely in central Africa, western East Africa and through the savanna zone to West Africa. However, despite this wide distribution, it is considered to be rare and endangered throughout much of its range. Although numbers are slowly increasing in South Africa, there is concern that animals have been imported from West Africa and this could lead to genetic contamination of the local populations.

Habitat: Roan Antelope require open or lightly wooded grassland with medium to tall grass and access to water. They avoid areas with short grass.

Behaviour: Live in small herds (5–12) usually led by an adult bull. Larger herds (30–80) have been recorded. Nursery herds, consisting of cows and young animals, occupy fixed areas that are defended by dominant bulls from approaches by other bulls. The herd itself is usually led by a cow, which becomes dominant over the other cows and juveniles. The bull is responsible for breeding and keeping competitors away and the lead cow selects the feeding and resting areas. Two-year-old bulls are driven away from the herd by the herd bull and join together to form small bachelor herds. Adult bulls (5–6 years old) move off to live alone or to take over nursery herds. Most activity takes place during the day.

Food: Roan Antelope are principally grazers, selecting medium or long grasses. They rarely browse. Will seek out areas of new grass after fires.

Reproduction: Calves may be dropped at any time of the year after a gestation period of about 280 days. Shortly before the birth the cow moves away from the herd and remains in bush cover until the calf is born. For the first few days the cow remains close to the calf, but then rejoins the herd, only visiting her calf in the early morning and late afternoon. When it is between 2 and 6 weeks old the calf joins the herd. Although its facial markings are similar to those of the adults, its body colour is light to rich rufous-brown.

Roan Antelope cow; note the slender horns and horse-like appearance, which has resulted in the scientific name.

Roan Antelope bull displays large, curved horns and distinctive black and white facial markings.

Roan Antelope

120 mm

Front

Hippotragus niger
■ Historical distribution

■ Sable Antelope *Hippotragus niger*

Shoulder height 1.35 m; tail 50 cm; mass 180–270 kg (bulls average 230 kg). Average horn length (bull) 102 cm; record horn length (southern Africa) 140.7 cm.

Identification pointers: Large size; contrasting black or dark-brown upperparts with pure white underparts; long, transversely ridged, back-curved horns in both sexes. Different body colour from Roan Antelope (page 212), with a somewhat lighter build, longer horns and no tuft of hair at the tip of the ear.

Description: The adult bull Sable Antelope is shiny black with sharply contrasting white underparts and inner thighs. Cows and younger bulls are usually reddish brown above. The black-and-white facial markings are conspicuous. The face is mainly white, with a broad black blaze from the forehead to the nose and a black stripe from below the eye almost to the muzzle. There is an erect, fairly long mane running from the top of the neck to just beyond the shoulders. The ears are long and narrow but lack the tufted tips found in Roan Antelope. Both sexes carry horns but those of the bull are longer and more robust. The transversely ridged horns rise up from the skull and then sweep backwards in a pronounced curve.

Distribution: Restricted to the north-eastern parts of southern Africa but even here, distribution is patchy and not continuous. It occurs as far north as southern Kenya and marginally in south-eastern Angola. An isolated population occurs in northern Angola, but is considered to be a separate subspecies, the so-called Giant Sable (*H. n. variani*). No recent counts have been made in Botswana or Zimbabwe, and within Namibia wild-ranging herds are restricted to the extreme north-east, although a small number of Sable Antelope has been introduced into Etosha National Park. Sable populations in Kruger National Park have declined by 70 per cent in the past 15 years, and it has been predicted that they will continue to decline into extinction in that park. Most herds are intensively managed on private game farms, as Sables fetch high prices as breeding stock and the bulls are sought-after as hunting trophies.

Habitat: Sable are usually associated with dry, open woodland with medium to tall grass. They avoid dense woodland and short grassveld. Water is essential.

Behaviour: Sable Antelope live in herds usually numbering from 10–30 individuals but occasionally larger groups come together. Territorial bulls establish themselves in territories overlapping those of nursery herds (cows and young animals). The nursery herds move within a fixed home range. During the rut the bull tries to keep the cows within his territory. As with Roan Antelope, a cow takes over leadership of a nursery herd. Young bulls grow up within bachelor herds, only seeking out their own territories in their fifth or sixth year. Most Sable Antelope activity takes place in the early morning and late afternoon.

Food: Sable Antelope are principally grazers but will take browse, particularly in the dry season. Regular access to drinking water is essential.

Reproduction: Sable Antelope is a seasonal breeder, dropping its calves between January and March, although this varies according to area. A single reddish-brown calf, weighing 13–22 kg, is born after a gestation period of about 270 days. The cow leaves the herd to give birth and the calf remains hidden for up to 2 months before joining the other animals. After each suckling, only once or twice a day, the calf moves to a new hiding-place and in this way reduces the chances of being found by a predator.

General: A pair of Sable Antelope horns collected in 1898 from Kruger National Park measured 140.7 cm, exceeding the currrent official South African record of 127.6 cm by more than 13 cm. A Giant Sable (*H. n. variani*), from northern Angola, holds the overall record horn length for the continent of 164.7 cm.

Sable Antelope in a mixed herd. Herd sizes range from 10–30 animals, but larger groups are known.

A Sable Antelope bull tests a cow's readiness to mate. There is a notable colour difference between the sexes.

Sable Antelope

115 mm

Front

Oryx gazella
■ Historical distribution

■ Gemsbok (Oryx) *Oryx gazella*
Shoulder height 1.2 m; mass 240 kg (bull), 210 kg (cow).
Average horn length 85 cm; record horn length (Kalahari) 125.1 cm.
Identification pointers: Heavily built with short, thick neck; distinct black facial and body markings; long, black, horse-like tail; long, straight horns.

Description: Heavily built with a thick neck and distinct black-and-white markings on head, body and legs; long horse-like tail. Body colour greyish-fawn, separated from white underparts by black streak along flanks. Black patches on upper part of legs and along top of rump. Black stripe runs down front of neck. Calves fawn and lack black body markings. Both sexes carry long, almost straight, transversely ridged, rapier-like horns; those of bull are shorter and more robust.

Distribution: Arid north-west of subregion, extending north into Angola. Another separate population in East Africa. Reintroduced widely in south.

Habitat: Open, dry country but also open woodland, grassveld and dune country. Availability of water is not an essential habitat requirement.

Behaviour: Gregarious, occurring in herds of about 15, sometimes more, particularly during rains. They occur in mixed herds (consisting of bulls, cows and young of different ages) or nursery herds (cows and young); solitary bulls are often seen. A territorial bull will herd a mixed or nursery herd into his territory and only he will mate with receptive cows. Gemsbok are usually forced by their hostile environment to be nomadic, moving to fresh vegetation growth following rain.

Food: Although mainly grazers they also include browse, seed-pods and fruits such as tsamma melons in their diet.

Reproduction: Single calf dropped after a gestation of about 264 days, usually linked to seasonal rainfall. The calf hides and will move with the mother at night to a new resting-place. Calves usually 3–6 weeks old before joining the herd.

Kobus ellipsiprymnus

■ Waterbuck *Kobus ellipsiprymnus*
Shoulder height 1.3 m; tail 35 cm; mass 250–270 kg (bulls).
Average horn length 75 cm; record horn length (South Africa) 99.7 cm.
Identification pointers: Large size; broad white ring around rump; coarse, shaggy grey-brown coat; long, ringed, forward-swept horns of the bull.

Description: Waterbuck are large, robust antelopes with coarse, long coats. The body colour is grey-brown with either grey or brown being dominant, scattered through with grey or white hairs. A broad white ring encircles the rump and a white band is present from throat to the base of the ears. The flanks are lighter in colour than the back and the hair around the mouth, nose and above the eyes is white. The ears are short, rounded, white on the inside with a black tip. The tail is quite long with a black tuft of hair at the tip. Only the bull has the long, heavily ringed horns that curve backwards and then forwards towards the tips.

Distribution: Waterbuck occur patchily in eastern southern Africa and then northwards through East Africa to southern Somalia.

Habitat: Always associated with water, preferring areas with reed-beds or tall grass as well as woodland. They will utilize open grassland adjacent to cover.

Behaviour: Gregarious, occurring in herds of 5–10, sometimes up to 30. Nursery herds may move through territories of several bulls. Younger bulls form bachelor herds. Often detected by the strong musky scent given off by their oily hair.

Food: Principally grass but also take browse.

Reproduction: A single calf may be dropped at any time of the year but mostly in summer; the gestation period is about 280 days. After 3–4 weeks in hiding the calf begins to follow the mother and joins the herd.

The distinctively marked Gemsbok cannot be confused with any other species; both sexes carry long, straight horns.

Waterbuck bull and cows. The broad white ring encircling the rump is diagnostic, and only the bull has horns.

Gemsbok

110 mm

Front

Waterbuck

90 mm

Front

Back

Kobus lechwe

Lechwe *Kobus leche*

Male: shoulder height 1 m; tail 34 cm; mass 100 kg.
Female: shoulder height 96 cm; tail 34 cm; mass 80 kg.
Average horn length 70 cm; record horn length 93.98 cm.
Identification pointers: Chestnut upperparts and white underparts; black lines on front of forelegs (absent in Puku); long, ridged, forward-pointing horns of the ram much longer than those of Puku. Semi-aquatic habitat sets Lechwe aside from other species. Different in appearance from Sitatunga (see page 210).

Description: Hindquarters of the Lechwe are noticeably higher than the shoulders and its muzzle is quite short. Upperparts are bright chestnut and the underparts from chin to belly are white. There are conspicuous black lines down the front of the forelegs. Only the ram has the long, strongly ridged, lyre-shaped horns. The tail has a tip of black hair.

Distribution: In the subregion, Lechwe is restricted to the Okavango and Chobe areas of northern Botswana and the Caprivi Strip, Namibia.

Habitat: Floodplains and seasonal swamps; rarely ventures more than 2–3 km from permanent water.

Behaviour: Next to the Sitatunga, the Lechwe is the most water-loving antelope. It takes readily to water, both to feed and when threatened. It usually occurs in herds of up to 30 individuals, but occasionally many thousands may be seen together. Rams form small territories within which they keep small groups of ewes for mating. Small groups of non-territorial rams congregate on the edges of the mating grounds. Ewe herds with their young move freely between ram territories. Lechwe are active during the early morning and late afternoon, lying up during the heat of the day and at night. Although quite slow on land, they can move rapidly in shallow water and swim readily.

Food: Almost entirely semi-aquatic grasses.

Reproduction: Most calves in the Okavango Swamps are born during the period from October to December, but they may be dropped at any time of the year. A single calf weighing approximately 5 kg is born after a gestation period of about 225 days. Calves remain hidden for the first 2–3 weeks.

Kobus vardonii

Puku *Kobus vardonii*

Shoulder height 80 cm; tail 28 cm; mass 74 kg (ram), 62 kg (ewe).
Average horn length 45 cm; record horn length 56.2 cm.
Identification pointers: Can be distinguished from Lechwe by the absence of black markings on the front of the forelegs and by the shorter horns of rams. Very restricted southern African distribution.

Description: The upperparts of this medium-sized antelope are golden-yellow with slightly paler sides. The underparts are off-white, as are the throat, the sides of the muzzle and around the eyes. The legs are uniform brown in colour, and the tail is golden-yellow. Only the ram has the relatively short, stout, lyre-shaped, well-ringed horns.

Distribution: In subregion, occurs only on Pookoo Flats and vicinity of the Chobe River, Botswana, but widely scattered through central and East Africa.

Habitat: Open flatland adjacent to rivers and marshes but usually not on open floodplains favoured by Lechwe.

Behaviour: Herds of Puku usually number from 5–30. Adult rams defend small territories for short periods, during which time they attempt to herd the ewes, which will, however, move across the territories of several rams.

Food: Predominantly grasses.

Red Lechwe ram and ewes. Note the bright chestnut-brown colour. Inset: The Lechwe ram has lyre-shaped horns.

Puku ram, showing lyre-shaped horns.

A herd of Puku ewes on the alert.

Lechwe

80 mm

Front

Puku

67 mm

Front   Back

219

Reproduction: Puku young may be dropped at any time of the year but in the south of its range there is a peak in births during the dry winter months. The gestation period is approximately 240 days. The lamb (<6 kg) hides for the early part of its life and, on joining the herd, usually moves with the other lambs as the mother/lamb bond is weak in comparison with other antelope species.

Redunca fulvorufula

■ Mountain Reedbuck *Redunca fulvorufula*
Shoulder height 72 cm; tail 18 cm; mass 30 kg.
Average horn length 14 cm; record horn length 25.4 cm.
Identification pointers: Grey-fawn upperparts; white underparts; bushy tail, grey above and white below; short, forward-curved horns of male. May be confused with Grey Rhebok (page 222) where they occur together, but the horns of the latter are straight and vertically set, and not forward-curved. Similar to Common Reedbuck but smaller, and has no dark-brown line on front of the forelegs; different habitat.
Description: Upperparts grey-fawn and underparts white. Hair on the head and neck is usually more yellow-fawn. Bushy tail, grey-fawn above, white below, is held vertically when animal flees, prominently displaying white under-surface, Ears are long and narrow. Only male has short, stout, forward-curved horns.
Distribution: Patchy distribution in eastern parts of subregion.
Habitat: The Mountain Reedbuck is restricted to mountainous and rocky areas. Preference for broken hill country with scattered bush, trees or grassy slopes but avoids steep rock-faces. Water is essential.
Behaviour: Territorial rams occupy their areas throughout the year but small groups of 2–6 ewes and young are unstable and move from herd to herd and over several ram territories. Bachelor groups may also be observed. This species is active both at night and during the day but lies up during the hottest hours.
Food: Grasses.
Reproduction: Breeding takes place throughout the year with a birth-peak in the summer months. A single lamb with a mass of 3 kg is born after a gestation period of approximately 242 days. The ewe gives birth to the lamb under cover and away from the group. The lamb remains hidden for 2–3 months before joining the other group members.

Redunca arundinum
■ Historical distribution

■ Common (Southern) Reedbuck *Redunca arundinum*
Shoulder height 80–95 cm; tail 25 cm; mass 50–70 kg.
Average horn length 30 cm; record horn length 46.68 cm.
Identification pointers: Forward-curved horns of the ram; white, bushy underside of tail is prominent when the animal is running away. Differs from Mountain Reedbuck in being larger, having black lines on front surface of forelegs, and by ram having considerably longer horns. Habitat requirements of the two species are different and they are rarely found together.
Description: Medium-sized antelope with brown or greyish-fawn upperparts, although head and neck are slightly lighter. Underparts are white. The short, bushy tail is grey-fawn above and white below. There is a vertical black stripe on the forward-facing surface of forelegs. Ears are broad and rounded and white on the inside. Only the ram has horns and they are curved forward and transversely ridged from the base for two-thirds of their length.
Distribution: Reedbuck has patchy distribution dictated by availability of suitable habitat, and is restricted to east and north of subregion. It has been eradicated in a number of areas, including extreme northern Namibia, although it still occurs in low

A Mountain Reedbuck ram.

A Mountain Reedbuck ewe.

Common (Southern) Reedbuck ram.

Common (Southern) Reedbuck ewe.

Mountain Reedbuck

43 mm

Front   *Back*

Common Reedbuck

65 mm

Front   *Back*

numbers in parts of the Caprivi Strip. It is also now absent from the coastal plain of South Africa's Eastern Cape province; but some historic records indicate that it might once have extended into the Western Cape. The highest densities reached in the subregion are in the Greater St. Lucia Wetland in KwaZulu-Natal.

Habitat: The Common Reedbuck requires tall-grass areas and reed-beds as well as permanent water. It avoids dense bush areas. They occur at altitudes ranging from near sea-level to about 2 000 m in South Africa.

Behaviour: Usually in pairs or family groups but up to 20 individuals on occasion. A pair occupies a territory, which is defended by the ram. Both nocturnal and diurnal. Loud alarm whistle emitted through the nostrils when the animal is disturbed, or by rams advertising their territories.

Food: Reedbuck are predominantly grazers but do sometimes take browse.

Reproduction: Birth peak in summer. Gestation 220 days. A single lamb weighs 4,5 kg, stays hidden for 2 months, and then accompanies the ewe; both join the ram after 3–4 months.

Pelea capreolus
Grey Rhebok has a patchy distribution; the red line denotes the limit of its total range.

■ Grey Rhebok *Pelea capreolus*

Shoulder height 75 cm; tail 10 cm; mass 20 kg.
Average horn length 20 cm; record horn length 30.16 cm.

Identification pointers: Woolly grey coat; long, narrow ears; large black nose; straight, upright horns of ram. May be confused with Mountain Reedbuck (see page 220) where the two species occur together, but the latter's horns curve forwards at the tip.

Description: Gracefully built antelope with a grey, thick, woolly coat. The underparts are pure white. The short, bushy tail is grey above and white underneath and at the tip. Ears are long and narrow. Only the male has the vertical, almost straight horns. The large black nose has a somewhat swollen appearance.

Distribution: Restricted to South Africa, Lesotho and Swaziland. This antelope has a patchy, discontinuous distribution and, despite its relatively large size, its range is not accurately known. There is a small population in the Huns Mountains (*Hunsberg*) in extreme south-western Namibia, close to the South African border. The largest population unit is located within the Drakensberg of KwaZulu-Natal. Relatively high numbers occur in the southern wheatlands of the Western Cape. It extends as far into the arid north-west as the Richtersveld and southwards into the Kamiesberg, but only in small numbers. There is a substantial population in the Karoo National Park and adjacent areas of the Nuweveld escarpment.

Habitat: Usually hill or mountain country, but also occurs in the wheatlands of the southwestern Cape, particularly in the Bredasdorp and Swellendam districts.

Behaviour: Normally in small family parties consisting of a territorial adult ram, several ewes and their young. Active by day. Gives vent to a sharp snort at regular intervals when disturbed or alarmed. Runs with rocking-horse motion displaying white underside of tail as warning signal.

Food: Grasses and browse, the latter most important seasonally.

Reproduction: Single lambs born in the wet season; gestation period 260 days.

Grey Rhebok rams have straight horns and a bushy, white-tipped tail.

Grey Rhebok ewes lack horns.

A pair of young Grey Rhebok in the wheatlands of the Western Cape.

Grey Rhebok

45 mm

Front

Connochaetes gnou

Black Wildebeest
horn development

6 months

12 months

24 months

36 months

48 months

(after W. von Richter, 1971)

■ **Black Wildebeest** *Connochaetes gnou*
Shoulder height 1.2 m; mass 100–180 kg.
Average horn length 62 cm; record double horn length (tip to tip) 74.62 cm.
Identification pointers: Overall black appearance; long, white, horse-like tail; characteristic horn shape, extensive facial 'hair-brush'. Could be confused with Blue Wildebeest (page 226) but the ranges do not overlap, except where introduced. The white tail is characteristic of this species.

Description: More dark brown than black, but from a distance the Black Wildebeest does look black. Long, white, horse-like tail contrasts with body colour. Somewhat grotesque in appearance: shoulders are higher than rump and it has a large, broad-snouted head. Face covered in brush-like tuft of hairs which points outwards and there is long hair on throat and on chest between forelegs. Erect mane runs from top of neck to shoulders. Horns of cow are thinner and less robust than those of bull. They bend steeply downward, forward and upward; in mature bulls horn base forms a 'boss' over top of head.

Distribution: Formerly distributed over a wide area of central South Africa, but brought to the brink of extinction last century. Numbers are now some 18 000 in total, with perhaps 11 000 in South Africa. Widely reintroduced even beyond former range. Some of the largest populations are located in Golden Gate Highlands National Park (>400) in the Free State and Mountain Zebra National Park (>300), near Cradock, in the Eastern Cape. There are more than 3 000 in various Free State provincial reserves, but by far the largest numbers (7 500) are kept on private land in that province. Of major concern is hybridization with Blue Wildebeest, and a number of populations are considered to be of dubious purity. A number of game farms run both species on the same property. Considerable numbers (± 7 000) are kept in Namibia, far outside of their traditional range.

Habitat: Low karoid scrub and open grassland.

Behaviour: Bulls set up territories and, during rut will attempt to 'herd' cows within their areas. Herds, consisting of cows and their young, normally wander freely over bull territories. Bulls mark their territories with urine, droppings and scent secretions, reinforcing the effect by performing elaborate displays. Bachelor herds consist of bulls of all ages. Although, in the wild, wildebeest tend to flee from humans, in captivity they can be extremely dangerous. We have recorded several cases of people being attacked by captive animals, which can inflict serious wounds in these encounters.

Food: Principally grasses but browse on occasion. Browse becomes particularly important during the dry winter months. This varies from area to area, but probably ranges from 5–30 per cent of intake during this time. On some game farms, access to grasses is limited, and browse intake may be higher than usual. Drinking water essential.

Reproduction: The majority of calves are dropped during the midsummer months but the peak period varies in different areas. A single calf (average 14 kg), dropped after a gestation of about 250 days, can move with the herd shortly after birth.

General: Also known as the White-tailed Gnu, the latter part of the name coming from the characteristic nasal call 'ge-nu'.

Black Wildebeest. Note the overall black appearance and the upward-curving horns; heavier in the bull than in the cow.

Black Wildebeest bull, showing the characteristic facial 'hair-brush' and long, horse-like white tail.

Black Wildebeest

90 mm

Front

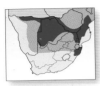

Connochaetes taurinus
■ Historical distribution

Blue Wildebeest
horn development

3 months

7 months

10 months

16 months

24 months

36 months

(after J. Kingdon, 1982)

■ **Blue Wildebeest** *Connochaetes taurinus*
Male: shoulder height 1.5 m; tail 60 cm; mass 250 kg.
Female: shoulder height 1.3 m; tail 60 cm; mass 180 kg.
Average horn length 60 cm; record horn length 86.05 cm (measured, like that of Black Wildebeest, from tip to tip along both horns).
Identification pointers: Forequarters higher and heavier than hindquarters; dark grey with some brown in younger animals and cows, with darker, vertical stripes on neck and chest; broad snout; superficially buffalo-like horns, but much lighter than African Buffalo (page 202). Distinguished by black tail (as opposed to white tail of Black Wildebeest, page 224).

Description: Blue Wildebeest has lightly built hindquarters and is more robust at the shoulders. The head is large with a broad snout. Adult animals are dark grey tinged with brown, and in certain light conditions a silvery sheen is discernible. A number of vertical, darker stripes are present from the neck to just behind the rib-cage; it is frequently referred to as the Brindled (brown-streaked) Gnu for this reason. There is a mane of long black hair down the back of the neck and a beard of black hair on the throat. The front of the face is almost black, although an area of brown hair may be present at the horn base, particularly in younger animals. The calf is rufous fawn with a darker face and a dark vertebral stripe. Both sexes have horns, although those of the cow are less robust. The horn bases form a boss over the top of the head and the horns themselves grow outwards, turn sharply up and then inwards. The tail is black and horse-like.

Distribution: Largely restricted to the northern areas of southern Africa but it has been introduced widely to reserves and farms further south. It extends from northern Namibia into southern Angola and western Zambia, with an isolated population in the Luangwa Valley. There is a break in distribution, with a separate population occurring in Tanzania and Kenya. In recent years, there has been a massive decline in numbers in Mozambique, as well as serious reductions in numbers in Botswana. In the former country, this can be ascribed to hunting levels and in the latter, because of the network of veterinary fences that criss-cross the country, preventing access to traditional migration routes.

Habitat: Preference for open savanna woodland and open grassland. Access to drinking water is essential.

Behaviour: Although Blue Wildebeest occur in herds of up to 30 individuals, much larger concentrations may be observed, numbering many thousands. These are formed during migrations to new feeding-grounds but the smaller herd units maintain their identity. Such mass movements still take place in Botswana but the erection of veterinary cordon fences in that country have disturbed a number of the traditional routes. Territorial bulls defend a zone around their cows, even when on the move. A bull may have between 2 and 150 cows with their young within his territorial control. Cows may move through the territories of a number of bulls and mate with more than one. Outside the mating season, the cow herds move freely and are not herded by territorial bulls. Bachelor herds are usually found around the edge of the main concentration. Blue Wildebeest are active by day but seek out shade during the hottest hours.

Food: Essentially grazers, showing a preference for short green grass.

Reproduction: The mating season is usually from March to June, with most calves dropped from mid-November to end-December, although this varies in different areas and may be influenced by factors such as drought or early rains. A single calf, weighing about 22 kg, is born after a gestation period of approximately 250 days. The calf is able to run with the mother a few minutes after birth.

Blue Wildebeest have to drink on a regular basis. They usually move in herds of up to 30 individuals.

Blue, or Black-bearded, Wildebeest cow and calves, drinking in Mkuzi Game Reserve, South Africa.

A Blue Wildebeest bull in the Kalahari.

Blue Wildebeest

100 mm

Front

Alcelaphus buselaphus
■ Historical distribution

Red Hartebeest
horn development

0–3 months

3–9 months

9–8 months

18–30 months

30–36⁺ months
(after O.B. Kok, 1975)

Alcelaphus lichtensteinii

■ **Red Hartebeest** *Alcelaphus buselaphus*
Shoulder height 1.25 m; tail 47 cm; mass 150 kg (bull), 120 kg (cow).
Average horn length 52 cm; record horn length 74.93 cm.
Identification pointers: Much higher at shoulder than at rump; golden-brown colour with black leg markings; long face with black blaze; unusual horn shape. Similar to Lichtenstein's Hartebeest (see below) but distributions do not overlap (see maps), and Tsessebe (page 232), but their horns are differently shaped.
Description: High-shouldered, awkward-looking antelope with long, pointed head. Body colour fawn to golden-brown, but darker from shoulders down centre of back to rump, particularly in bulls. Rump and upper thighs paler than rest of body. Black blaze down front of face and black markings on all four legs. Tail is pale at base, with black hair over remainder. Horns in both sexes; those of bull are heavier but both are set close together at the base, curving forwards and out and then twisting in and back.
Distribution: Now restricted to arid western parts of subregion, but formerly found as far south as Cape Town. Reintroduced widely within former range.
Habitat: Open savanna country and open woodland. Drinking water not essential.
Behaviour: Normally in herds numbering from about 20 to several hundred, occasionally thousands; larger groups usually forming at onset of summer rains. In arid areas, travels great distances in search of fresh grass. Adult bulls are territorial. Harem herds consisting of cows, young animals and a territorial bull occupy the best grazing, with bachelor herds having to make do with what is left. Mostly active by day.
Food: Mainly grasses but also browse, depending on season and conditions.
Reproduction: Single calf born away from herd, after gestation period of 240 days, usually in early summer. It remains hidden until it is strong enough to keep up with the other animals.

■ **Lichtenstein's Hartebeest** *Alcelaphus lichtensteinii*
Shoulder height 1.25 m; tail 48 cm; mass 170 kg (bull).
Average horn length 52 cm; record horn length 61.92 cm.
Identification pointers: Higher at shoulders than rump; yellow-tawny body colouring; characteristic Z-shaped horn. Compare with Tsessebe (page 232) where range overlaps.
Description: A clumsy-looking antelope with its shoulders higher than its hindquarters. Yellow-fawn body with slightly darker 'saddle' from shoulders to rump. Flanks and underparts are lighter with an off-white area on rump. Dark stripe runs down front of forelegs. Tail base is white but remainder of tail is covered in longish black hair. Both sexes have horns flattened at base, strongly ringed, except at the tips, with a Z-shaped curvature similar to those of Red Hartebeest.
Distribution: Occurs in Mozambique and south-eastern Zimbabwe. Introduced to Kruger National Park from Malawi.
Habitat: Savanna woodland where it abuts on vleis or floodplains. Access to surface water is essential.
Behaviour: Small herds of up to 10 individuals; occasionally larger groups. A territorial bull stays with a number of cows and calves within a fixed area. Bachelor herds subsist in less favourable habitat. Mainly active by day but partly nocturnal.
Food: Grasses, but occasionally browse from a range of tree species.
Reproduction: Single calf weighing about 15 kg is born after a gestation period of 240 days, usually in September. Can follow mother soon after birth but usually lies up between feeds; makes no attempt to hide.

A Red Hartebeest cow with a calf of approximately nine months old; the difference in horn development is evident.

Lichtenstein's Hartebeest has a limited distribution and occurs in small numbers in southern Africa.

Red Hartebeest

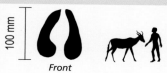

100 mm

Front

Lichtenstein's Hartebeest

■ *Damaliscus pygargus dorcas*
■ *Damaliscus pygargus phillipsi*

■ **Bontebok** *Damaliscus pygargus dorcas*
Shoulder height 90 cm; mass 62 kg (ram).
■ **Blesbok** *Damaliscus pygargus phillipsi*
Shoulder height 95 cm; mass 70 kg (ram).
Average horn length (both subspecies) 38 cm; record horn length 52.39 cm (Blesbok), 42.55 cm (Bontebok).
Identification pointers: Bontebok has a rich, dark-brown body colour with pure white buttocks, open white blaze from muzzle to between horns; Blesbok has a reddish-brown colour with pale brown buttock patch, white blaze on muzzle broken by brown between the eyes. No other hartebeest-like antelope has white on the face.
Description: The Bontebok and Blesbok are separate and distinct subspecies of *Damaliscus pygargus*. The differences between the two are outlined in the table below. Both subspecies are higher at the shoulder than at the rump and have long, pointed heads with both sexes carrying simple lyre-shaped horns. They are thus similar in general appearance to the other hartebeests and the Tsessebe. The ewe's horns are more slender than those of the ram.

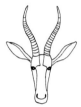

Bontebok showing continuous facial blaze

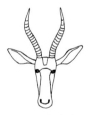

Blesbok showing broken facial blaze

	Bontebok	**Blesbok**
Body colour	Rich, dark brown with purple gloss, particularly rams; darker on sides and upper limbs	Reddish-brown; no gloss
Face	White blaze usually unbroken but narrows between eyes (This character not 100%)	White blaze usually broken by brown band between eyes (This character not 100%)
Buttocks	Always white	Usually pale but rarely white
Limbs	Lower part usually white	Rarely as white as in Bontebok
Horns	Usually black on upper ringed surface	Usually straw-coloured on upper ringed surface

Distribution: Bontebok historically restricted to the Bredasdorp and Mossel Bay areas of Western Cape. After near-extinction, now safe on several reserves and private farms. Largest single population occurs in De Hoop Nature Reserve near Bredasdorp. Blesbok occur throughout the central grasslands of the Free State, and in Eastern Cape, as well as marginally in KwaZulu-Natal. Both have been moved extensively outside their traditional range. (Largely uncontrolled transportation of the two subspecies into areas outside their traditional ranges has resulted in hybridization, where herds have been deliberately or accidentally mixed. This has resulted in an unknown number of populations being labelled as suspect as far as subspecies purity is concerned.)
Habitat: Bontebok: coastal plain within Cape fynbos vegetation zone; require short grass, water and some cover. Blesbok: open grassland with water.
Behaviour: Both Bontebok and Blesbok are diurnal, but are less active during hotter midday hours. Both characteristically stand head-down in groups facing the sun. Territorial Bontebok rams hold their areas throughout the year and ewe/lamb groups numbering some 6–10 wander at will through adjoining territories. Ewe groups are herded during January–March rut. Bachelor herds usually establish

Young Bontebok showing early stage of horn development.

Bontebok ram, showing glossy dark-brown colour.

Bontebok ewe showing continuous facial blaze.

Blesbok ram with characteristic broken blaze.

Bontebok
Blesbok

62 mm

Front

231

home ranges away from those held by territorial rams. Blesbok ewes move in harem herds numbering from 2–25, each herd attended by a territorial ram. Unlike Bontebok, where herd structure remains largely unchanged throughout the year, Blesbok do not occupy the same home range continuously, but come together in large mixed herds during the dry winter months.

Food: Grasses but will browse occasionally.

Reproduction: Most Bontebok lambs born September–October with a few being dropped as late as February. Most Blesbok lambs born November–January with a peak in December. Gestation period is approximately 240 days and the lamb has a mass of 6–7 kg at birth. It is pale fawn to creamy in colour and can run with the mother within 20–30 minutes of birth.

Damaliscus lunatus

Tsessebe *Damaliscus lunatus*

Shoulder height 1.2 m; tail 45 cm; mass 140 kg (bull), 126 kg (cow). Average horn length 34 cm; record horn length 46.99 cm.

Identification pointers: Higher at shoulder than rump; characteristic horn shape; head dark in contrast to reddish-brown body. See Red Hartebeest and Lichtenstein's Hartebeest (both page 228) where distributions overlap.

Description: Rather hartebeest-like in general appearance, with long face and sloping back. Upperparts dark reddish-brown with distinct purplish sheen, Bulls darker than cows. Head, lower shoulder and upper parts of legs darker in colour than rest of body. Lower parts of legs are brownish-yellow, with pale-fawn tail base and inner thighs. Black tassel on end half of tail. Both sexes have horns; lyrate and ringed except at the tip.

Distribution: Occurs patchily in north and north-eastern areas of subregion. Large herds of Tsessebe are never encountered in the subregion, but herds numbering in the thousands sometimes gather on the floodplain woodlands fringing the Bangweulu Swamp in north-eastern Zambia.

Habitat: Open savanna woodland with adjacent grassland and surface water.

Behaviour: Small herds of 5 or 6 individuals but sometimes number up to 30 or more, especially near water or favourable grazing. A territorial bull maintains a defended area, within which the cows and young animals live permanently.

Food: Grasses.

Reproduction: Single young, with a mass of 10–12 kg, born after gestation of 240 days, usually October–December. Calves run with the herd shortly after birth.

Aepyceros melampus

Impala *Aepyceros melampus*

Shoulder height 90 cm; tail 28 cm; mass 50 kg (ram), 40 kg (ewe). Average horn length 50 cm; record horn length 80.97 cm.

Identification pointers: Long, graceful, lyrate horns of the ram; black tuft of hair above the hoof on the rear surface of hindleg; thin black line down centre of white tail and vertical black line on each buttock.

Description: Medium-sized, lightly built antelope. Upperparts reddish-fawn becoming paler on sides; chest, belly, throat and chin are white. Tail is white with central black line on upper surface, and each buttock has vertical black blaze. Tuft of black hair on lower rear edge of hindleg is a characteristic unique to the Impala. Ears are black-tipped. Only rams carry the long graceful lyrate horns.

The Black-faced Impala (*Aepyceros melampus petersi*) of northern Namibia differs at subspecies level from the eastern populations of Impala (*A. melampus melampus*); black blaze down front of face of petersi is distinctive.

Distribution: Widespread in north-eastern areas of subregion and northwards

The Tsessebe is decreasing in numbers throughout its southern African range.

The Impala ram has lyre-shaped horns and tuft of black hair above the hoof.

A pair of watchful Impala ewes: note the black-tipped ears.
Inset: Black-faced Impala ewe.

Tsessebe
90 mm

Front

Front
47 mm

Impala

233

to Kenya. In South Africa, Impala have been widely introduced into areas far outside their natural range, including parts of the semi-arid Karoo, where they do particularly well. The greatest numbers occur in Limpopo, Mpumalanga and KwaZulu-Natal. An isolated subspecies, the Black-faced Impala (see 'Description' on page 232), is found in north-western Namibia and extending into Angola.

Habitat: Open or light savanna woodland; avoids open grassland unless there is scattered bush cover. Absent from mountains. Surface water must be available.

Behaviour: Rams are extremely vocal during the mating season and give vent to growls, roars and snorts. They are only territorial during the rut, from January to May, spending the rest of the time in bachelor herds. The home range of a breeding herd, consisting of ewes and young animals, may overlap with the territories of several territorial rams. Rams separate harem herds of 15–20 ewes (with their young) for mating. This disrupts the composition of the herds but they reunite at the conclusion of the rut. Bachelor herds tend to occupy areas away from the breeding herds. Impala are active mainly during the cooler daylight hours but there is some nocturnal activity.

Food: Short grasses and browse; proportions vary with area and season.

Reproduction: Single lamb, weighing approximately 5 kg, is born in early summer after gestation of 196 days.

Note: In the 1960s, the Black-faced Impala was threatened with extinction within its limited Namibian and Angolan range, and some 180 were captured and released in the south-west of Etosha National Park. They have since spread throughout the park and numbers are approaching 2 000 individuals. Common Impala have been introduced onto surrounding game farms and hybridization has taken place between the two subspecies.

Antidorcas marsupialis
■ Historical distribution

■ **Springbok** *Antidorcas marsupialis*
Shoulder height 75 cm; tail 25 cm; mass 41 kg (ram), 37 kg (ewe).
Average horn length (ram) 35 cm; record horn length (ram) 49.22 cm.
Identification pointers: Dark-brown band separating upper- from underparts; white head with brown stripe through eye to corner of mouth; short lyrate horns in both sexes; broad white crest on back visible when pronking.

Description: Hindquarters of this distinctive antelope appear to be slightly higher than shoulders. Dark red-brown band along flanks separates fawn-brown upperparts from white underparts. Head is white with a brown stripe running through eye to corner of upper lip. A large white patch on rump is bordered by brown stripe. A long-haired, white dorsal crest extends from the midpoint of the back to the rump; this is normally seen only when the crest is erected, for example, during 'pronking'. The pronk is a jump performed with stiff legs accompanied by arching of the back. Tail is white with tuft of black hairs at tip. Both sexes have heavily ridged, lyre-shaped horns but ram's are thicker and longer.

Distribution: More arid western areas of subregion and into Angola. Now one of South Africa's most important game-farming animals.

Habitat: Open, arid plains. Surface water not essential.

Behaviour: Normally in small herds but when moving to new feeding-grounds may congregate in herds of many thousands. Small herds may be mixed or consist of rams only; solitary rams are frequently encountered. Springbok rams are territorial and when in rut will herd ewe groups; they do not, however, remain in their territories throughout the year. Springbok are active during the cooler daylight hours but also partly at night.

Food: Grass and browse; will dig for roots and bulbs.

A 'creche' of Impala fawns rests in the shade during the heat of the day.

A Springbok ram; the dark band along the flank is clear.

A Springbok ewe; both sexes have lyrate horns.

Springbok

58 mm

Front

Reproduction: A single lamb weighing about 3.8 kg is born after a gestation period of about 168 days, usually during rains. Joins herd after 2 days.

General: Springbok are farmed for their venison and skins. Aberrant Springbok with white or black coats appear from time to time, and are often selectively bred by farmers as they fetch high prices at sales of game animals.

Madoqua damarensis

■ Damara Dik-dik *Madoqua damarensis*

Shoulder height 38 cm; tail 5 cm; mass 5 kg.

Average horn length 8 cm; record horn length 11.43 cm.

Identification pointers: Small size; elongated nose; crest of long hair on forehead. No similar species occur within southern African distribution range.

Description: Very small; characterized by having elongated, very mobile nose. Upperparts yellowish-grey with grizzled appearance; neck paler than shoulders and flanks. Underparts white to off-white. Tuft of long hair on forehead is erected when the Dik-dik is alarmed or displaying. Rams have short, spike-like horns that slope back at angle of facial profile.

Distribution: Central and north-western Namibia and into south-western Angola. A separate East African population is known as *Madoqua kirkii* (Kirk's Dik-dik).

Habitat: Damara Dik-dik show a strong preference for fairly dense, dry woodland. They penetrate deep into the Namib Desert along riverine woodland. Bush-covered hillsides and adjacent scrub are also occupied.

Behaviour: Usually single, in pairs or in small family parties. Pairs establish communal dung middens within home range; territorial. Nocturnal and diurnal.

Food: Although they are chiefly browsers they do take some grass during the rainy season. They will utilize leaves, pods and flowers knocked down by larger species, such as Elephant and Kudu.

Reproduction: After a gestation period of approximately 170 days, a single fawn with a mass of 620–760 g is dropped during the summer months.

Neotragus moschatus

■ Suni *Neotragus moschatus*

Shoulder height 35 cm; tail 12 cm; mass 5 kg.

Average horn length 8 cm; record horn length 13.34 cm.

Identification pointers: Very small size; constantly flicking white-tipped tail; pink-lined, translucent appearance of ears. Much smaller than Sharpe's Grysbok (page 242); while white flecks on the upperparts distinguish Suni from similar-sized Blue Duiker (page 244).

Description: Tiny, elegant antelope with rich rufous-brown upperparts flecked with white hairs, and white underparts. Two slightly curved white bars on throat. Above each hoof is narrow dark band. Tail fairly long and is dark brown above with a white tip and is regularly flicked from side to side. Pink-lined ears give the appearance of being almost transparent. Only ram has horns and these are quite thick, prominently transversely ridged and slope backwards in line with facial profile. Prominent gland in front of each eye of ram.

Distribution: Widespread in Mozambique, but occurs only marginally in northern KwaZulu-Natal, and south-east and north-east Zimbabwe. Because of the marginal nature of this antelope's range, there are only three substantial populations in South Africa: Thembe Elephant Reserve (>3 000); Phinda Resource Reserve (500) and False Bay Park (350), all in KwaZulu-Natal. There is probably a total of about 5 000 Suni in South Africa.

Habitat: Dry thickets and riverine woodland with dense underbrush.

Damara Dik-Dik ewe. Note the elongated, mobile nose. Inset: *Damara Dik-dik ram has short spike-like horns.*

Only the Suni ram carries short, straight and heavily ringed horns. Inset: *A Suni ewe; these animals frequent dry thickets.*

Damara
Dik-dik

21 mm

Front   *Back*

23 mm

Front   *Back*

Suni

Behaviour: Usually occur in pairs or small groups consisting of one adult ram and up to 4 ewes. Chiefly nocturnal but are probably also active during early mornings and late afternoons. When disturbed they take off in a rapid zigzag resembling that of a startled hare. They follow regular pathways and use communal dung-heaps.

Food: Principally browse, but take a wide range of plant food.

Reproduction: Single fawn (750 g) is born at any time of the year; gestation about 180 days. Remains hidden for several weeks, only emerging to suckle.

Oreotragus oreotragus

■ Klipspringer *Oreotragus oreotragus*
Shoulder height 60 cm; tail 8 cm; mass 10 kg (ram), 13 kg (ewe).
Average horn length 8 cm; record horn length (South Africa) 16.19 cm.
Identification pointers: Stocky appearance; short muzzle; walking on hoof-tips; associated with rocky areas where it displays great agility.

Description: A small, stocky antelope with coarse, spiny hair. Heavily built appearance is caused by hair standing on end instead of lying flat as with other antelope. General colour yellow-brown to grey-yellow, with an overall grizzled appearance. Underparts, chin and lips are white. Ears are rounded, broad and bordered with black. Only the ram has horns; these are short, widely separated at the base, vertically placed and ringed only near base. Characteristically walks on the tips of hoofs, the only antelope to do so.

Distribution: Wide but patchy distribution in rocky habitats.

Habitat: Rocky habitat only, crossing open plains between isolated rock outcrops.

Behaviour: Occur in pairs or small family groups. Adult ram is territorial. Extremely agile in moving across rocky terrain and up steep rock-covered slopes. Frequently stop to look back when running from a disturbance and both sexes give loud nasal alarm whistles. Use communal dung-heaps, which are usually situated on flat areas. Active in morning and in later afternoon but throughout day when cool.

Food: Predominantly browse, but grass taken occasionally.

Reproduction: Klipspringer probably give birth at any time of the year. A single lamb weighing about 1 kg is born after a gestation period of 210 days (some give this as low as 150 days). The lamb remains hidden for 2–3 months after birth.

General: Popular opinion has it that the Klipspringer's coarse, bristly, hollow hair has a cushioning function when the animal falls. However, it is more likely that it serves as a heat regulator. Klipspringer hair was once prized for stuffing saddles.

Raphicerus campestris

■ Steenbok *Raphicerus campestris*
Shoulder height 50 cm; tail 5 cm; mass 11 kg.
Average horn length 9 cm; record horn length 19.05 cm.
Identification pointers: Small size; large ears; clearly demarcated reddish-fawn upperparts and white underparts; very short tail; only ram has short, vertical horns. Could be confused with Oribi, but the latter is larger, has smaller ears, longer neck, a black tail tuft and the Oribi ram's horns are ridged for part of their length. Also see Cape and Sharpe's Grysbok (both page 242).

Description: Small, elegant, large-eyed antelope, normally rufous-fawn above but varies from pale fawn to reddish-brown. Underparts including insides of legs are pure white, and there is a white patch on throat and above eyes. Very short rufous-fawn tail. Only ram carries short, sharp-pointed, smooth-surfaced, vertical horns.

Distribution: Widespread in subregion; separate population in East Africa. The East African range is much smaller than that of the southern African populations, being restricted to southern Kenya and the adjacent area of Tanzania. It is believed that the original separation of the species was a consequence of the

The Klipspringer ram has short, widely separated horns.

The Klipspringer ewe does not carry horns.

The Steenbok ram carries straight, sharp-pointed, smooth-surfaced vertical horns; the ears and eyes are large.
Inset: A Steenbok ram testing an ewe for readiness to mate.

Klipspringer

20 mm

Front

Steenbok

40 mm

Front   Back

dry climatic conditions that prevailed during the Pleistocene and linked north and south, being replaced by a higher rainfall regime that created the wooded belt across southern central Africa. This dense woodland, known as Miombo, was unsuitable for Steenbok, which retreated from this area, or died out.

Habitat: Open country, with some cover. In arid areas inhabit dry river-beds.

Behaviour: Occur singly or in pairs. Territorial. Unlike other small antelope, Steenbok defecate and urinate in shallow scrapes dug by front hooves, then covered. These latrines, or toilet sites, appear to be mainly located around the perimeter of territories, and serve a marking role. Steenbok have glands between the hooves, on the throat and in front of each eye; it is presumed the secretions from these glands also play a role in marking territories. Steenbok lie up in cover during the heat of day, feeding in the early morning and late afternoon; they are also active at night, particularly in areas where they suffer disturbance.

Food: Mixed feeders taking grasses, browse, seed-pods and fruit; digs for roots and bulbs with the front hoofs, but browse is the most important food source.

Reproduction: Single lamb, approximately 900 g, born after gestation of 170 days at any time of the year, but usually summer. Remains hidden up to 3 months.

Ourebia ourebi

█ Oribi *Ourebia ourebi*

Shoulder height 60 cm; tail 6–15 cm; mass 14 kg.

Average horn length 10 cm; record horn length 19.05 cm.

Identification pointers: Steenbok-like but larger; yellow-orange rufous above, white below; short, black-tipped tail; long neck. The ram has erect, partly ridged horns, unlike the smooth horns of the Steenbok ram.

Description: Largest of the 'small' antelope. Upperparts rufous yellow-orange and underparts white. White hair extends onto front of chest. Relatively long neck, medium-sized ears and short tail with distinguishing black tip. Has pale throat patch and off-white areas on either side of nostrils and above eyes. Hair on back and underparts may have a curly appearance, particularly during winter. Only ram has horns and these are short, erect and partly ridged.

Distribution: Widely separated areas in eastern and northern parts of subregion. Widespread in sub-Saharan Africa.

Habitat: Open short grassland with taller grass patches for cover.

Behaviour: Occur in pairs or small parties consisting of one ram and up to four ewes. The ram is vigorously territorial. Communal dung-heaps serve a territorial marking function. When disturbed Oribi give a sharp whistle or sneeze and run off rapidly with occasional stiff-legged jumps displaying black-tipped tail. Inquisitive, however, and will turn to look back at source of disturbance after running a short distance. Also lies down in taller grass if disturbed, with head erect; in this position they are difficult to detect.

Food: Principally grazers but occasionally browse, with a marked preference for short grass, moving if grass becomes too long. Independent of drinking water.

Reproduction: Births have been recorded throughout the year but the majority of lambs are dropped during the wet summer months. A single lamb is born after a gestation period of about 210 days. The lamb remains hidden for as long as 3–4 months before joining the group.

Note: Oribi are endangered in South Africa. The largest populations (totalling some 3 000 individuals) occur in the Drakensberg fringes and KwaZulu-Natal Midlands. Small populations in Eastern Cape number perhaps 500 antelope. Threats include destruction of, or changing, habitat, poor veld-burning practices, illegal hunting with dogs and increased predation by Black-backed Jackal and Caracal.

Steenbok ewes do not carry horns; both sexes have a pale to white ring around the eye.

An Oribi ewe showing the short, black tail and the fairly long dorsal hair. Inset: Only the Oribi ram carries horns.

Oribi

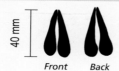

40 mm

Front   Back

Raphicerus melanotis

■ Cape Grysbok *Raphicerus melanotis*
Shoulder height 54 cm; tail 5.5 cm; mass 10 kg.
Average horn length 8 cm; record horn length 13.34 cm.
Identification pointers: Similar to Sharpe's Grysbok (see below) but distribution ranges do not overlap (see maps). Brown underparts and rufous-brown upperparts flecked with white distinguish it from Steenbok (page 238).
Description: A small, squat antelope characterized by rufous-brown upperparts abundantly flecked with white hairs. Flanks and neck have fewer white hairs and underparts are lighter brown than upperparts. Tail very short and grey-brown ears are proportionately large with white hairs on inside. Only ram has short, smooth, slightly back-angled horns. Pair of 'false hoofs' above the fetlock.
Distribution: Restricted to a narrow belt along south-western and southern coastal belt and the adjacent interior.
Habitat: An inhabitant of relatively thick scrub-bush, it is almost entirely restricted to the fynbos vegetation. It is found in a variety of situations, from scrub-covered sand-dunes to wooded gorges on mountain slopes. In the areas where it enters the extreme southern Karoo, it can be found along rivers and on scrub-covered hillsides. It is frequently found along the fringes of agricultural land where belts of natural vegetation remain.
Behaviour: Mainly nocturnal but active in early morning and late afternoon if not disturbed, or on overcast and cool days. Usually single except when mating or when ewes are tending lambs. Males territorial; range size dictated by season.
Food: It is mainly a browser but will take fresh grass. In the south-western Cape vineyards it is considered to be a nuisance as it eats the young grapes and terminal buds. Also feeds in rooibos tea plantations.
Reproduction: Although lambs may be dropped at any time of the year, most are born from September to December. A single lamb is born after a gestation period of approximately 180 days.

■ Sharpe's Grysbok *Raphicerus sharpei*
Shoulder height 50 cm; tail 6 cm; mass 7.5 kg.
Average horn length 6 cm; record length 10.48 cm (6.35 cm for subregion).
Identification pointers: Similar to Cape Grysbok but distribution ranges do not overlap (see maps). The white freckling and buff underparts distinguish it from the Steenbok (page 238). Although larger and distinct in other ways, it could possibly be confused with Suni (page 236) where ranges overlap.

Raphicerus sharpei

Description: Small, stoutly built antelope with reddish-brown upperparts liberally flecked with white hairs. Incidence of white hairs diminishes down sides and legs. Underparts are buff-white, and area around mouth and eyes is off-white. Only the ram has the short, sharp, slightly back-angled horns. 'False hoofs' are normally absent (see Cape Grysbok, above).
Distribution: Restricted to the north-eastern parts of southern Africa, and then northwards into Malawi, Zambia, Tanzania and southern Congo.
Habitat: Sharpe's Grysbok requires good vegetation cover, preferring low thicket with adjacent open patches of grass. It is also found on vegetated rocky hills and in the scrub at their base.
Behaviour: Sharpe's Grysbok is almost entirely nocturnal but can be seen in the coolness of the early morning and late afternoon. Although usually seen singly, it is possible that a pair may live in loose association within a home range. The rams are probably territorial. Because of its largely nocturnal activity and secretive nature, very little is known about this small antelope.

Cape Grysbok ram; note the white flecked coat.

Sharpe's Grysbok ewe.

Sharpe's Grysbok ram, showing the reddish-brown coat flecked with white hairs.

Sharpe's Grysbok

34 mm

Front

34 mm

Front *Back*

Cape Grysbok

243

Food: Mostly browse but also grass. It will take fruits, berries and pods.

Reproduction: Lambs may be dropped at any time of the year but more are probably born during the wet summer months than in any other season. A single lamb is born after a gestation period of approximately 200 days.

Cephalophus natalensis

■ Red Duiker *Cephalophus natalensis*
Shoulder height 43 cm; tail 11 cm; mass 14 kg.
Average horn length 6 cm; record horn length 10.48 cm.

Identification pointers: Uniform rich reddish-brown coat; small size; black-and-white tipped tail; prominent crest on top of head. Lacks the white flecking of either Sharpe's Grysbok or Suni (page 236). Walks with a 'hunchback' gait.

Description: A small, thickset antelope with relatively short legs. The general colour is rich reddish-brown, with underparts being slightly paler, and chin and throat paler than rest of the body. Although short, the tail is the same colour as the body at the base, with a well-developed tuft of mixed black-and-white hairs. A long crest is present on top of the head, sometimes obscuring the short horns. Both sexes have horns, which slope backwards at the same angle as the face.

Distribution: Occurs along the eastern coastal plain with an isolated population in the Soutpansberg range of northern South Africa. It occurs as far north as southern Sudan and Somalia.

Habitat: Forest and dense woodland with permanent water.

Behaviour: Because of the dense habitat that it favours, and its secretive nature, little is known about this duiker's behaviour. It is usually solitary but it seems probable that a pair may live in loose association within the same home range. The dung pellets are deposited in specific areas and there are often many small piles of currant-sized pellets at these sites. Mainly active in daylight.

Food: They are browsers, taking leaves, shoots, fruits and berries.

Reproduction: Fawns are probably dropped at any time of the year but peak in the summer months. Single fawn (<1 kg) after gestation of about 210 days.

Cephalophus monticola

■ Blue Duiker *Cephalophus monticola*
Shoulder height 30 cm; tail 8 cm; mass 4 kg.
Average horn length 3 cm; record horn length 7.3 cm.

Identification pointers: Smallest southern African antelope; grey to brown coloration with blue-grey sheen. Short horns in both sexes. Skulking nature.

Description: The smallest antelope occurring in southern Africa. The upperparts vary from slate-grey to dark brown with a grey-blue sheen and the underparts are white or off-white. A constantly wagging tail is characteristic of this duiker. The tail is quite long, bushy and black, bordered with white. Short horns are present in both sexes but these are often hidden by the crest of hair on top of the head.

Distribution: Apart from a population in Mozambique and eastern Zimbabwe, the Blue Duiker is only found in the subregion in a narrow belt along the coast from George in the south to KwaZulu-Natal. It occurs widely in central and equatorial Africa and patchily in East Africa.

Habitat: Blue Duiker are confined to forests and dense stands of bush. They utilize open glades when feeding. Water is an essential habitat requirement.

Behaviour: It usually occurs singly, or in pairs during courtship. It is very timid and is rarely seen, its dung-pellet heaps usually being the only indication of its presence. The level of disturbance probably influences times of activity but it is known to feed both at night and during the day. It uses regular pathways to feeding- and drinking-sites.

Red Duiker ewe; note the short black-and-white tail and slit-like gland in front of the eye.

The Blue Duiker's large preorbital gland is used for scent-marking.

The Blue Duiker is the smallest of the duikers; the colouring varies from slate-grey to dark-brown and the underparts are white to off-white.

Red Duiker

30 mm

Front

Blue Duiker

24 mm

Front   Back

245

Food: The Blue Duiker is a browser, and includes fruits and berries in its diet.
Reproduction: The young are born throughout the year with a possible peak in the summer months. A single lamb weighing approximately 400 g is born after a gestation period of about 200 days; some sources say as low as 165 days.

Sylvicapra grimmia

■ **Common Duiker** *Sylvicapra grimmia*
Shoulder height 50 cm; tail 12 cm; mass 18 kg (ram), 21 kg (ewe).
Average horn length 11 cm; record horn length (South Africa) 18.1 cm.
Identification pointers: Crest of long hair usually present on top of head; uniform grey-brownish colouring of upperparts and paler underparts; usually black blaze (vertical stripe) on face; fairly short tail – black above and white below. Ears are long and somewhat narrow.
Description: Uniform grey-brown to reddish-yellow upperparts, with paler (sometimes white) underparts. Black blaze of variable length on face. Short tail, black above and white below. Front surfaces of slender forelegs are dark brown or black. On top of head there is usually a crest of long hair. Ram has well-ringed, sharp-pointed horns.
Distribution: Found throughout subregion.
Habitat: Wide range of habitats but prefers scrub and bush-covered country.
Behaviour: Usually single but sometimes pairs. Active in early morning and late afternoon but also at night. Lies low when disturbed but on too-close approach takes off at a fast zigzag run. Home ranges extend from 6 to 27 ha.
Food: Wide variety of browse species; also agricultural crops; some animal food.
Reproduction: Single 1.6-kg lamb may be born in any month after 190 days.

DEER | Family Cervidae

■ **European Fallow Deer** *Cervus dama* (introduced)
Shoulder height 90 cm; mass (male) 95 kg.
Identification pointers: Distinctive white spotting; males carry branched antlers for much of the year. Restricted to enclosed farms, but numerous escapes.
Description: Variable in colour and patterning, with the summer coat being rich yellowish-fawn above, spotted boldly in white. White stripe along each flank. Underside of tail and surrounding areas conspicuously white. Underparts and inner leg areas are pale. Winter coat duller and hair longer. Males carry antlers shed during midsummer months to make way for new set.
Distribution: Introduced from Europe to private farms in South Africa.
Habitat: Open woodland to scrub or grassland.
Behaviour: Adult buck establish territories during the rut and form harem herds. Outside rut sexes are separate.
Food: Principally browse but also grass.
Reproduction: Usually single fawn born in summer, but sometimes twins.

Introduced species: In recent years, serious efforts have been made to eradicate the Himalayan Tahr from the Table Mountain range in Cape Town. By 2006 only a handful of animals remained and efforts to remove them are ongoing.

Other problem introductions to be watched are feral populations of Barbary Sheep in the Karoo, and Mouflon elsewhere. Both species are ideally suited to semi-arid conditions and escapes are highly likely.

Common, or Grey, Duiker ram.

Common Duiker ewe.

Fallow Deer doe in summer coat.

Fallow Deer stags shed their antlers in autumn.

Fallow Deer doe in winter coat.

Common Duiker

38 mm

Front

65 mm

Front   *Back*

Fallow Deer

Key to Marine Mammals maps:
- ■ *Common or frequent distribution*
- ■ *Rare or occasional distribution*
- ? *Unknown distribution*
- ✖ *Strandings on the mainland*

MARINE MAMMALS

SEALS | Order Carnivora

FUR SEALS | Family Otariidae

Only three species of fur seal have been recorded from southern African waters, one as a permanent resident and the others as rare vagrants. The Antarctic Fur Seal (*Arctocephalus gazella*) is recorded from the Southern Ocean islands that fall under South African jurisdiction (namely the Prince Edward Islands) and one individual recently recorded from South Africa.

Arctocephalus pusillus
Crosses indicate principal breeding grounds.

■ **Cape Fur Seal** *Arctocephalus pusillus*
Male: length 2.2 m; mass 190 kg. Female: length 1.6 m; mass 75 kg.
Identification pointers: Large size; only seal likely to be encountered in southern African waters, along west coast and as far east along south coast as East London. Males lack crest on top of head found in Sub-Antarctic Fur Seal.
Description: Males much larger than females (up to 300 kg in summer), with powerfully developed necks. When moving on land hindlimbs are brought forward to support some of body mass and forelimbs bend out and slightly backwards. Dark brown to golden brown but tend to be darker. Coarse outer hair of bulls may be greyish-black with a tinge of brown. Females tend to be more brownish-grey. Newborn pups have black velvety coat.
Distribution: Offshore islands and along parts of the mainland of the western and southern coastline to Port Elizabeth but rarely as far as East London.
Behaviour and Reproduction: Within southern African waters there are estimated to be well over one million fur seals in some 25 breeding colonies. In mid-October mature bulls move to the breeding sites to establish territories and these are actively defended against rival bulls. The cows arrive several weeks later to give birth. A territorial bull establishes a harem of several cows. Mating takes place about 5 or 6 days after the cow has given birth. The territories and harems break up before the end of December. Can dive to at least 200 m.
Food: Shoaling fish such as pilchards; other fish, squid and crustaceans.

Arctocephalus tropicalis

■ **Sub-Antarctic Fur Seal** *Arctocephalus tropicalis*
Male: total length 1.8 m; mass 120–165 kg. Female: total length 1.4 m; mass 50 kg.
Identification pointers: Yellow-brown face and chest lighter than rest of body and contrast with brown upperparts. Males have crest and cape of long hair on top of head – a feature not found in Cape Fur Seal.
Description: Similar in form to Cape Fur Seal but differs in colouring. The upperparts are variable grey-brown to brown, with the head, shoulders and flippers being darker and the face and chest being yellow-brown or creamy brown. Mature bulls have a crest and cape of long hair on the head and shoulders.
Distribution: They occur in sub-Antarctic waters and haul out on small oceanic islands such as Gough and the Prince Edward islands. Vagrants occasionally haul out on the coastline of South Africa and Namibia.
Behaviour and Reproduction: This species does not breed within southern African waters. Behaviour, however, is similar to that of Cape Fur Seal. Most pups are born in mid-December.
Food: Squid and fish seem to be of equal importance, but crustaceans are occasionally taken.

A Cape Fur Seal cow in an onshore breeding colony. Inset: *Note the pointed ears.*

Sub-Antarctic Fur Seals breed on islands in the southern Atlantic, but occasionally come ashore along our coastline.
Inset: *Antarctic Fur Seals are known to haul out on the Prince Edward Islands in the Southern Ocean.*

Cape Fur Seal

Sub-Antarctic Fur Seal

Antarctic Fur Seal

TRUE SEALS | Family Phocidae

Three species of true seal have been recorded along the coastline of southern Africa, but all as rare vagrants. Leopard Seal (page 252) has only been recorded twice on the southern African mainland. Weddell Seal (*Leptonychotes weddellii*) has never been recorded on the southern African mainland but there is a record from the South African-administered Marion Island, in the South Atlantic Ocean. As there are records from Uruguay and Australia, it is possible that the Weddell Seal could, in time, be recorded on the South African coastline.

Mirounga leonina

■ Southern Elephant Seal *Mirounga leonina*

Male: total length 4.5–6.5 m; mass 3 500 kg. Female: total length 3.0–4.0 m; mass 350–800 kg.

Identification pointers: Massive size, particularly in the case of bulls; bulls also have swollen, prominent snout.

Description: This is the largest of all living seals. The massive bulls have a short, prominent, bulbous proboscis, which projects from just below the eye and hangs over the mouth. This organ can be inflated during threat displays. Fur colour is usually greyish-brown to brown but in mature males, and before the moult, the fur takes on a yellowish-brown colour. Old bulls are usually heavily scarred on the head and shoulders from territorial fighting.

Distribution: This seal has a circumpolar distribution, largely restricted to a belt of sub-Antarctic waters extending to the southern tip of South America. Vagrants occasionally beach on the southern African coastline. More than 50 records.

Behaviour and Reproduction: The Elephant Seal moults on land, remaining there throughout the duration of the moult. Adult bulls spend much of the winter at sea. In spring they haul out on island beaches for mating. Mature bulls arrive first to establish the territories in which they will keep their harems of cows. The pregnant cows haul out shortly after the bulls and the pups conceived the year before are born within about one week of their arrival. The females come on heat 2–3 weeks after the pups are born and are mated by their harem bull.

Food: Southern Elephant Seals feed mostly on squid and fish but some crustaceans are also taken. When hunting, they can dive to depths of 1 200 m and remain submerged for more than an hour.

Lobodon carcinophagus

■ Crabeater Seal *Lobodon carcinophagus*

Total length 2.3–2.7 m; mass 250 kg.

Identification pointers: Sleek, long body; usually silvery-grey but no prominent markings; distinctly serrated edge to each cheek-tooth. Vagrants in southern African waters, with less than 20 records.

Description: This slender and agile seal has a general body colour of silvery grey-fawn with paler underparts. Numerous brown markings are scattered on the shoulders and sides of younger animals. The flippers are darker than the rest of the body. The fur becomes creamy-white towards the moult and older animals become paler with age. The cheek-teeth have up to 6 cusps each and have a distinctive saw-like profile. When the jaws are closed the teeth interlock neatly and are used to sieve out the small crustaceans upon which this seal feeds.

Distribution: Crabeater Seal is by far the most abundant seal in the world and is confined to the pack-ice zone around Antarctica. Hauls out rarely on the southern African coast.

Behaviour and Reproduction: It is estimated there are between 30 and 50 million Crabeater Seals in Antarctica. Despite their abundance, the harsh environment

Southern Elephant Seal bull: note the short, prominent proboscis from which the common name is derived.

Crabeater Seal is mainly found in the pack-ice zone around Antarctica, rarely hauling out in southern African waters.

Southern Elephant Seal

Crabeater Seal

251

in which they live makes them extremely difficult to study and therefore little is known about them. In contrast to Fur Seals and Elephant Seals, during the breeding season Crabeater Seals associate in family pairs, comprising mother and newborn pup, with an attendant bull waiting nearby for the female to come into oestrus after the birth. Between September and November, the pups are born on ice-floes. Outside of the breeding season, Crabeater Seals form large or small groups of both sexes.

Food: Despite their name, Crabeater Seals do not eat crabs but feed almost exclusively on krill, a small crustacean that abounds in Antarctic waters. Their technique is to swim into a krill shoal with open mouth and then close their jaws, forcing the water out between closely fitting teeth and swallowing the krill that remains in the mouth. Feed mostly at night. Some squid and fish also eaten.

Hydrurga leptonyx

■ Leopard Seal *Hydrurga leptonyx*
Male: total length 3.5 m; mass 300 kg. Female: total length 4.0 m; mass 450 kg.
Identification pointers: Sleek; silvery-grey above, white below; numerous dark spots especially on throat, shoulders and sides; only two records from the coast of southern Africa.

Description: These are slender, agile seals, with silvery-grey fur on the upperparts and (usually) white fur on the underparts. There is a liberal scattering of darker grey to black spots, particularly on the sides, throat and shoulders. The head is long and slender and it has a large 'gape'.

Distribution: Predominantly a species of the Antarctic pack-ice, but in winter and spring it moves towards the sub-Antarctic islands.

Behaviour and Reproduction: The Leopard Seal is a solitary species, which spends summer and autumn around the pack-ice and which tends to disperse towards the small mid-oceanic islands of the sub-Antarctic in winter and spring. Little is known about its reproduction.

Food: Leopard Seal takes a wide variety of food items, predominantly penguins, but also fish, squid and krill, and the young (possibly also adults) of other seals.

■ Weddell Seal *Leptonychotes weddellii*
Total length 2.8–3.0 m; mass 360–400 kg.
Identification pointers: Not as streamlined as Crabeater Seal; relatively small head; dark brown-grey to almost black above; white streaks and splashes on sides; underparts mainly white.

Description: Stoutly built, with rather small head. Upperparts are dark and sides are flecked and splashed with pale-grey to white. Underparts are predominantly white to pale-greyish blotched. Female slightly larger than male.

Distribution: This seal is largely restricted to the inshore rim of Antarctica. It is the most southerly occurring of the seals. One live specimen found on Marion Island, a South African possession. Records from Uruguay, Chile, New Zealand and Australia indicate that, in time, it might beach on the South African mainland.

Behaviour and Reproduction: Difficult to assess, but probably number at least 500,000. Pregnant cows concentrate from August, dropping single pups in September or October. In winter, most time is spent in the water under the ice. Breathing holes are kept open by regular sawing with the teeth.

Food: Mainly fish.

Penguins comprise a major part of the Leopard Seal's diet.

Leopard Seals live amongst the pack ice of Antarctica, moving towards the sub-Antarctic islands in winter and spring.
Inset: *Weddell Seal occurs mainly in Antarctica.*

Leopard Seal

Weddell Seal

253

WHALES & DOLPHINS | Order Whippomorpha |
Suborder Cetacea

Baleen or Whalebone Whales | Infraorder Mysticeti
Nine species of baleen whales have been recorded off the coastline of southern Africa.

RORQUALS (PLEATED WHALES) | Family Balaenopteridae
Long, slender, streamlined whales with flattened heads, pointed flippers and a small, back-curved dorsal fin set far back along body. Rorquals are characterized by a large number of grooves, or pleats, running longitudinally from throat and chest to upper abdomen.

Balaenoptera acutorostrata

■ **Dwarf Minke Whale** *Balaenoptera acutorostrata*
Total length 8 m; mass 6–8 t.
Identification pointers: Smallest of the rorquals; white patch on upper flipper surface. Flippers of Humpback Whale (page 258) are much longer and usually more white. Indistinct blow.
Description: This, the smallest of the rorquals, has 1–3 ridges running along top of head. Upperparts are dark blue-grey to almost black, with lighter-coloured whitish underparts. Flippers sometimes have a bright white patch on upper surface, extending on to body, and very occasionally are wholly white. Tail-flukes are rarely raised above the water. 52–60 throat grooves.
Distribution: Worldwide. Infrequently off southern African coast and rarely comes to shore; usually off continental shelf.
Behaviour: Singly or in pairs but larger groups at feeding-grounds.
Food: Krill and to a lesser extent small fish and squid.
Reproduction: Approximately 2-m calf born after 10-month gestation period.
Note: Antarctic Minke Whale (*Balaenoptera bonaerensis*) slightly larger, to 10 tons, females to almost 10 m. Similar to Dwarf but lacks white flipper patch. Tends to remain well offshore and does not extend as far north into tropical waters. Relatively recently added to the subregion's mammal inventory, but probably a case of being overlooked in the past.

Balaenoptera edeni
Dark blue indicates
population concentrations.

Balaenoptera borealis

■ **Bryde's Whale** *Balaenoptera edeni*
Total length 12–14 m; mass 13 t (to 24 t).
■ **Sei Whale** *Balaenoptera borealis*
Total length 15–16 m; mass 14–16 t (to 26 t).
Identification pointers: Medium to large size; Bryde's Whale has three ridges on top of head; only one in Sei Whale. Two forms of Bryde's Whale have been recognized in South African waters, a smaller, resident form and a larger form that is migratory and stays in deeper water beyond the continental shelf. (Globally, Bryde's Whale may yet be found to be a complex of species.)
Description: Sei Whale is a slender blue-black whale with white band from chin to abdomen, broadening dorsally. Throat grooves stretch back to flippers. Bryde's Whale similar but light-grey underparts. The main distinguishing character is that there are 3 ridges on head of Bryde's Whale from around the blowholes to the tip of the snout, and only one (the median ridge common to most baleen whales) on the head of the Sei Whale. These whales submerge gently and their flukes and flippers do not show when they dive down from the surface. Bryde's Whale usually has around 45 throat grooves; Sei Whale has 60–65 throat grooves.

Dwarf Minke Whale, the smallest of the rorquals, has a white patch on the upper flipper surface.

Bryde's Whale has three ridges on the top of the head, extending from around the blowholes to the tip of the snout.

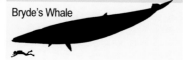

Dwarf Minke Whale

Bryde's Whale

Sei Whale

255

Distribution: Sei Whale worldwide but Bryde's largely restricted to tropics and adjacent waters. Some Bryde's resident off southern African coast. Sei Whale is a deep-water species and rarely observed from land.

Behaviour: Both species are usually encountered in small pods of about 5 or 6 individuals but both may form groups numbering more than 100. Bryde's Whale is often seen close inshore.

Food: Both species feed on planktonic crustaceans and small fish, with Bryde's Whale off the west coast, for example, taking shoaling fish such as pilchards.

Reproduction: Sei Whale calves, born in June and July, measure about 4.5 m at birth; those of Bryde's Whale are about 50 cm shorter at birth. Bryde's Whale may be a seasonal breeder, but the inshore form is aseasonal.

Balaenoptera physalus

■ Fin Whale   *Balaenoptera physalus*
Total length 25 m; mass 40–50 t (to 90 t).

Identification pointers: Large size; dark upperparts and light to white underparts with the right lower jaw being white, the left black. Rear end raised before diving but flukes not raised above water. Fin appears after the blow.

Description: Second-largest living mammal. Unique colour pattern. Upperparts are dark grey and underparts lighter or white, but right lower jaw, right front baleen plates and undersides of flippers and flukes are white; left half of lower jaw is black and left-side baleen plates are bluish-grey. The asymmetrical colour pattern of the lower jaw gives it a somewhat twisted or lop-sided appearance. There are 50–60 throat grooves.

Distribution: Worldwide. Not usually seen offshore.

Behaviour: Occurs in groups of 6–15, but very rarely up to 100.

Food: Krill, fish and squid.

Reproduction: One 6.5-m calf born in warmer waters during winter.

Balaenoptera musculus

■ Blue Whale   *Balaenoptera musculus*
Total length 25–33 m; mass 100–120 t (to 160 t).

Identification pointers: Massive size; blue-grey colour with lighter mottling. When diving, performs a smooth, even roll with no humping; the tail-flukes emerge shallowly and briefly. Fin only shows in dive.

Description: Largest mammal on Earth. Upperparts blue-grey mottled with light-grey spots; underparts of body and under-surface of flippers much lighter in colour. There are 88–94 throat grooves. Dorsal fin small and set very far back; not exposed while blowing but may be seen when whale dives. Flukes show briefly just above surface when diving. Blow may reach a height of 12 m.

Distribution: Worldwide.

Behaviour: Usually occurs singly or in groups of 3 or 4 but up to 50 have been seen together. Southern hemisphere populations migrate to Antarctic waters in summer to feed on krill, returning to warmer waters in the winter to breed.

Food: Various species of krill, especially *Euphausia superba*.

Reproduction: A single calf, up to 7 m, weighing 2.5 t, born during early winter after a gestation of 11 months.

Fin Whale

Sei Whale has 60–65 throat grooves.

Fin Whale has dark grey upperparts and white underparts.

Blue Whale, the largest mammal in the world, can measure over 30 m – nearly one-third the length of a football field.

Blue Whale

Megaptera novaeangliae
Dark blue indicates the migration routes between Antarctica and the tropical breeding grounds.

Humpback Whale tail fluke (*top*) and flipper (*above*).

■ Humpback Whale *Megaptera novaeangliae*

Total length 15 m; mass 35–45 t.

Identification pointers: Very long flippers, white below, and variable black or white or both above; body dark above, light to white below including flukes. Dorsal fin shows when blowing; when diving, flukes raised high above water. Often shows flippers and jumps clear of water.

Description: Humpback easily distinguishable from other rorquals because of less streamlined appearance, small dorsal fin situated further forward than in other members of this group, knobbly head and extremely long flippers which may measure up to one-third of body length. Leading edges of flippers are serrated and may be partly or entirely white. Upperparts of Humpback are dark-grey to black and underparts are usually dark although throat grooves are white. 30 or fewer throat grooves – considerably fewer than in other baleen whales.

Distribution: Worldwide. Occurs off the coast in midwinter and in spring.

Behaviour: In the southern hemisphere they migrate from their Antarctic feeding-grounds to overwinter and breed in tropical waters. They remain in warmer waters for a short period before moving southwards again.

Food: Mainly krill/plankton feeders, but they also take shoaling fish.

Reproduction: Calves are born in tropical waters during winter after a gestation period of almost one year. At birth, the calf measures about 4.5 m; during the first 10 months of life, it doubles in length.

RIGHT WHALES | Families Balaenidae and Neobalaenidae

Right Whales, of which one species occurs in southern African waters, were so called because they are slow-moving and were easily caught by early whalers; when killed they floated, allowing the whalers to tow the carcasses to land, hence they were the 'right' whales to hunt. They are characterized by their large heads with arched jaw-line and smooth ungrooved throat.

Eubalaena australis
Although these whales can be expected in waters off much of southern Africa, the main concentration is located between Cape Town and Port Elizabeth, from May to October.

■ Southern Right Whale *Eubalaena australis*

Total length 14–18 m; mass 60 t (to 180 t).

Identification pointers: Large size; no dorsal fin; lumpy white growths on head; broad-tipped flippers; very large flukes; overall dark colour with occasional white patches on underparts; no throat grooves. Blows when much of back exposed, and when diving the flukes are clear of water. Flippers often seen. V-shaped blow. Frequently seen close inshore in South Africa.

Description: This is a relatively easy whale to identify. There is no dorsal fin, there are no grooves or pleats on the throat, the flukes are large and pointed at the tips and the head is very large with a deeply arched jaw-line. The head and back are more or less on the same level. The flippers are broad-tipped. A distinguishing character is the presence of numerous white callosities on the head; the largest (the 'bonnet') is situated at the front of the snout. The overall body colour is dark grey-black with occasional white markings on the underparts.

Distribution: Circumpolar north and south of the tropics. This is the easiest large whale to observe close inshore in South African waters (from May to December). Some of the best viewing sites are Hermanus (Walker Bay), the inshore trough at De Hoop Nature Reserve near Bredasdorp, Mossel Bay (especially from Reebok and Tergniet) and Plettenberg Bay, particularly off Robberg Peninsula. It is now known that some (several hundred) Southern Right Whales move up the West coast, especially off St. Helena Bay, and remain here into the summer and even autumn; there is an abundance of plankton in this area.

The Humpback Whale has characteristic long flippers, with a serrated leading edge.
Inset: Humpback Whales often jump clear of the water, an action known as breaching.

Southern Right Whale. Inset: The distinguishing white callosities on the head are clearly visible.

Humpback
Whale

Southern
Right Whale

Southern Right Whale tail fluke (*top*) and flipper (*above*).

Behaviour: A typical pod of Southern Right Whales usually consists of fewer than 6 individuals and is normally a family unit. A regularly monitored and steadily increasing population is frequently seen in sheltered bays off the southern and western coast of South Africa. Southern Right Whales move north into southern African coastal waters from about May to October, spending the summer and autumn months in their Antarctic feeding-grounds. They glide and roll on the surface, when the flippers and flukes are clearly visible, and not infrequently jump or 'breach' clear of the water – a sight once seen, never to be forgotten.

Food: Plankton.

Reproduction: Calves, some 6 m long, are born in southern African waters from about June to September with an August peak in sheltered bays.

PYGMY RIGHT WHALE | Family Neobalaenidae

Caperea marginata

■ **Pygmy Right Whale** *Caperea marginata*
Total length 6 m; mass 4–5 t.

Identification pointers: Small size and similar appearance to Southern Right Whale but note possession of dorsal fin and absence of white head callosities. No throat grooves. When it rises to breathe, usually only the head breaks the surface and then it sinks quietly back without exposing back.

Description: The smallest of all the baleen whales, with an arch to the lower jaw like that of the Southern Right Whale; the head, however, is comparatively small. Unlike Southern Right Whale, Pygmy Right Whale possesses a dorsal fin, but as the flukes of this species are never raised above water; the fin is rarely seen. The overall colour is dark grey-blue, with a paler band around the neck. There are no callosities on the head.

Distribution: Circumpolar distribution south of the tropics. Rarely seen off the southern African coast.

Behaviour: Usually seen in pairs or small groups. It frequently associates with other whale species.

Food: Plankton (including copepods and amphipods) skimmed off the surface.

Reproduction: Virtually unknown.

TOOTHED WHALES & DOLPHINS | Infraorder Odontoceti

Thirty-two species of toothed whales and dolphins have been recorded off the coasts of southern Africa.

BEAKED WHALES | Family Ziphiidae

Nine species of beaked whales have been recorded from southern African waters but most are known from very few specimens and sightings. For convenience, the nine species have been divided into two groups below.

Berardius arnuxii

■ **Arnoux's Beaked Whale** *Berardius arnuxii*
Total length 10 m; mass 9 t.
■ **Southern Bottlenose Whale** *Hyperoodon planifrons*
Total length 7 m; mass 3 t (to 6 t).
■ **Cuvier's Beaked (Goose-beaked) Whale** *Ziphius cavirostris*
Total length 6–7 m; mass 3.5 t.

Hyperoodon planifrons

260

Pygmy Right Whale is the smallest of the baleen whales.

Arnoux's Beaked Whale has a prominent forehead 'melon'.

The Southern Bottlenose Whale has a bulging, dome-like forehead, or 'melon' and a prominent beak.

Pygmy Right Whale

Southern Bottlenose;
Cuvier's Beaked
Whale

Arnoux's Beaked Whale

261

Ziphius cavirostris

Identification pointers: Cuvier's Beaked Whale with white beak, head and back to just behind dorsal fin; head only slightly swollen. Southern Bottlenose Whale with very swollen head or 'melon'. Nothing distinctive about Arnoux's Beaked Whale, but if a stranded specimen should be encountered, note that it is our only beaked whale with two pairs of teeth in the lower jaw and our only beaked whale in which the female has visible teeth.

Description: Arnoux's Beaked Whale is a medium-sized, dark-grey or black whale with paler underparts. The beak and forehead 'melon' are prominent. Both sexes have two pairs of teeth close to the tip of the lower jaw, which protrudes beyond the tip of the upper jaw. The front teeth are about 8 cm long; the back ones are shorter. This species is known from four records in southern African waters, one a specimen stranded near Port Elizabeth.

Southern Bottlenose Whale is smaller than Arnoux's, with a prominent beak; its bulging dome-like forehead rises vertically above the beak and is rounded onto the back. Dorsal fin is fairly prominent, situated well back and slightly curved at the tip. The colour of the upperparts is bluish-grey and the throat and belly are off-white or grey. Males have only one pair of teeth in the lower jaw; in the females the teeth do not erupt through the gums.

Cuvier's Beaked Whale has a stubby beak and the domed head or 'melon' is poorly developed. This species may be separated from other species by the fact that the snout, head and back to just beyond the dorsal fin are white, while the rest of the body is usually grey to black. The male has a single pair of teeth, each about 7 cm long, at the lower jaw tip; the female's teeth do not erupt through the gums.

Distribution: Only Cuvier's Beaked Whale has a worldwide distribution in temperate and tropical seas, although it is absent from Arctic and Antarctic waters. Southern Bottlenose Whale and Arnoux's Beaked Whale are only found in the southern hemisphere, south of the Tropic of Capricorn.

Behaviour: Cuvier's Beaked Whale is an animal of deep waters and is usually seen alone or in small groups of 2–7. Also a deep-water whale, Arnoux's Beaked Whale is usually solitary although 6–10 (to 50) individuals may on occasion be seen together. Southern Bottlenose Whale in small tight-knit groups.

Food: Arnoux's Beaked Whale and Southern Bottlenose Whale feed predominantly on squid and cuttlefish; Cuvier's Beaked Whale also takes fish, crabs and starfish.

Reproduction: Calves of the Southern Bottlenose Whale and Cuvier's Beaked Whale are apparently born in the summer months.

Mesoplodon densirostris

Mesoplodon grayi

■ **Blainville's Beaked Whale** *Mesoplodon densirostris*
Total length 5–6 m; mass 1 t (to 1.5 t).
■ **Gray's Beaked Whale** *Mesoplodon grayi*
Total length to 5.6 m; mass 1 t.
■ **Hector's Beaked Whale** *Mesoplodon hectori*
Total length 4 m; mass 1 t.
■ **Strap-toothed (Layard's) Beaked Whale** *Mesoplodon layardii*
Total length 6 m; mass 1.5–2 t.
■ **True's Beaked Whale** *Mesoplodon mirus*
Total length 5 m; mass 1–2 t.
Identification pointers: See descriptions for specific pointers.
Description: All five southern African species in the genus *Mesoplodon* are very difficult to identify in the field. This is compounded by there being considerable variation in body colour within any one species. Only an examination of the males' teeth can ensure positive identification; like most beaked whales, female

Cuvier's Beaked Whale has a stubby beak and a poorly developed domed head, or 'melon'; the dorsal fin is small.

Blainville's Beaked Whale can be identified by the upward-curving jaw.

Arnoux's Beaked Whale

Southern Bottlenose Whale

Hector's Beaked Whale

Blainville's Beaked Whale

Layard's Beaked Whale

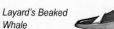

Blainville's Beaked Whale

Hector's Beaked Whale

263

Mesoplodon hectori

Mesoplodon layardii

Mesoplodon mirus

Indopacetus pacificus

Mesoplodon whales lack visible teeth. The species most likely to be seen in southern African waters is Blainville's Beaked Whale; the male of this species can be identified by a massive upward extension of each side of the lower jaw. One tooth is situated about midway along each jaw, at the apex of the extended portion but, although each tooth is about 10 cm long, only a small portion is visible above the jaw.

Gray's Beaked Whale is usually dark grey above and whitish or light grey below; its head is almost flat on top and is not markedly swollen.

Hector's Beaked Whale is only sketchily known from 6 or 7 skulls and incomplete specimens found worldwide.

Strap-toothed Beaked Whale is blackish above but there is a grey area from the distinct (but not large) 'melon' to a point half-way along the back. The underparts are also black but the front half of the beak, the throat, and a patch around the genital area are white. The male is clearly identified by the two, 6-cm-broad, curved, tusk-like teeth, one to each lower jaw, which protrude from the jaw and curve over the top of the beak; these teeth apparently prevent the mouth from opening more than a few centimetres.

True's Beaked Whale has a smallish but clearly bulbous 'melon' and its single pair of small teeth is situated at the tip of the lower jaw. It has a distinctive colour pattern, being blackish overall but white on the lower jaw, around the genital area and on the posterior section of both upperparts (including the dorsal fin) and underparts (including underside of the tail-flukes). The edges of the jaw and throat are speckled with blackish on a light-grey background.

Distribution: Gray's and Strap-toothed Beaked Whales are confined to the seas of the southern hemisphere south of the Tropic of Capricorn. Although little is known of Hector's Beaked Whale, it appears to have a circumpolar distribution in the colder waters of the southern hemisphere. True's and Blainville's Beaked Whales both occur in the northern and southern hemispheres; Blainville's appears to prefer tropical waters while True's Beaked Whale is found in both subtropical and temperate waters.

Behaviour: Although available information is scanty, True's Beaked Whale is thought to occur in pairs or as a cow with calf; Blainville's Beaked Whale is normally seen in groups of 3–6 and Gray's Beaked Whale in groups of 6 or more. All species are usually associated with deeper waters.

Food: Squid appears to be the principal food but fish is included in the diet of at least Blainville's Beaked Whale. Some beaked whales, certainly Strap-toothed, also eat crustaceans.

Reproduction: Very little known.

Note: Longman's Beaked Whale, also called Tropical Bottlenose Whale, (*Indopacetus pacificus*), is known from very few specimens. Two skulls have been collected in South Africa, at Blythesdale Beach and Sodwana Bay, KwaZulu-Natal (see map). Apparent sightings of this species in the Indian and Pacific oceans include tight groups of 5–20 but up to as many as 100. The beak and forehead 'melon' are often exposed when travelling on the surface at speed.

Gray's Beaked Whale is dark-grey, with a flat head.

True's Beaked Whale has a small forehead 'melon'.

Strap-toothed (Layard's) Beaked Whale has a grey area across the back and some of the frontal underparts.

Hector's Beaked Whale is seldom encountered; it appears to inhabit colder waters.

Gray's Beaked Whale

Strap-toothed (Layard's) Beaked Whale

True's Beaked Whale

265

SPERM WHALES | Families Kogiidae and Physeteridae

All three members of these two families have been recorded from southern African waters. Characterized by having square heads and by the possession of teeth on the lower, but not the upper jaw. They derive their name from the large spermaceti organ situated in a depression in the upper part of the front of the skull. Spermaceti wax is believed to assist in regulating the whales' buoyancy in deep diving and may also focus sound used in echolocation.

Family Kogiidae

Kogia breviceps

■ **Pygmy Sperm Whale** *Kogia breviceps*
Total length 3 m; mass 350–500 kg.
■ **Dwarf Sperm Whale** *Kogia sima*
Total length 2.6 m; mass 160–350 kg.
Identification pointers: Difficult to tell apart but head shape and body size should separate them from any other species. 'False gill' marking of Pygmy Sperm Whale is characteristic, as is the mid-back placement of the larger dorsal fin of the Dwarf Sperm Whale.

Kogia sima

Description: Species similar in appearance but differ considerably in size. Snout area swollen and projects beyond lower jaw, a feature that gives these two small whales a somewhat shark-like appearance. Dorsal fin of Dwarf Sperm Whale is large and situated half-way down the back, whereas that of the Pygmy Sperm Whale is smaller and situated further down the back. Both dark grey above and white to pinkish-white or light grey below. White 'false gill' marking is often present on head of Pygmy Sperm Whale.
Distribution: Both species have an extensive distribution within the tropics, but extend into the temperate seas of both northern and southern hemispheres.
Behaviour: Both species may be seen singly or in small groups, the Dwarf Sperm Whale in schools of up to 10 individuals.
Food: Principally squid, fish and crabs.
Reproduction: Little known; gestation period may be 9–11 months.

Family Physeteridae

Physeter catodon

■ **Sperm Whale** *Physeter (macrocephalus) catodon*
Total length 10–18 m; mass (males) 40 t.
Identification pointers: Cannot be mistaken for any other species. Large size; high, blunt snout; dorsal hump instead of fin; forward blow.
Description: Unmistakable profile with enormous square head, blunt snout and relatively small, undershot jaw. Head occupies nearly one-third of total length and contains vast spermaceti organ. No true dorsal fin but there is a distinct dorsal hump about two-thirds of way along back; behind this in male is usually a line of 4–5 smaller humps. Flippers short and stubby; tail-flukes broad and powerful. Males larger than females. Body skin has a series of longitudinal corrugations. Upperparts are dark grey-blue to black; underparts are paler. Skin around lips is usually white, with occasional white patches on the body. Blowhole is at tip of front of head and angled forward, giving a characteristic blow at an angle of approximately 45°. Sperm Whales occasionally breach or leap from the water.
Distribution: Worldwide, with preference for deep waters.
Behaviour: Sperm Whales descend to great depths to feed and stay down for lengthy periods. Accurate sonar tracking has shown that they can certainly reach

Sperm Whale tail fluke

The Pygmy Sperm Whale's snout gives it the appearance of a shark. Note the white 'false gill' marking on the head.
Inset: The dorsal fin of the Dwarf Sperm Whale is situated halfway down the back.

The Sperm Whale has a characteristic large square head and blunt snout, and longitudinal corrugations along the body.

Pygmy Sperm Whale   Dwarf Sperm Whale

Sperm Whale

at least 1 200 m (probably up to 3 000 m); long dives, of between 1 and 2 hours, are on record. Adult bulls hold harems, forming groups of 20–30 individuals. The species is not currently under threat of extinction: one estimate puts the southern hemisphere stocks of Sperm Whales at some 350,000.

Food: Mostly squid, but also fish and crustaceans.

Reproduction: Calves in subregion are born November–June with a peak in February and March. After a gestation period of almost 15 months, a calf is born, measuring about 4 m and weighing some 800 kg.

WHALE DOLPHINS, PILOT WHALES, KILLER & FALSE KILLER WHALES | Family Delphinidae

This is a diverse group of small whales and dolphins, of which 20 species have been recorded in southern African waters. They can be divided into four main groups on the basis of their general appearance, namely:
1. No dorsal fin; beak present (1 species)
2. Blunt or rounded heads; beak absent; dorsal fin present (8 species)
3. Beak present, but very short; dorsal fin present (3 species)
4. Long beak; dorsal fin present (8 species).

1. No dorsal fin; beak present

Lissodelphis peronii
Rarely occurs inshore, but a population is present off southern Namibia.

■ **Southern Right Whale Dolphin** *Lissodelphis peronii*
Total length 2 m (males to 3 m); mass 60 kg (to 115 kg).
Identification pointers: Small size; only dolphin with no dorsal fin; black above and white below; white beak, forehead, flippers and underside of tail-flukes.
Description: This small dolphin is unique in that it has no dorsal fin, and the back curves smoothly from the tip of the nose to the tail. It is further characterized by having a black dorsal surface and white underparts, with a clear dividing line between these colours along the side. The white coloration is continuous from the underside of the tail-flukes along the belly and flanks onto the flippers, throat and beak; it extends over the whole beak onto the forehead.
Distribution: From Tropic of Capricorn southwards to about 50°S.
Behaviour: This is usually a deep-sea species but it occasionally comes close inshore. Normally school size varies from about 20–100 but over 1 000 have been observed together. Poorly known.
Food: Fish and squid.
Reproduction: Unknown.

2. Blunt or rounded heads; beak absent; dorsal fin present

Orcinus orca

■ **Killer Whale** *Orcinus orca*
Male: total length 7.5 m (to 9.5 m); mass (up to) 8 t. Female: total length 5.5 m; mass (up to) 3 t.
Identification pointers: Large size; prominent dorsal fin; distinctive black-and-white markings; characteristic white oval patch behind eye; rounded head.
Description: This species is unmistakable with its large size, heavy build, blunt or rounded head, large paddle-like flippers, bold black-and-white coloration and very tall dorsal fin. The fin of the male may be up to 2 m in height and is erect and

The Southern Right Whale Dolphin has no dorsal fin.

The Killer Whale has very distinctive black-and-white coloration and a large dorsal fin.

Southern Right Whale Dolphin

Killer Whale

Killer Whale dorsal fin; male (*top*) and female (*above*).

sometimes forward-pointing, while the female fin is smaller, and more shark-like in form. They are jet-black above, and white below from the chin to the vicinity of the anus and sometimes beyond. A short 'arm' of white extends from the ventral area onto the side in an angle towards but not reaching the tail. There is a characteristic oval white spot just above, and stretching a short way back from the eye. A greyish patch or saddle is usually present on the back behind the fin.

Distribution: World-wide, but most common in colder waters.

Behaviour: Usually encountered in pods of from 3–30 individuals; they hunt in packs, hence the name 'wolves of the sea'.

Food: Wide variety of vertebrate food, including fish, birds, seals, dolphins and even large whales. Only cetacean to prey on warm-blooded species.

Reproduction: Gestation period 12 months. At birth, measures 2.1–2.7 m.

Pseudorca crassidens

■ False Killer Whale   *Pseudorca crassidens*

Male: total length 5.8 m; mass 2 t. **Female:** total length 4.6 m; mass 1.2 t.

Identification pointers: Dark and slender; dark grey to black with no distinctive markings or white scars from interspecific fighting (see Risso's Dolphin, page 274); prominent, centrally situated dorsal fin; flippers pointed, narrow with 'elbow'. At a distance it could be mistaken for Killer Whale (page 268), Pilot Whale (page 272), Pygmy Killer Whale or Melon-headed Whale (page 274) – but all of these have distinctive white or pale markings. For further differences see individual species accounts. The False Killer Whale is the largest species likely to be seen sporting in the bow-waves of ships.

Description: This is a long and slender species with a slightly rounded head; the upper jaw projects slightly over the mouth. The flippers are pointed and narrow with a distinct bend or 'elbow'. Dorsal fin is situated at about mid-back and is prominent, narrow and strongly curved; it is never as strongly developed as in the Killer Whale. Overall colour is dark-grey to black with a narrow grey blaze ventrally. The common name is presumably derived from the fact that these whales have a wide gape and well-developed teeth.

Distribution: False Killer Whales are found worldwide in all tropical and temperate seas, usually in deep water.

Behaviour: Usually travel in small family pods but several such pods may come together to form larger groups of 20–50. This species appears to be prone to stranding; the first recorded stranding in southern Africa was of 108 individuals on the beach at Kommetjie, near Cape Town, in 1928. Among other strandings, 58 died at St Helena Bay, north of Cape Town, in 1936, and 65 stranded and died on the same 1 500-m stretch of beach in 1981. Often swims with mouth open.

Food: Squid and large pelagic fish.

Reproduction: Said to produce young at any time of year but possibly summer, with gestation periods of about 15 months.

Feresa attenuata

■ Pygmy Killer Whale   *Feresa attenuata*

Total length 2.4 m; mass 170 kg.

Identification pointers: Much smaller than either Killer or False Killer Whale; rounded head with white lips and chin patch; could be confused with Melon-headed Whale (page 274) but the latter species' head is curved into a 'parrot beak' and the white of its lips does not extend onto chin.

Description: Pygmy Killer Whale has a slender tapered body, with a compressed, narrow and rounded head. Dorsal fin is long, pointed, with the tip curved towards the tail. The flippers are relatively short and rounded at the tip. Much of the body

Right: *The False Killer Whale is a long, slender species with a slightly rounded head and a prominent dorsal fin situated at mid-back.*

The Pygmy Killer Whale has a slender, tapered body and a long, thin dorsal fin that is curved towards the tail.

Pygmy Killer Whale

False Killer Whale

is black, although the sides may have a greyish tinge, and a pale-grey anchor-shaped blaze is situated between the flippers. There is a large white anal patch and this may stretch almost back to the tail. They have white lips and a white patch at the tip of the chin as an extension of the white on the lips.

Distribution: Found in warmer deep waters worldwide.

Behaviour: This species hunts in groups of from about 10–50 individuals. It rarely moves close inshore and is essentially a species of the open sea.

Food: Fish and squid, and it has been suggested that it may also hunt dolphins.

Reproduction: Poorly known.

Globicephala macrorhynchus

Globicephala melas

■ **Short-finned Pilot Whale** *Globicephala macrorhynchus*
Total length 6 m; mass 1.5–3 t.

■ **Long-finned Pilot Whale** *Globicephala melas*
Total length 5-7 m; mass 2–4 t.

Identification pointers: Prominent fin, slightly forward of mid-body; rounded head with prominent 'melon'; dark or black dorsal surface and sides, with a grey patch behind dorsal fin of Long-finned Pilot Whale. White anchor-shaped blaze along belly of Long-finned; dark-grey anchor-shaped blaze in Short-finned Pilot Whales. Distinguished from False Killer Whale by that species' more tapered head, narrow, more pointed fin and all-black back. False Killer Whale frequently sports in bow- and stern-waves of boats but this is extremely rare in the case of the pilot whales. Short-finned Pilot Whale is most likely to be seen off the east coast of the subregion and Long-finned Pilot Whale off the west coast.

Description: Difficult to tell apart. They are long, thin and rather cylindrical with blunt, rounded and bulbous heads; this 'melon' is usually better developed in old males. Head of Short-finned more prominent and rounded than that of Long-finned. Flipper form is characteristic: in the Long-finned, the flippers are long (18–27 per cent of body length) and pointed, with a distinct bend or 'elbow'; in the Short-finned they are 15–18 per cent of body length and lack the 'elbow'. Prominent and back-curved dorsal fin of both is set slightly forward of body midpoint. Upperparts of both dark grey or black but there is distinct pale-grey patch situated behind dorsal fin in Long-finned. White anchor-shaped blaze runs from throat to belly in Long-finned; Short-finned dark-grey anchor-shaped blaze is only on belly, from between flippers to anal region.

Distribution: Short-finned Pilot Whale occurs worldwide in warmer waters. The Long-finned has two populations, one south of the Tropic of Capricorn and the other in the North Atlantic.

Behaviour: Both species come together in large schools, but group size may vary from fewer than 10 to several hundred individuals; several thousand Long-finned Pilot Whales have been observed together. Often float on the surface.

Food: Predominantly squid, but also fish.

Reproduction: Gestation lasts about 16 months in both species.

The Short-finned Pilot Whale has a grey patch behind the dorsal fin, and a prominent, rounded head.

The Long-finned Pilot Whale has a distinct 'elbow bend' on the flippers, and a white blaze on the belly.

Short-finned Pilot Whale

Long-finned Pilot Whale

273

Peponocephala electra

■ Melon-headed Whale *Peponocephala electra*
Total length 2.7 m; mass 180 kg.

Identification pointers: Fairly slender with prominent centrally situated fin; overall dark uppersides and flanks without markings; rounded head; white lips but no white chin patch, as found in the fairly similar Pygmy Killer Whale (page 270). Presumably very rare in southern African waters.

Description: A fairly long and slender whale, which superficially resembles the Long-finned Pilot Whale; despite the implication of its common name, however, the swelling on the head is not as pronounced as that of the pilot whales, the head more closely resembling that of False Killer Whale. The front of the head has a 'parrot-beak' appearance. The fin is prominent, about 25 cm high, and strongly curved and set more or less in mid-back. Overall body colour is dark-grey to black, with a white or pale-grey ventral anchor-shaped patch between the flippers and throat and a lighter coloured patch around the anal and genital area. The lips are white but there is no white chin patch as in Pygmy Killer Whale.

Distribution: Worldwide in warm waters. Only once known to have stranded on South African coast.

Behaviour: Very little is known, but schools from around 20 to several hundred individuals have been recorded, mainly in deep waters.

Food: Probably squid and fish.

Reproduction: In the southern hemisphere, calves are born between August and December after a gestation period of about 12 months.

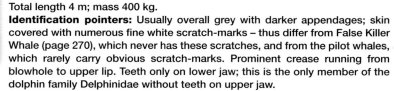

Grampus griseus

■ Risso's Dolphin *Grampus griseus*
Total length 4 m; mass 400 kg.

Identification pointers: Usually overall grey with darker appendages; skin covered with numerous fine white scratch-marks – thus differ from False Killer Whale (page 270), which never has these scratches, and from the pilot whales, which rarely carry obvious scratch-marks. Prominent crease running from blowhole to upper lip. Teeth only on lower jaw; this is the only member of the dolphin family Delphinidae without teeth on upper jaw.

Description: Similar in appearance to the Pilot whales. It is robustly built in front of a tall, thin, back-pointing fin situated in mid-back, but behind the fin the body tapers and narrows rapidly towards the tail. There is no beak and the head bulges slightly. This species can be easily identified at close range as it is the only species with a deep crease down the centre of the head, from the blowhole to the upper lip. The flippers are fairly long (but shorter than in the pilot whales) and pointed and the flukes are broad and deeply notched. This dolphin is dark grey above and pale grey below, with dark-grey flippers, dorsal fin and tail-flukes. With increasing age, the body may become paler, to almost white on the belly, face and anterior portion of the back. Fin, flukes and flippers retain their dark colour with age; however, there is considerable variation in overall colour. The body is usually criss-crossed with numerous fine white lines produced by teeth of fellow members of this species during fights; perhaps also by squids.

Distribution: This species is found worldwide but avoids colder waters.

Behaviour: Between 3 and 30 individuals make up the normal school but larger groups have been observed. Found mainly in deep waters along and beyond the continental shelf.

Food: Squid.

Reproduction: Calves are apparently born during the summer after a gestation period of about 12 months. They have a length at birth of 1.5 m.

The Melon-headed Whale is fairly slender, with a centrally situated dorsal fin, an overall dark cololur, and white lips.

Risso's Dolphin has a deep crease down the centre of the head, from the blowhole to the upper lip. The grey skin is usually covered in scratches, either from fighting or from encounters with squid, a favoured prey.

Melon-headed Whale

Risso's Dolphin

3. Beak present, but very short; dorsal fin present

Three species occurring in southern African waters have short but clearly visible beaks: they are Heaviside's Dolphin, Dusky Dolphin and Fraser's Dolphin.

Cephalorhynchus heavisidii

■ **Heaviside's Dolphin** *Cephalorhynchus heavisidii*
Total length 1.3 m (to 1.7 m); mass 40 kg (to 70 kg).
Identification pointers: Small size; distinctive black-and-white markings; flattened, broad head; stocky body. Only likely to be seen off the west coast of southern Africa. Should not be confused with any other species.
Description: Heaviside's Dolphin is easily distinguishable from the other two dolphins with short beaks because of its small size and stocky appearance. In addition it has black upperparts, which contrast with white areas on the lower throat, chest and abdomen, with white extending from the throat towards the eye, and from above the flipper towards the eye. Another broad white band extends from the abdomen in a shallow sweep across the flank back towards the tail to a round-ended point just beyond the back line of the fin. The fin is broad-based and triangular. The head is broad and flat, without a real beak, although from a distance the flattened head could appear to have such an extension.
Distribution: Apparently restricted to cold waters of Benguela Current off southern Africa's west coast, although recent records to Plettenberg Bay on south coast.
Behaviour: Little known, but it is said to form small schools only, usually very close inshore. Commonly interact with boats.
Food: Squid and bottom-dwelling fish.
Reproduction: Unknown.

Lagenodelphis hosei

Lagenorhynchus obscurus

■ **Fraser's Dolphin** *Lagenodelphis hosei*
Total length 2.6 m; mass 130–190 kg.
■ **Dusky Dolphin** *Lagenorhynchus obscurus*
Total length 2.1 m; mass 115 kg (40–90 kg average).
Identification pointers: Fraser's Dolphin: dark above, white below, separated by two stripes, a lighter upper stripe broadening over upper hindquarters and a darker lower stripe from corner of mouth and through eye to anus.
   Dusky Dolphin: dark above, whitish below and grey along flanks with two dark blazes from black upperparts extending into the grey in broad backward- and downward-pointing sweeps. Fin has pale concave edge behind. Both species have short beaks. Both species rare in southern African waters.
Description: Both species have definite, very short beaks. Typical dolphin appearance but flippers and fin of Fraser's are shorter than those of Dusky Dolphin. Fraser's Dolphin is dark grey-blue above (from head to three-quarters along back beyond the fin), pinkish-white below, with two parallel stripes along body length creating a boundary between dark upper- and light underparts. Upper stripe, pale grey to cream, runs from above and in front of eye along the side to below the fin where it widens over the upperparts behind the fin as a light-grey area extending to the tail. More prominent lower stripe, black or dark grey, runs from the beak through the eye along the flank to the anus. Throat, chin and rest of the underparts are white. Edge and tip of lower jaw are usually black. Dusky Dolphin has dark-grey to black upperparts, flippers and flukes, the fin having a light-grey to white margin to its trailing edge. Underparts are white and between upper- and underparts is a broad band of light-grey along the flanks. Intruding into the grey of the flanks are two backward-pointing blazes of blackish coloration extending downwards from blackish upperparts. No other species should be confused with Dusky Dolphin.

Heaviside's Dolphin is small and stocky, with black upperparts. A white band extends from the abdomen towards the tail.

Fraser's Dolphin is dark grey-blue above and pinkish-white below with two parallel stripes running the length of the body.

The Dusky Dolphin has dark-grey to black upperparts, flippers and flukes and white underparts, separated by a band of light-grey along the flanks.

Heaviside's Dolphin	Fraser's Dolphin	Dusky Dolphin

Distribution: Dusky Dolphin has a circumpolar distribution south of the Tropic of Capricorn. Fraser's Dolphin is apparently restricted to tropical waters on both sides of the equator.

Behaviour: Both species usually observed in small groups but Fraser's has been recorded in schools of up to 500, even thousands, and Dusky as many as 300, but these large groups are probably temporary. Dusky Dolphin is more coastal than Fraser's Dolphin, often accompanying ships and riding the bow-waves.

Food: Both species feed on squid and fish.

Reproduction: The calves of Dusky Dolphin are apparently unusually small and are born after a gestation period of about 9 months. Other than this, nothing is on record for the two species.

4. Long-beak; dorsal fin present

Sousa chinensis

■ Humpback Dolphin *Sousa chinensis*
Total length 2.8 m; mass 280 kg.

Identification pointers: Long prominent hump supporting dorsal fin.

Description: Easily distinguished from other long-beaked dolphins by long thickened ridge along the middle of the back, supporting a pointed dorsal fin. Dark-grey to black upperparts fade gradually to off-white underparts.

Distribution: Largely restricted to coastal areas of Indian Ocean and extreme western Pacific Ocean. Unlikely to be seen west of the Gouritz River.

Behaviour: School size 1–30 (average 7); shallow coastal waters.

Food: Fish, mostly from reefs near rocky coastlines, squid and crustaceans.

Reproduction: Calves at any time of year but peak in summer.

Stenella attenuata

■ Pantropical Spotted Dolphin *Stenella attenuata*
Total length 2.3 m; mass 100 kg.

Identification pointers: Long, dark beak with white lips; dark-grey body spotted with white.

Description: Prominent, curved dorsal fin, long flippers and marked ventral keel towards end of tail-stock. Dark slate-grey above, paler to pinkish below; fin, flippers and flukes are dark. Blackish circle around eye connected to blackish line around beak base, extending further as dark band from jaw to flipper. Beak black with pink or white lips. Numerous white spots on body, particularly on sides and underparts posterior to genital aperture. Young animals have few or no spots.

Distribution: Worldwide in tropics; in subregion only likely to be seen off east coast from KwaZulu-Natal northwards. Mainly oceanic and along continental shelf.

Behaviour: Large schools (100 +). Surface-feeder. Commonly bow-rides.

Food: Squid and fish.

Reproduction: 11-month gestation period.

Stenella coeruleoalba

■ Striped Dolphin *Stenella coeruleoalba*
Total length 2.3 m; mass 130 kg.

Identification pointers: Distinctive light and dark longitudinal striping. Stripes appear to commence around eye and diverge from each other posteriorly.

Description: Upperparts usually dark greyish-blue, with or without a brownish tinge; on death darkens to deep blue. White underparts. Black stripe from eye along side to anus and another dark stripe from eye to flipper. V-shaped lighter band runs above main side stripe, its shorter upper arm running towards fin and longer lower arm extending to tail.

The Humpback Dolphin has a prominent ridge, or hump, below a small dorsal fin.

Pantropical Spotted Dolphin, or Spotted Dolphin, has a darkish circle around the eye, and numerous white spots on the body.

Humpback Dolphin

Pantropical Spotted Dolphin

Distribution: Worldwide from southern continental tips northwards to northern hemisphere. Most likely to be encountered off the southern and eastern coastal areas of southern Africa although generally in deeper waters and not considered to be a coastal dolphin.
Behaviour: Large schools (over 100 individuals). Surface-feeder.
Food: Squid, fish and crustaceans (crabs, lobsters and shrimps).
Reproduction: Gestation of around 12 months. Cows calve at 3-year intervals.

Stenella longirostris

■ Long-snouted (Spinner) Dolphin *Stenella longirostris*
Total length 2.1 m; mass 75 kg.
Identification pointers: Habit of 'spinning' while jumping out of water.
Description: Very long rostrum or beak, and long, pointed flippers. Upperparts dark grey-brown with pale-grey to white underparts, spotted with small darker areas. Difficult to identify on appearance but its striking behaviour is diagnostic: individuals from its large schools periodically hurl themselves into air, twisting and spinning their bodies along longitudinal axis – thus the name Spinner Dolphin.
Distribution: Worldwide in tropical waters. Very few records off southern Africa.
Behaviour: Schools of 30 to several hundreds. Deep-water feeder.
Food: Predominantly squid.
Reproduction: Newborn calves measure less than 1 m long. Calving interval just over 2 years.

Tursiops aduncus

■ Indian Ocean Bottlenosed Dolphin *Tursiops aduncus*
Total length 2.4 m; mass 120–190 kg.
Identification pointers: Dark grey and plain coloured, with no distinctive identifying features. Smaller than the next species.
Description: Robust with tall, curved fin and medium-length beak that is wide and rounded at the tip. Lower jaw projects slightly beyond upper jaw. Usually dark-grey back with paler grey sides and ventral area. Thin pale line usually runs from eye to flipper.
Distribution: Coastal waters of Indian Ocean, extending to China and Australia.
Behaviour: Large schools of several hundreds (20–50 usual). Inshore and deep sea.
Food: Mostly fish, but also squid.
Reproduction: Gestation 12 months; newborn calves about 1 m long.

Tursiops truncatus
Dark blue indicates two
separate populations,
one inshore and the
other in deep water,
which apparently rarely
intermingle.

■ Atlantic Ocean Bottlenosed Dolphin *Tursiops truncatus*
Total length 3.2 m; mass 200 kg.
Identification pointers: Dark grey and plain coloured, with no distinctive identifying features.
Description: As for Indian Ocean Bottlenosed Dolphin, above.
Distribution: Widespread; found in North Sea and Mediterranean Sea, as well as both the North and South Atlantic.
Behaviour: Large schools, numbering up to several hundred (usual 25 +). Occur both inshore and in deeper seas.
Food: Fish and squid.
Reproduction: Gestation period 12 months; calving interval perhaps 2 years.
Note: Some scientists believe the Indian Ocean and Atlantic Ocean Bottlenosed Dolphins are the same species.

Striped Dolphin has distinctive light and dark stripes, with a black stripe running along the side from the eye to the anus.

The Long-snouted (Spinner) Dolphin has a very long beak.

Bottlenosed Dolphins are dark grey and plain coloured and it is hard to distinguish one species from the other.

Striped Dolphin	Long-snouted (Spinner) Dolphin	Indian Ocean Bottlenosed Dolphin	Atlantic Ocean Bottlenosed Dolphin

Delphinus delphis
Dark blue indicates main
deep water range; pale
blue occasional incursions
between the continental
shelf and the mainland.

Delphinus capensis

Steno bredanensis

■ **Short-beaked Common Dolphin** *Delphinus delphis*
■ **Long-beaked Common Dolphin** *Delphinus capensis*
Short-beaked Common Dolphin is a deep water species; the Long-beaked Common Dolphin is now recognized as the inshore species.
Total length 1.6–2.3 m; mass 150 kg.
Identification pointers: Clear 'figure-of-eight' pattern along flanks.
Description: Sleek and streamlined; pointed flippers and a prominent back-curved fin. Rostrum or beak is long. Dark grey to brown-black above and pale grey below. Characterized by having elongated 'figure-of-eight' or 'hour-glass' pattern on each side, from eye to tail-flukes. Colouring of 'hour-glass' variable but section from eye to mid-body is commonly brown-grey (occasionally tinged yellow), while hind section usually pale grey. Thin black line from corner of mouth to flipper. Long-beaked Common Dolphin similar in appearance to Short-beaked.
Distribution: Worldwide in tropical and warm temperate waters, both in deep water and inshore. In the subregion, Short-beaked is most frequently seen off south and east coasts, rarely inshore. Long-beaked, common inshore, is often found in large schools (up to 5 000).
Behaviour: Short-beaked is usually found in schools of about 20 but can be up to several hundreds or even thousands. Feeds in deeper waters.
Food: Squid; cuttlefish; small schooling fish.
Reproduction: Newborn calves around 85 cm long.

■ **Rough-toothed Dolphin** *Steno bredanensis*
Total length 2.4 m; mass 140 kg.
Identification pointers: Dark puplish-grey above; white throat and belly; flanks blotched with pinkish-white.
Description: Centrally placed sickle-shaped fin. Dark grey above with white throat and belly as far as genital area. Dark flanks blotched with pinkish-white.
Distribution: Only three records from southern Africa. Found worldwide in the deep waters of tropical, subtropical and warm temperate seas.

Common Dolphins are fast, graceful swimmers. Inset: *These dolphins are known for leaping out of the water.*

Rough-toothed Dolphin has a centrally placed sickle-shaped dorsal fin and dark flanks blotched with pinky-white.

Short-beaked Common Dolphin	Long-beaked Common Dolphin	Rough-toothed Dolphin

DUGONG | Order Sirenia | Family Dugongidae

Dugong dugon

■ **Dugong** *Dugong dugon*
Total length 2.5–3 m; mass 350–500 kg.
Identification pointers: Cigar-shaped body with flippers and tail flukes. Completely aquatic; found only in shallow waters.
Description: Entirely aquatic, never coming on land. Forelimbs are paddle-like flippers; no hindlimbs. Large, fleshy, boneless tail flattened horizontally. Skin greyish-brown with sparsley scattered bristles; upperparts slightly darker than underparts. Front of mouth and lower lip covered with short, thick bristles.
Distribution: In subregion restricted to sheltered areas along Mozambique coast but stragglers occasionally seen in northern KwaZulu-Natal. It occurs from the south-west Pacific, including New Caledonia, Micronesia, Philippines, Taiwan, New Guinea, Australia and westwards along the coastlines of countries fringing the Indian Ocean. Some of the highest populations are to be found off the tropical coastline of Australia. Shark Bay, on that country's west coast, is estimated to be home to as many as 10,000 Dugong. Elsewhere, it is hunted heavily for its palatable meat and many populations are in decline, or have disappeared completely. Other reasons for declines include silting over of sea grass beds that form the bulk of its food, disturbance at feeding grounds and pollution.
Habitat: Shallow, sheltered waters close to the coastline.
Behaviour: Although usually seen singly, in pairs or in family parties, groups of up to 30 have been recorded in southern Africa. They are slow swimmers (2 knots) but can achieve speeds of up to 5 knots to escape danger; able to remain submerged for over 5 minutes although the average dive lasts for just over a minute.
Food: Several species of sea grass in sheltered shallow bays and lagoons. They can consume up to 15% of their body mass during each feeding day.
Reproduction: Single young (rarely twins) born November–January. Gestation period apparently 11 – 13 months and new-born young weigh up to 35 kg but usually less. The mother suckles the young for up to 18 months, and the calf drinks the milk underwater.
Note: One other member of the Order Sirenia occurs in Africa, the West African Manatee (*Trichechus senegalensis*). Unlike the Dugong, which is purely coastal marine, the Manatee is found in shallow coastal waters and estuaries, and moves deep into the interior along major rivers such as the Congo, Benoue, Niger and Volta. Two other manatee species occur in the Americas.

The Dugong, an entirely aquatic mammal, inhabits shallow coastal waters and lagoons where it feeds on sea-grass.

Dugong

SKULLS

On occasion all there is to view of an animal is its skeletal remains, of which the most recognizable part is the skull, and this can be identified to a particular species. In some cases, even a cursory examination will show whether a skull belonged to a male or female. This section will aid identification and enhance knowledge with regard to the dentition and skull form of the species.

The measurements shown are averages (in mm) for total length.Where relevant, horns have been included, as they are often a clue to an animal's gender.

GIANT GOLDEN MOLE
Chrysospalax trevelyani
42 mm   pg 30

FOUR-TOED SENGI
Petrodromus tetradactylus
56 mm   pg 34

SOUTHERN AFRICAN HEDGEHOG *Atelerix frontalis* 47 mm   pg 38

GREATER RED MUSK SHREW *Crocidura flavescens* 26 mm   pg 42

WAHLBERG'S EPAULETTED FRUIT-BAT *Epomophorus wahlbergi* 42 mm   pg 48

COMMERSON'S LEAF-NOSED BAT *Hipposideros commersoni* 32 mm   pg 52

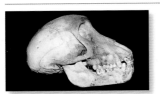

SAVANNA BABOON
(female) *Papio cynocephalus ursinus* 177 mm   pg 78

SAVANNA BABOON
(male) *Papio cynocephalus ursinus* 240 mm   pg 78

VERVET MONKEY
(female) *Cercopithecus pygerythrus* 100 mm pg 80

SYKES'S MONKEY
(male) *Cercopithecus albogularis* 108 mm pg 82

THICK-TAILED (GREATER) GALAGO *Otolemur (Galago) crassicaudatus* 72 mm   pg 84

SOUTHERN LESSER GALAGO *Galago moholi*
40 mm   pg 84

GROUND PANGOLIN [1]
Manis temminckii
82 mm   pg 86

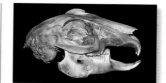

CAPE HARE
Lepus capensis
88 mm   pg 88

SCRUB HARE
Lepus saxatilis
95 mm   pg 88

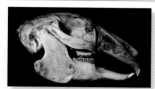

SMITH'S RED ROCK RABBIT *Pronolagus rupestris* 84 mm   pg 90

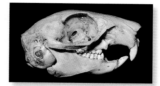

SOUTHERN AFRICAN GROUND SQUIRREL
Xerus inauris 60 mm   pg 92

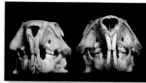

(Left) **DAMARA GROUND SQUIRREL**; (right) **SA GROUND SQUIRREL**   pg 94

TREE SQUIRREL
Paraxerus cepapi
44 mm   pg 96

SPRINGHARE
Pedetes capensis
90 mm   pg 100

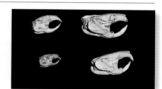

RODENT MOLES (Mole-rats)
Family Bathyergidae   pg 100

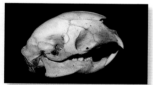

CAPE PORCUPINE
Hystrix africaeaustralis
150 mm   pg 102

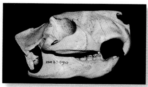

GREATER CANE-RAT
Thryonomys swinderianus
85 mm   pg 104

DASSIE RAT
Petromus typicus
34 mm   pg 106

CAPE SHORT-TAILED GERBIL *Desmodillus auricularis* 36 mm   pg 112

AFRICAN MARSH RAT
Dasymys incomtus
35 mm   pg 118

VLEI RAT
Otomys irroratus
38 mm   pg 130

BAT-EARED FOX
Otocyon megalotis
118 mm   pg 134

BLACK-BACKED JACKAL
Canis mesomelas
170 mm   pg 136

CAPE CLAWLESS OTTER
Aonyx capensis
134 mm   pg 140

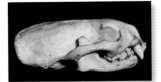

AFRICAN STRIPED WEASEL *Poecilogale albinucha* 48 mm   pg 142

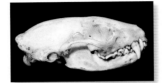

STRIPED POLECAT
Ictonyx striatus
62 mm   pg 144

BANDED MONGOOSE
Mungos mungo
70 mm   pg 144

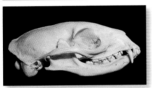

MELLER'S MONGOOSE
Rhynchogale melleri
90 mm   pg 146

SELOUS'S MONGOOSE
Paracynictis selousi
90 mm   pg 148

SMALL GREY MONGOOSE
Galerella pulverulenta
68 mm   pg 148

LARGE GREY MONGOOSE
Herpestes ichneumon
98 mm   pg 150

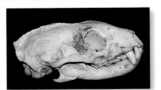

WATER (MARSH) MONGOOSE *Atilax paludinosus* 110 mm   pg 152

DWARF MONGOOSE
Helogale parvula
48 mm   pg 154

WHITE-TAILED MONGOOSE *Ichneumia albicauda* 108 mm   pg 154

YELLOW MONGOOSE
Cynictis penicillata
60 mm   pg 156

SURICATE (MEERKAT)
Suricata suricatta
62 mm   pg 156

SKULLS

SA LARGE-SPOTTED GENET *Genetta tigrina*
92 mm — pg 158

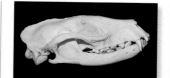

AFRICAN CIVET
Civettictis civetta
150 mm — pg 160

AFRICAN PALM CIVET
Nandinia binotata
90 mm — pg 162

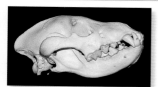

BROWN HYAENA
Parahyaena brunnea
263 mm — pg 164

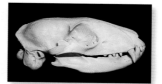

AARDWOLF
Proteles cristatus
135 mm — pg 166

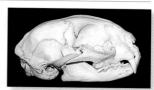

AFRICAN WILD CAT
Felis silvestris lybica
95 mm — pg 168

SMALL SPOTTED CAT
Felis nigripes
84 mm — pg 168

SERVAL
Leptailurus serval
124 mm — pg 170

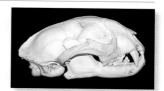

CARACAL
Caracal caracal
135 mm — pg 170

CHEETAH
Acinonyx jubatus
170 mm — pg 172

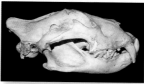

LION (male)
Panthera leo
420 mm — pg 174

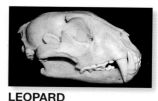

LEOPARD
Panthera pardus
210 mm — pg 176

AARDVARK
Orycteropus afer
198 mm — pg 178

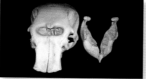

ELEPHANT *Loxodonta africana* (mandible on right)
1136 mm — pg 180

ROCK DASSIE (HYRAX)
Procavia capensis
90 mm — pg 182

289

TREE DASSIE (HYRAX)
Dendrohyrax arboreus
90 mm   pg 186

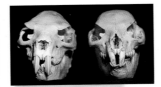

ROCK DASSIE MALE
(*left*) AND FEMALE (*right*)
Procavia capensis   pg 182

HARTMANN'S MOUNTAIN
ZEBRA *Equus zebra*
hartmannae 560 mm   pg 188

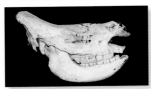

SQUARE-LIPPED
RHINOCEROS *Ceratotherium*
simum 750 mm   pg 192

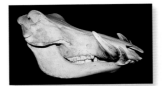

COMMON WARTHOG
Phacochoerus africanus
385 mm   pg 194

BUSHPIG
Potamochoerus larvatus
372 mm   pg 196

HIPPOPOTAMUS
Hippopotamus amphibius
642 mm   pg 198

GIRAFFE
Giraffa camelopardalis
540 mm   pg 200

GREY RHEBOK (ram)
Pelea capreolus
284 mm   pg 222

SUNI (ram)
Neotragus moschatus
118 mm   pg 236

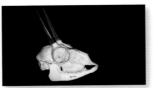

KLIPSPRINGER (ram)
Oreotragus oreotragus
155 mm   pg 238

ORIBI (ram)
Ourebia ourebi
149 mm   pg 240

CAPE GRYSBOK (ewe)
Raphicerus melanotis
142–149 mm   pg 242

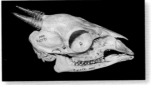

BLUE DUIKER
Cephalophus monticola
122 mm   pg 244

COMMON DUIKER (ram)
Sylvicapra grimmia
170 mm   pg 246

GLOSSARY

Alpha male/female The dominant male or female within a social group; often the only breeders.
Anterior Of or near the head; also at or near the front.
Aquatic Living in or near water.
Arboreal Adapted for life in trees.
Baleen Comb-like structures in mouths of baleen whales, used for filtering plankton from the water.
Bifurcated Forked or divided into two branches.
Biome An ecological region, usually extensive, characterized by a dominant type of plant life.
Biotic zone A geographical area which, in terms of its ecological character and the nature of its life forms, is recognized as a coherent ecosystem distinguishable from its adjacent areas.
Canine The tooth that lies between the incisors and premolars, usually cone-shaped and pointed and used as part of the killing apparatus in many carnivores.
Cheek-teeth Molar and premolar teeth lying behind the canines or incisors. Also called carnassials.
Crepuscular Active during the twilight hours of dawn and dusk.
Diurnal Active during the daylight hours.
Dorsal The back- or upper-surface.
Drey A domed nest of leaves and twigs constructed by some species of tree squirrels.
Ecosystem Unit of the environment within which living and non-living elements interact.
Ecotone The zone between two major ecological communities.
Endangered Refers to a species that is facing a very high risk of extinction.
Endemic Native to a particular country, region or restricted area.
Exotic Not native to a country or region but introduced from other countries or areas. Also 'alien'.
Feral Having reverted to a wild state.
Flehmen Grimace in which an animal's lips are pulled back, the teeth are exposed and the nose wrinkled, usually associated with males sniffing urine from an oestrus female.
Foraging Searching for or seeking out food.
Fossorial Burrowing animals, adapted to spend most, or part, of their life underground or in burrows.
Genus A taxonomic group containing one or more species.
Gestation The period between conception and birth in which offspring are carried in the uterus.
Gregarious Living together in groups, herds or colonies.
Guano Accumulations of droppings, usually used of bird and bat colonies.
Herbivore Animal that feeds principally on plants. Large mammalian herbivores may be classed as 'grazers' (subsisting largely on grasses) or 'browsers' (subsisting largely on woody or herbaceous plants).
Home range The area covered by an animal in the course of its day-to-day activities.
Incisors Sharp-edged front teeth, usually in both the upper and lower jaws.
Insectivore A mammal that subsists largely on insects.
Interfemoral membrane The thin membrane situated between the hindlegs of bats.
Introduced (also alien, exotic) Species brought by man from areas where it occurs naturally to areas where it has not previously occurred. Some introductions are accidental, others deliberate.
Lateral At the side or sides.
Midden (latrine) Place where droppings (scats) are regularly deposited.
Molar Tooth adapted for grinding food, situated at the back of the jaws.
Moult The process in which old hair is shed to make way for new hair.
Nocturnal Active during hours of darkness.
Nuchal patch A contrasting patch of hair in the nape (between and behind the ears).
Oestrus (heat) Period during which female animals are sexually receptive to males.
Omnivore An animal that feeds on both plant and animal food.
Order A taxonomic group which contains one or more families of species.
Pelage Hair covering or coat.
Plankton Mainly microscopic organisms, both plant and animal, that drift or float in the surface layers of the sea or fresh water.

Pod A group of whales with some kind of social structure.

Post-partum oestrus Renewed ovulation and mating within hours or days of giving birth.

Predator An animal that preys on other live animals for its food.

Pre-orbital gland Gland in front of the eye socket.

Rare A loose term for a species that is uncommon or whose numbers have recently decreased, but which is not endangered; not a recognized conservation category.

Riparian In close association with rivers and river-bank habitats.

Rooting behaviour Digging at roots with feet and snout.

Ruminant Mammal with a specialized digestive system typified by behaviour of chewing the cud; an adaptation to digesting the cellulose walls of plant cells.

Rut Period of sexual excitement (in male animals) associated with the mating season.

Scats Faeces or droppings.

Scavenger Animal that feeds on dead or decaying organic matter.

Scrotum The pouch that contains the testes in most mammals.

South African Red Data Book A publication listing and describing the conservation status of species of a particular taxon (for example, mammals, birds or plants) that are vulnerable or endangered.

Species A group of interbreeding individuals of common ancestry, reproductively isolated from all other groups.

Subterranean Living underground.

Taxonomy The classification of organisms into logical groups.

Terrestrial Living on land.

Territory A restricted area inhabited by an animal, usually for breeding purposes, and actively defended against other individuals of the same species.

Tragus (pl. tragi) Small cartilaginous process situated in the external ear-opening of most species of bat.

Ungulate Mammal which has its feet modified as hoofs (of various types).

Vibrissae (s. 'vibrissa') Prominent coarse hairs or whiskers, usually on the face.

Vulnerable Referring to a species that faces a high risk of extermination in the medium-term future.

Withers Area behind the neck and between the shoulders of an animal.

SUGGESTED FURTHER READING

Dorst, J. & Dandelot, P. 1983. *A Field Guide to the Larger Mammals of Africa*. Macmillan, Johannesburg.

Haltenorth, T. & Diller, H. 1984. *A Field Guide to the Mammals of Africa including Madagascar*. Collins Publishers, London.

Mills, G. and Hes, L. 1997. *The Complete Book of Southern African Mammals*. Struik Winchester, Cape Town.

Skinner, J.D. and Chimimba, C.T. 2005. *The Mammals of the Southern African Subregion*. Cambridge University Press, Cambridge.

Stuart, C. & Stuart, T. 2006. *Field Guide to the Larger Mammals of Africa*. Struik Publishers, Cape Town.

Stuart, C. & Stuart, T. 1992. *Southern, Central and East African Mammals: a Photographic Guide*. Struik Publishers, Cape Town.

Stuart, C. & Stuart, T. 1994. *A Field Guide to the Tracks and Signs of Southern and East African Wildlife*. Struik Publishers, Cape Town.

Stuart, C. & Stuart. T. 1995. *Africa: a Natural History*. Southern Book Publishers, Halfway House.

Stuart, C. & Stuart, T. 1996. *Africa's Vanishing Wildlife*. Southern Book Publishers, Halfway House.

ORGANIZATIONS CONCERNED WITH MAMMAL STUDIES

■ Non-government organizations

Mammal Research Institute
University of Pretoria, Tshwane 0002, South Africa. www.up.ac.za/academic/zoology
Founded in 1966, this semi-autonomous organization operates within the Dept. of Zoology at the University of Pretoria. Its highly qualified staff and postgraduate students undertake mammalogical research.

Small Mammals Research Group
Department of Zoology, University of Cape Town, Rondebosch 7701. www.zoology.uct.ac.za
Networks locally and internationally with other academic and research organizations, and also offers consultancy services to public and private sector concerns. Staff undertake a variety of research, teaching and review projects as well as provide information and advice. Fees are levied for certain services.

The Wildlife and Environment Society of Southern Africa
P O Box 44189, Linden 2104, South Africa. www.wildlifesociety.org.za
The Society is concerned with the conservation of southern African wildlife, wild places and natural resources for all the people of the subcontinent.

Bat Conservation International
P O Box 162603, Austin TX 78716, United States of America. www.batcon.org
Bat Conservation International was founded in 1982 by Dr Merlin D. Tuttle. Its purpose is to document and publicize the value and conservation needs of bats, to promote bat conservation projects and to assist with bat management initiatives worldwide. BCI has been instrumental in protecting some of the world's most important bat populations and has members in 40 countries. It welcomes contact with people who have an interest in bats.

Endangered Wildlife Trust
Private Bag X11, Parkview 2122, South Africa. www.ewt.org.za
The Endangered Wildlife Trust has three main aims: to maintain essential ecological processes and life-support systems; to preserve genetic diversity and to ensure that no form of life becomes extinct through ignorance or apathy; and to ensure the sustainable utilization of species and ecosystems.

Worldwide Fund for Nature (South Africa)
P O Box 456, Stellenbosch 7600, South Africa. www.panda.org.za
The South African branch of the Fund raises finance for the conservation of wildlife and the natural environment. Through the support of the South African public, this organization has been able to create or help develop numerous parks and nature reserves.

African-Arabian Wildlife Research Centre
P O Box 6, Loxton 6985, South Africa. aawrc@yebo.co.za
Originally started in 1986 as the African Carnivore Survey, the Centre has been developed to monitor the carnivores and other biota of Africa and, most recently, the Arabian Peninsula. Although its principal aim remains the compilation of available information on mammalian carnivores and promoting their conservation, it now looks at many additional conservation issues.

Marine Biology Reseach Institute
Department of Zoology, University of Cape Town, Rondebosch 7701. www.zoology.uct.ac.za
The institute undertakes multi-discipline research into related activities and inhabitants, including marine mammals, co-ordinated through the School of Marine Science.

Chipangali Wildlife Trust
P O Box 1057, Bulawayo, Zimbabwe.
The Trust has four basic aims: conservation of wildlife; conservation education; stimulation of environmental awareness; and conservation research. It is currently involved in a study of the duikers of Africa.

Kalahari Conservation Society
P O Box 859, Gaborone, Botswana. www.kcs.org.bw
The Kalahari Conservation Society aims to promote knowledge of Botswana's rich wildlife resources and its environment; encourage research; and promote sound conservation policies in that country.

Swaziland National Trust (Nature Conservation Division)
P O Box 75, Mbabane, Swaziland. www.sntc.org.sz

■ National and provincial conservation organizations

South African National Parks (Sanparks): P O Box 787, Tshwane 0001. www.sanparks.org
Gauteng: Directorate of Nature Conservation, Private Bag X209, Tshwane 0001.
Limpopo: Department of Environmental Affairs and Tourism, P O Box 217, Polokwane 0700.
Mpumalanga: Department of Environmental Affairs, Private Bag 11233, Nelspruit 1200.
North West Province: Dept. of Agriculture & Environmental Affairs, P. Bag X6102, Mmabatho 8681.
KwaZulu-Natal: Ezemvelo, P O Box 662, Pietermaritzburg 3200.
Eastern Cape: Eastern Cape Nature Conservation, Private Bag X1126, Port Elizabeth 6000.
Western Cape: CapeNature, Cape Nature House, Belmont Park, Belmont Road, Rondebosch, Cape Town. Private Bag X29, Rondebosch 7701. www.capenature.org.za
Northern Cape: Nature Conservation Service, Private Bag X6102, Kimberley 8300.
Free State: Department of Agriculture and Environment Affairs, P O Box 517, Bloemfontein 9300.

Botswana: Ministry of Environment, Wildlife and Tourism, P O Box 131, Gaborone, Botswana.
Namibia: Ministry of Environment and Tourism, Private Bag 13306, Windhoek, Namibia. www.met.gov.na
Lesotho: Lesotho National Parks (Conservation Division), P O Box 92, Maseru 100, Lesotho.
Zimbabwe: Dept. National Parks & Wildlife Management, P O Box 8365, Causeway, Harare, Zimbabwe.

■ Museums with resident mammalogists

Iziko South African Museum www.iziko.org.za
25 Queen Victoria Street, Cape Town; PO Box 61, Cape Town 8000, South Africa.
Transvaal Museum www.nfi.org.za | www-tm.up.ac.za
Paul Kruger Street, Tshwane; PO Box 413, Tshwane 0001, South Africa.
National Museum www.nasmus.co.za
Aliwal Street, Bloemfontein; PO Box 266, Bloemfontein 9300, South Africa.
Port Elizabeth Museum www.gardenroute.co.za/pe/museum
Beach Road, Humewood; PO Box 13147, Humewood 6013, South Africa.
Amathole Museum Albert Road, King William's Town;
PO Box 1434, King William's Town 5600, South Africa.
National Museum (Namibia) PO Box 1203, Windhoek, Namibia. www.natmus.cul.na
National Museum (Zimbabwe) PO Box 240, Bulawayo, Zimbabwe.

PHOTOGRAPHIC CREDITS

All photographs in this book have been taken by the authors, with the exception of those listed below. Copyright rests with the individual photographers.
ABPL = Anthony Bannister Photo Library.

ABPL/Anthony Bannister: 237 (bottom main)
ABPL/Clem Haagner: 237 (bottom inset)
ABPL/Joan Ryder: 165 (bottom)
ABPL/Lorna Stanton: 85 (bottom)
ABPL/Nigel Dennis: 225 (top)
Doug Allen/naturepl.com: 253 (top)
P. K. Anderson: 285
Daryl and Sharna Balfour (Wildphotos): 149 (top right)
Tony Bruton: 109 (top left)
John Carlyon: 53 (top and bottom right), 101 (top left and right), 131 (bottom right), 137 (bottom), 249 (inset), 251 (top and bottom), 253 (bottom inset)
Nigel Dennis/Images of Africa: 157 (bottom main), 201 (top), 227 (bottom right)
U. de V. Pienaar: 147 (bottom main)
N. Dippenaar: 41 (bottom)
Andrew Duthie: 93 (top left)
Th. Engel: 149 (inset bottom left)
Chris and Monique Fallows: 283 (top inset)
Ken Findlay: 259 (top inset, bottom inset)
Pat J. Frere: 187 (bottom right)
Roger Fussell/Big Sky Lodges: 149 (inset bottom right)
Ian Gaigher: 161 (bottom main)
Mike Griffin (MET Namibia): 31 (bottom right), 43 (bottom right), 71 (top), 101 (centre right), 115 (top left, middle right), 127 (centre left), 129 (top inset, bottom)
Todd Kaplan/Wildlife Campus: 99 (bottom left)
Pam Laycock: 55 (top)
Ian Manning: 211 (centre left)
W. Massyn: 63 (top right), 73 (inset bottom), 77 (bottom left)
Nature Picture Library: 253 (bottom)
Brent Naudé-Moseley: 123 (bottom main)
Rory Nefdt: 61 (centre right)
Harald Nicolay: 159 (bottom inset)
Helmut Niebuhr: cover (main image)
I. L. Rautenbach: 55 (bottom), 61 (bottom left), 63 (bottom right), 69, 73 (inset top), 75 (top, bottom left)
Ernest Seamark: 77 (top left)
Peter Taylor: 57 (top right), 77 (bottom right)
Merlin Tuttle: 47 (top right, bottom left), 49 (bottom, bottom inset)
Harry van Rompaey: 163 (top left)
John Visser: 43 (bottom left), 71 (bottom); 249 (bottom)
Jane Waterman: 95 (top)
Alan Weaving: 243 (bottom)
Lloyd Wingate: 61 (top right), 63 (bottom left), 75 (top)

INDEX TO AFRIKAANS COMMON NAMES

INDEX TO AFRIKAANS COMMON NAMES

INDEX TO GERMAN COMMMON NAMES

INDEX TO SCIENTIFIC NAMES

KEY:
ORDER – CAPITALS
Family – **bold**
Species – *italics*

INDEX TO ENGLISH COMMON NAMES